The Whole Gospel
according to
the Universal Theater of God's Kingdom

The Whole Gospel according to the Universal Theater of God's Kingdom

Any Handy Metaphor Will Do

Written and Edited by
CATHERINE WHITTIER HUBER

Written and Illustrated by
LYNN C. MCCALLUM

RESOURCE *Publications* • Eugene, Oregon

THE WHOLE GOSPEL ACCORDING TO THE UNIVERSAL THEATER OF
GOD'S KINGDOM
Any Handy Metaphor Will Do

Copyright © 2011 Catherine Whittier Huber and Lynn C. McCallum. All rights reserved. Except for brief quotations in critical publications or reviews, no part of this book may be reproduced in any manner without prior written permission from the publisher. Write: Permissions, Wipf and Stock Publishers, 199 W. 8th Ave., Suite 3, Eugene, OR 97401.

"Revised Standard Version of the Bible, copyright 1952 [2nd edition, 1971] by the Division of Christian Education of the National Council of the Churches of Christ in the United States of America. Used by permission. All rights reserved."

"New Revised Standard Version Bible, copyright 1989, Division of Christian Education of the National Council of the Churches of Christ in the United States of America. Used by permission. All rights reserved."

With deep appreciation to Mohr Siebeck Gmbh & Co. KG, Tubingen, Germany, publisher of the Huck-Lietzmann *Synopsis,* Ninth Edition, 1936—which originally inspired the numbering scheme found in the Appendix of this volume—for granting permission for it to be used here for the purpose of cross-referencing the synoptic gospels with these "Universal Theater of God's Kingdom" translations.

Resource Publications
An Imprint of Wipf and Stock Publishers
199 W. 8th Ave., Suite 3
Eugene, OR 97401

www.wipfandstock.com

ISBN 13: 978-1-60899-824-1

Manufactured in the U.S.A.

In loving memory of

The Reverend Lynn Chiles McCallum

(1942–2010)

who truly blessed many people

with his presence and delightful sense of humor.

Contents

*One Act Play
**Illustration

Preface • xv
Abbreviations • xvii

Chapter I: A Handful of Previous Productions • 1

A Man for Whom Faith was a Terrible Trial *(Genesis 22:1-14)*
Theophany in the Bush *(Exodus 3:1-6)*
Elijah Bread *(I Kings 17:8-16)*
**Baal Cake
Isaiah Rap *(Isaiah 28:14-22)*
The "Fleeing as You Fled" Song *(Zechariah 14:4-9)*

Chapter II: Nativity • 9

In the Beginning *(John 1:1-18)*
The Annunciation of Anonymous *(Luke 1:26-38)*
The Next Generations' Magnificat *(Luke 1:39-56)*
Jesus is Born in Context *(Matthew 1:18-25)*
A Bright, Life-Saving Idea *(Matthew 2:13-23)*

Chapter III: A Voice in the Wilderness • 16

The Qumran Computation *(Luke 3:1-6)*
*The Wild Man of Judea *(Luke 3:7-18)*
**Dead-weight Rocks

Chapter IV: In the Galilee Theater • 26

Jésus ben Dios in Spring Training *(Luke 4:1-13)*

**Spring Training Bus
The Galilee Theater *(Matthew 4:12–23)*
The Galilee School District *(John 1:43–51)*
The Roman Empire Board of Education *(Mark 1:21–28)*
Doctor Jesus *(Mark 1:29–39)*
The Lake of the Human Heart *(Luke 5:1–11)*
The Way-to-Be Attitudes *(Matthew 5:1–12)*
The Holy Script-yours *(Matthew 5:13–20)*
Three Rulis Dramatis *(Matthew 5:21–37)*
Commentary on the Script of the Competition *(Matthew 5:38–48)*
The Rock or Sand Sermon *(Matthew 7:21–27)*
Invigorating the Paralyzed at Home *(Mark 2:1–12)*
Dr. Jesus Eats with Patients and Orderlies *(Matthew 9:1–9)*
Computer-Savvy Bishop Jesus *(Matthew 9:9–13)*
**Hacker Jesus
Chef Jesus' Culinary Magic Show *(Matthew 9:35–10:15)*
Jesus' School of Servanthood *(Matthew 10:24–33)*
Shredding Illusions of Domestic Tranquility *(Matthew 10:34–42)*
John the Journalist *(Matthew 11:2–11)*
Jesus' Jokes are Easy *(Matthew 11:25–30)*
**Bird in Hand is De-Light
The "Bread of God's Presence" Bread Company *(Mark 2:23–28)*
The Sermon on the Level *(Luke 6:17–26)*
The "Just A Few Good Men" Men's Club *(Luke 7:36–50)*
St. Pious in the Suburbs *(Luke 7:36–50)*
The Incredible Skulk *(Luke 8:26–39)*
Jesus' Rap Song *(Mark 3:22–25)*
To Un-Clog Your Ears *(Matthew 13:1–9; 18–23)*
Headline News from Trying Times *(Matthew 13:24–30; 36–43)*
Like a Book of Common Prayer *(Matthew 13: 31–33; 44–49a)*
**Seeking Readers
**Immersed in the Text
Farmer Jesus' Metaphorical Seeds *(Mark 4:25–34)*
**God Sows
**Disciples' Row
The Women's Issue *(Mark 5:22–43)*
The Gospel of the Prairie *(Mark 6:7–13)*
Head Chef Jesus *(Mark 14:13–21)*

Camp Eerie *(Matthew 14:22–33)*
Dog Tired *(Matthew 15:21–28)*
**Dog Tired
**Canine-type Female
**Criminetly!
**Shamelessly Groveled
**Nipped Him Back
**Wrapped His Arms
Man with Attention Deaf-icit Disorder *(Mark 7:31–37)*
In the Chapel of the Consoling Christ *(Luke 9:18–24)*
The Demise of the Fairy Tale God *(Matthew 17:1–9)*
All Saints' Way Out in the Mountains *(Matthew 17:1–9)*
Bishop Jesus and the Unwilling Spirit *(Mark 8:27–38)*
Infant Formula: INAMA *(Mark 9:30–37)*
Bishop Jesus Cuts Some Clergy Down *(Mark 9:38–48)*
Two to Tango *(Matthew 18:15–20)*

Chapter V: The Lukan Theater Wing • 90

You're in God's Army Now *(Luke 9:57–62)*
In the Army of the Dog *(Luke 10:1–20)*
**The Cynic
The Good Un-Churched Fellow *(Luke 10:25–37)*
Jesus' Lesson Plan at Mary's and Martha's *(Luke 10:38–42)*
How to Pray to God on Your Cell Phone *(Luke 11:1–13)*
*Shop 'til You Drop *(Luke 12:13–21)*
The Graciously, Gracefully-Humored Person *(Luke 12:32–40)*
Pyromaniac-Arsonist Jesus *(Luke 12:49–56)*
The International Association of Fairly Good People *(Luke 13:1–9)*
*All People's Airline *(Luke 13:22–35)*
A Real Cause for Celebration *(Luke 15:1–15)*
Happy Hour *(Luke 17:5–10)*
Marshal Jesus Encounters the Dirty Men-yon *(Luke 17:11–19)*
**Marshal Jesus
**Happy Trails
Another One Bites the Dust *(Luke 18:1–14)*

Chapter VI: In the Judean Theater • 109

What? Am I a Lawyer? *(Mark 10:2–9)*

A Precocious Child *(Mark 10:17-27)*
The Factory of Absolute Fairness *(Matthew 20:1-16)*
Bart and Zack *(Luke 19:1-10)*
Nicodemus and Metanoia Man *(John 3:1-17)*
Anglo-Catholic Father Jesus *(John 4:5-26)*
***Anglo-Catholic Father Jesus*
***Woman at Holy Water Basin*
***Father Jesus Close-Up*
***Excuse me, Father*
**Holy Water Basin
***Encountering Each Other*
The Living Quail *(John 6:60-69)*
The Wild Card of Judea *(Matthew 21:28-32)*
Time to Vote in a Very Important Election *(Matthew 21:28-32)*
What Will that Bishop Do? *(Matthew 21:33-43)*
His Steadfast Love Endures Forever *(Matthew 21:33-43)*
The Absentee Landlord *(Luke 20:9-19)*
The Enemy Dressed in His Sunday Best *(Matthew 22:1-14)*
Jesus Answers in a Timely Fashion *(Matthew 22:15-22)*
*One Bride for Seven Brothers *(Luke 20:27-38)*
Jésus ben Dios and Dave "The Babe" King *(Matthew 22:34-36)*
Yogi Jesus and the Voices of Anxiety *(Matthew 23:1-12)*
*An Apocalyptic Coffee Hour Conversation *(Luke 21:5-19)*
The Bosom of God *(Mark 13:14-37)*
*The Presence of God is Coming to Town *(Matthew 14:37-44)*
*A Groom-Centered Wedding *(Matthew 25:1-13)*
*Mean Old Mommy *(Matthew 25:14-29)*
Two Types of Dead Meat *(Matthew 25:31-46)*

Chapter VII: The Johaninne Theater Wing • 149

The Country Wedding *(John 2:1-11)*
The Miracle at the Eucharist *(John 2:1-11)*
Light Perception *(John 9:14-38)*
Man with Strange Looking Spectacles *(John 9:14-38)*
I am the Backstage Door *(John 10:1-10)*
I am the Good Mother *(John 10:11-16)*
The Jerusalem National Gallery of Art *(John 10:22-30)*
***Jerusalem National Gallery of Art*

**Artist Jesus
Poor Old Russ *(John 11:7-44)*
*The Baptismal Font of Electrifying Power *(John 12:20-33)*
Terms of Endearment *(John 13:31-35)*
No Way! Yes, Way! *(John 14:1-14)*
Correspond and Collaborate with the Author *(John 14:1-14)*
Dr. Jesus of Nazareth, Medicine Man *(John 14:15-21)*
Dr. Spiritus Sanctus *(John 14:15-21)*
The First/Last Bank of Hope and Trust *(John 15:1-8)*
Prayer Jesus *(John 17:1-11)*

Chapter VIII: The Passion • 171

The Presiding Bishop of the Whole Church *(John 18:33-37)*
*A Passion Play in One Final Bet *(Luke 23:35-43)*

Chapter IX: Ongoing Appearances • 174

Two of the Women *(Matthew 28:1-10)*
*A WGIJ-TV Easter Broadcast *(Mark 16:1-8)*
The Sacristy of the Human Heart *(Luke 24:1-12)*
**Sacristy Door
**Clergy Types
**Preaching to the Choir
On the Road to Amaze-Us *(Luke 24:13-35)*
CSI: Jerusalem *(Luke 24-13-35)*
A Spooky Way to Handle Jesus *(Luke 24:36-48)*
A Certain Pillar of the Church *(John 20:1-18)*
Jesus Ascends Before Our Very Eyes *(Luke 24:49-53)*
The Whole World Communications Company *(Mark 16:9-20)*
The Last Curtain Falls *(Matthew 28:16-20)*
God's Great Love for the World *(John 20:19-23)*
On Pentecost Sunday *(John 20:19-23)*
Fishing in the Lake of the Human Heart *(John 21:1-14)*
**Something on the Horizon

Chapter X: Beginning Again • 196

How Strange and Beautiful *(Acts 8:26-40)*

Notes • 198
Appendix • 203

Songs

Chapter I
    The "Fleeing as You Fled" Song • 7

Chapter II
    The Gen-Y Magnificat • 13

Chapter III
    That Son of Resistance • 17
    Jesus Christ is Coming Our Way • 22
    Take Off the Garment of Your Sorrow • 23

Chapter IV
    Keep Me True to God's Spirit • 28
    Jesus is Our Doctor • 34
    The Devil May Struggle • 60
    Calm Down and Relax • 75

Chapter V
    You're in God's Army Now • 91
    Do Your Lamps Burn Long? • 98
    Pop Comes God's Kingdom • 98

Chapter VII
    The Queen of Love • 154

Preface

"Overtones are constantly being lost.
Let him approach polysemia cross-eyed, coin in hand."[1]

THIS LITTLE BOOK TOOK us about fifteen years to write—crafting, illustrating and creating props for each story week after week—and then at least another five years to figure out how to edit and share any of it outside of the context of worship. With only a few exceptions, each translation of the lectionary text appointed for a particular Sunday morning was used as the inner-most part of an interactive sermon delivered during that particular Sunday's worship at either St. Paul's in Oregon, Ohio, St. Timothy's in Trenton, Michigan or St. Andrew's in Toledo, Ohio, while The Rev. McCallum was serving as the rector in those parishes. Sadly, only a handful of Lynn's very large body of colorful drawings is reproduced here due to insufficient resources to photograph and present all of them at this time; the loss is surely to the reader for they lack much of their original vitality when reduced to grayscale and limited to so few examples.

In many ways, any one of these individual story-scripts reflects upon all of the other scripts in this collection, but perhaps none better than *The Jerusalem National Gallery of Art*, based on John 10:22–30, in which our beloved Performance Artist Jesus, standing right in the middle of the Great Masters' Hall next to the world-famous works of the likes of David Monet, Ezekiel Matisse, Elijah Lautrec, Moses DaVinci, Sarah O'Keefe, and Rebecca Rembrandt, gives a simple answer to all those who say to him, "How long will you keep us in suspense? If you are the Christ, tell us plainly" (John 10:24).

> The performance art that I perform for our Creator clearly and plainly expresses everything that there is to know about me, but you do not see it because you are not students of my creative art. My students are not the least bit confused about who I am and what I am doing and saying in my art form. And I know who they are because they are the ones who practice my technique. I continually inspire them with abundantly creative life without end and no one can take that away from me—or from them for that matter! My students are free gifts to me from My Father who is the greatest Performance Artist of All Time and Creation. My gift to them is this very same Source of creativity that will never end so that they too can perform the works that I perform—and even more so because I go to the Creator where I continue to share our Creator's creativity with them forever. The creativity our Creator has lavished upon me is the greatest re-story-izing art of all, and no one can take that away from the hand of the Artist God who gives it so freely. In this—God's own art form—the Creator of the Universe and I are one and the same! You see? *Now* you're really getting the picture![2]

We hope something in it will inspire you to seek and reveal the signs of God's great performance art as they are so wonderfully evidenced—not frozen and hanging on the walls of the world's museums to the past—but everywhere you go, look, and see God's gracious hand at work in the world today.

C. W. H.
December, 2010

They said to each other
"Did not our hearts burn within us while he talked to us on the road,
while he opened to us the scripture?"
Luke 24:32

Abbreviations

RSV   *The Bible,* Revised Standard Version
NRSV   *The Bible,* New Revised Standard Version
BCP   *The Book of Common Prayer,* Harrisburg: Morehouse Publishing, 1985.
UTGK   *The Whole Gospel according to the Universal Theater of God's Kingdom,* Huber and McCallum, Eugene: Wipf and Stock, 2011.

I

A Handful of Previous Productions

A MAN FOR WHOM FAITH WAS A TERRIBLE TRIAL

Devotion to God above all else was a terrible trial and a mighty struggle for the Father of Our Faith, but God called him the Father of Our Faith, and he responded from the depths of his heart, "that means me."

And then he heard his God say, "Take your beloved sense of humor, that innocent child of your innermost being, and go out into a dry and a humorless place, and make it a mighty sacrifice on the altar of my demands."

So the Father of Our Faith gathered up all his resources, as well as his beloved sense of humor, that precious child of his innermost being, and he went out into that dry and humorless place where he prepared to make it a mighty sacrifice on the altar of God's demands.

And then his beloved sense of humor, that much-loved child of his innermost being, cried out to him, "So what in the world are you planning to sacrifice on the altar of God's demands today?"

And the Father of our Faith lied through his teeth about his own plans when he said, "Oh, not to worry. Just a little something that God Almighty will supply himself, that's all." And then the Father of Our Faith actually started to intentionally murder his own beloved child, that funny sense of humor from his innermost being named "He Really Makes Me Laugh!"

But suddenly there appeared to be a brightly-energetic presence glimmering all around him and speaking directly into the depths of his innermost being, "Hey you, Father of Faith!" And he thought, "Uh oh, that means me!"

"Do not harm a hair on the head of that child of your innermost being who really makes me laugh, your most beloved sense of humor! For it is already much more than obvious that you are deeply devoted to the Lord your God and that you would even break your own heart if you thought that was what God wanted you to do to prove it!"

At which point the Father of Our Faith looked up from that experience with a brand-new and a brightly-energetic perspective! And, lo and behold, there it was! See? Now that's a real ram in the bush indeed!

So the Father of Our Faith took that absolutely free gift of God's great goodness and grace and shimmering insight and placed it on the altar; but not on some false altar of God's Demands, but on the true altar of God's Great Love instead.

And he called that place, "God Gives Really Delightful Gifts!" And that is exactly how it is still known even until this very day.

THEOPHANY IN THE BUSH

Now Moses was way out on the fringes of human habitation (out in the sticks, in the bushes, in the wilderness, in the wild, in the wildness) where he was tending to some ordinary, everyday, family business for his father-in-law, owner and operator of Jethro, Inc.

While in the course of tending to this ordinary business of looking for greener pastures, Moses unexpectedly stepped beyond the outmost reaches of ordinary, civilized, human experience and cultural influence, right on to the mountain dwelling-place of the Most Wholly Other High and Holy One, also known as the unpronounceable MWOHHO.

And behold! An extraordinarily bright flame heralded him from the midst of the bush giving Moses the bright idea to boldly announce to anyone who might be listening, "Wow! That's really weird! I think I'll stop and take a sidewise glance at that burning bush to see if I can discover why it hasn't been burnt to a crisp, which is surely what's normal and to be expected!"

Now when the MWOHHO saw that Moses had actually stopped and turned his full attention to where he was, the voice of the MWOHHO blazed out from the midst of the burning bush: "Moses! Moses!"

"Yikes! I'm here, Sir! Ma'am! Your Scary, Burning Brightness! At your disposal!" Moses flickered in response, stepping even closer.

"Keep your distance, Man! Have a little respect, for God's sake! And take off your shoes! For this wholly uncivilized, completely wild, and unfamiliar religious territory is home to the Most Wholly Other High and Holy One!"

First one shoe drops, and then the other.

"I Am: The One and Only Most High and Holy God; The One who enflamed the hearts and minds of all who came to this place long before you!"

To which Moses said, "Yikes!" and covered this sight from his eyes because he was afraid that he would completely burn up if he looked too closely and for too long. But it was too late, and his mind and his heart were already enflamed, and the whole world had been turned upside and inside out, and Moses was born again into the leader who brought God's people out of slavery all the way up to a very good view of the Promised Land.

ELIJAH BREAD

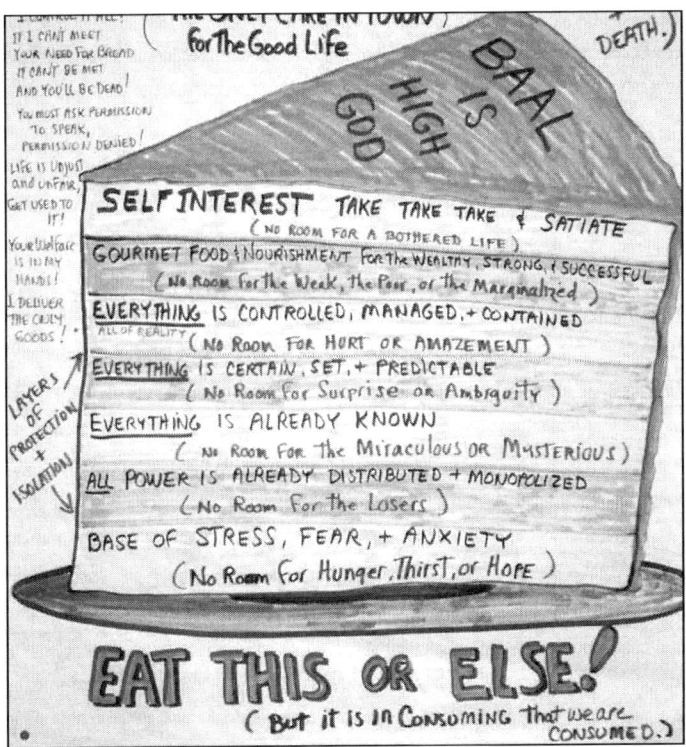

One time, right in the middle of the starvation diet and spiritual drought of a bankrupt royal system, the Lord God did not send his servant to the king's table to eat junk food, but instead, God sent his servant out to be fed by ravens, and then out to an even more foreign place, way out beyond the borders of the royal monopoly, to live there and to be fed by a nameless woman (as such women always are), who was a woman way out on the edge, a victim of the royal definers of human worth, barely existing on crumbs and debris, and courting despair; but yet a woman whom God had commanded to feed his servant whose very name means "The Ultimate Source of Life is God"!

When God's servant got to the woman, he clearly expressed his hunger and thirst as he said, "Woman, give me some water— in a cup would be good—if you will." Then while she was literally on her way to draw some water for him, The Ultimate Source of Life is God suddenly intervened and commanded, "And also a taste of that life giving stuff you hold in the palm of your hand," which really kind of scared the woman, so she turned to him and said, "God only knows I only have a drop of this and a morsel of that in two sorry little containers and not even enough time to do anything with it yet, and you, Sir, are interrupting my plan to go home and make a little ritual of death: one last, sad, final meal and deathbed for me and my son, and so as you can plainly see, I have nothing to give."

But God's servant said, as all good heralds and bearers of God's Life-Giving Presence always say, "Do not be afraid. Make your plans if you must, but first take your little of this and your little of that and do as God commands you: Give me a taste of the cake you would have baked me if you'd known I was coming! Then, after that, see how you feel about cooking-up something for you and your son out of these two simple ingredients you also have on hand: the abundance of food for the human soul and the deep compassion for the human condition that the Lord God is freely providing for you right this very minute, even as we speak here with one another. For these are the ingredients that will never run out whenever and wherever the True God Reigns as the Ultimate Source of Life."

And so, in this extraordinarily ordinary way, they were all fed from the very riches of God's grace which can never be contained, controlled or depleted, even until this day, as the servants of God continually feed and sustain one another according to the word of God as spoken by his servant whose very name means "The Ultimate Source of Life is God."

And so here is yet another reminder of some of the abundant life you hold in the palm of your hand: your compassion; your humility; your emptiness; your forsaken-ness; your poverty; your empty vessel-ness; your open-ness to being changed; your identification and solidarity with those who suffer want because you are in touch with your own needs; your capacity to be filled to overflowing with God's compassion; your capacity to allow God to create something new in you, which is also known as your creativity; your capacity to put yourself out for somebody else; your willingness to learn, your willingness to serve.

ISAIAH RAP

Listen-up you Pompous Liars who rule this land:

Because you say,
"We've got a deal with death!"
And because you sign a pact with Sheol,
Hell, because you make your bed of lies,
You think you've got it covered, well,
You say, "No harm can come to our Homeland
Security here is working Swell!"
You say you live in safety, well

Now hear the voice of God's Mouthpiece
For I will sell
You what God also has to tell!

The Lord Himself, that even
Higher Power will send a plague
On your parade,
A scourge on your self-serving days;
A purge of your death-dealings ways;
And drown your safety in the mud;
And sweep away your bed of lies;
And flood the shelter of your sin;
Then turn around and come again!

Your marriage to Death will be annulled;
The vows you made cannot withstand
The overwhelming
Passing-through,
The purging scourge.

You get it? Now you understand?
Watch out, I say!
My Lord God deals in truth
And all the rest pack lies!

He builds with tested, solid rock;
His own plumb line is in his hand
To righteousness and justice tied,
His love of justice does not slide!
And those who trust God
Do not panic, run away,
Or haste to hide!

But those who get the message now
Will surely faint and fall with fear;
You never really had it covered anyway,
That much is clear!

The living Lord will rise
To do his work;
His work is weird;
Created for all eternity,
Arriving now, arriving here,

God's absolutely-overwhelming love
Is an awesomely-incredible
Power to fear!

So do not lie or lie around,
Whatever else you say or do,
When God performs
God's mighty works,
Your lie might tell the truth on you!

For I have said truly what I have heard:
Each strange, invigorating, alien word
As I let sound God's purging planned
For every heart where God will land!

THE "FLEEING AS YOU FLED" SONG
Sung to the tune of "Jingle Bells."[1]

Refrain:

God is near, God is near,
God is on the Way!
O there won't be cold or frost
Or dark on that new-born day-hey!
God is near, God is near,
God is on the Way!
Even in the evening time,
There will be light of day!

Verses:

1) Fleeing as you fled
In the days of King Uzziah
Weeping and gnashing your teeth
Or laughing all the way
(Ha! Ha! Ha!)
His feet on the Mount of Olives
Making a very wide valley
O my God, will surely come with all the holy ones!

2) Withdrawing to the north
Withdrawing to the south
The mountain split apart
And the valley all stopped up
(Ha! Ha! Ha!)
Making a very wide valley
Reaching to Azal
Living waters shall divide and flow right through Israel!

3) Fainting fearful folks
Foreboding everywhere
Distress among the nations
Confusion in the air
(Ha! Ha! Ha!)
Stand up and raise your heads
Your redemption is drawing near
Look at the trees and sprouting leaves, and know that summer's here!

II

Nativity

IN THE BEGINNING

In the beginning was the sound and the sound composed the poem, and the poem composed the symphony, and this symphony plays in the silence, and the silence cannot stop it from playing.

Now, as you will recall, there was a promoter named John who advertised the composition of the symphony so that all might hear it. This promoter was not the composer or the composition of the symphony itself, of course, but he just told everybody when and where to tune in to hear its power and beauty because the symphony was going to be played on the radio soon.

Then the symphony was played on the radio but all the world heard was a lot of static noise and interference. And then the symphony was played in the concert halls, but, alas, even then, all the world heard was a lot of static noise and interference. But to those few who did somehow manage to hear it, the original composer of the music gave the power and beauty of the symphony itself, so that they might become his very own special orchestra and choir. Hallelujah! And then the sound became composed of flesh and blood moving around and among us in the noisy world. Hallelujah! And it was full of passion, and accent, and melody, and harmony. Hallelujah! And power, and definition, and grace, and beauty, and compassionate resonance. Hallelujah! And when we heard it playing, we heard how glorious it was indeed! Hallelujah!

THE ANNUNCIATION OF ANONYMOUS

Now on a certain day in the twelfth month of the two-thousandth Year of Our Lord, plus or minus ten years or so, an angel was sent by God to a certain nondescript town in the middle of the country—the name of which was a national joke—to a layperson who was interested in the art of preaching and discussing it with a local parish priest. Now that woman's name was surely Anonymous.

The angel came and said to her, "Blessings just come up like a storm and rain upon you, oh Lucky One! For God is with you all the way!" But she was really quite confused by the angel's weird appearance and very strange words suddenly coming to her right at the very moment when she most found herself at a complete loss for words. But the angel said to her, "Look, do not be too surprised neither overly-overwhelmed, Dear Anonymous One, for God is really very pleased to be doing you this small favor wrapped in swaddling clothes. For even right this very minute you are in the process of conceiving in your mind and knowing full well in your heart of hearts the name of the One you are to carry into the world with all of your actions and words, even as if of your very own body, and you are even now naming him: Jesus Christ your Lord, for he is indeed the Lord of Life and the Prince of Peace for whom your own heart and the whole world yearns."

But Anonymous was astounded and said to the angel, "How can what you say be true, even figuratively-speaking, since I am a layperson and completely anonymous to boot?" The angel said to her, "Look, the Holy Spirit will come upon you and completely overshadow you and inspire you with the power to bring to light God's own Word full of grace and life, Emmanuel, God with us. And your most profound proof of this is that your old friend, even in his old age, is also busy conceiving of new and abundant life in him, and he who has recently complained that he has been depressed is now fully alert and alive and awake to all the brilliant expressions of faith and joy in your immediate time and place—for nothing deeply and richly rewarding will be impossible with God!"

Then Anonymous said, "Here I am at my keyboard, Lord, and you are at the door to my heart. Let it proceed with me according to your Word." Then the angel let her get right down to her very strange work.

And then that Bright, New Angelic Presence immediately hurried to make itself known in that very same town, to a struggling, yet amazingly alive and engaging church, when the Bright, New, Angelic

Presence simply appeared and said to her, "Greetings, oh Favored One! The Lord is also with you!" But the church was much perplexed and not a little confused about what such a sudden, unexplained appearance and strange, cryptic greeting was supposed to mean, especially coming to her in the midst of a regular Sunday service, and speaking to her in the middle of an ordinary sermon for God's sake, and so she pondered about what sort of greeting this might be.

And the angel said to her, "Oh, Dear People, look; do not be afraid. God is delighted to appear among you and to bless you with life-giving and Holy Presence, for already, right here and now, you are deeply engaged in the process of conceiving in your minds and knowing in your heart of hearts the name of the One whom you are called to bear and carry throughout every aspect of your lives in this world: the very same Jesus Christ, the Lord of Life and the Prince of Peace for whom your own hearts and the whole world yearns. All honor and glory be to him for ever and ever. Amen."

And the church said to the angel, "How in the world can this be, especially here and now, in the midst of our often precarious finances and the ongoing roller-coaster of our lives and relationships; the ever-changing demands of people coming and going; and the busy, hassled, and scattered lives that we all lead? How in the world can this be when we are so small and inexperienced and have so few resources?"

But the Bright, Angelic Presence said to her, "Look, the Holy Spirit has come upon you and is overshadowing you to work its magic within you even as we speak, and blessing you with the power to bring into life God's very own word of grace and truth, Emmanuel, God with us. And even now, your aging pastor is also busy conceiving and laboring hard to bring new life into your very midst, even right in the middle of a sermon for God's sake, for with God, not even *that* is impossible!

And she said, "OK! OK! Alright already! We get it! Here we are, Lord! Let it be with us according to your Word!" So then the angel of the Lord let them proceed with their worship in peace, using an ancient confession of faith as found in their contemporary book of prayers.

THE NEXT GENERATIONS' MAGNIFICAT

But it wasn't very long until they found themselves right in back the midst of the gathering darkness when everyone was saying what an incredible decline there was in everything good and sweet and innocent and beautiful in the world. For it happened right in the midst of those dark days, when almost all of the elaborate churches, mosques, synagogues and other Temples to the Past had somehow inexplicably transformed themselves into huge, cold, empty caverns of gaping, joyless wonder reflecting nothing so much as the dreams and desires of the proud imaginations of the previous generations with their enormous sense of entitlement to everything on the earth; their incredible belief that the world was their oyster and the pearl within as well; the assumed righteousness of all who went before, including the parents of the population explosion, their living-and-breathing two-legged legacy of personal, providential benevolence so numerous and known as the Oblivious Children of the Entitlement, whose parents often called them, "So delightful! So adorable! So well-behaved!" and "So dutifully playing The Only Game in town in their own back yards: playing *House* because you've got to own a house to play this game; playing *Car* because you've got to have cars, of course; playing *Work* because you've got to have an identity, which, according to this game, depends upon having a job or an inheritance; playing *War* because everyone needs to have an enemy; and playing *School* because this game includes a lot of very important lessons to learn and to teach to the next generations all about how you've got to have a house, and a car, and a job, and a war, and a better school, and a bigger house, and an SUV and an ATV, and a better job, and a bigger war, and an expensive tank-like vehicle, and a better house, and, of course, an even better school to teach you all about *The Only Game in Town.*"

For it was right in the midst of these ominous, dark days when everyone was so terribly busy and anxiously spending more and more time and energy and resources on trying to hold the empire together; building and shoring-up all kinds of defenses; making-up more and more rules, harsher laws and greater punishments; building more and more secure prisons and hiring more and more security personnel, police, and militias, and sending troops out in all directions in ever wider circles, and ever-widening directions, when a certain, pregnant, young Gen-Y somehow managed to leap out of bed, throw on some clothes, and climb up the hill to her Ancient Old Uncle's house to hang-out with her favorite cousin, Gen-X, who, as it so wonderfully turned out, was also awake and pregnant with true hope for new life.

When Gen-X heard Gen-Y's cheerful voice calling-out for her to get up and greet the dawn of the new day, Gen-X's own little flicker of life suddenly leapt-up within her and broke out in full voice: "Oh Ssssweet! My Own Kindred Spirit! Dear Cousin! You grace me with your presence! You Bringer of Good News! You Bearer of Good Tidings! Come in! Come in! You Birth Mother of the Future! Of all generations! My Song and my Delight!" And then, right then and there, Gen-X burst into one of her favorite songs: "O My God! What if I had not believed that I would see the goodness of the Lord in the land of the living?! O hang-out, and await the Lord's pleasure; be strong, and [She] shall comfort your heart!" which was her own special cover of an old song of their favorite singer/songwriter, David "The King" King, from his #27th CD "Life with God," Cuts #13 and #14 (Psalm 27:13–14) named "Everything Old is New Again!"

And then Gen-Y immediately responded with the song in *her* heart, which later became famous under the title, "The Gen-Y Magnificat," sung to the tune of the famous Italian song, "O Sole Mio."[1]

> O Sole Mio! My heart is glad!
> My soul rejoices and is not sad!
> Tomorrow at last is here!
> The future's promise is very near!
>
> O Sole Savior! To you we bow!
> Your goodness present! Your strength, so wow!
> Your arm, the proud will scatter!
> The humble lift up! The time is now!
>
> O God of Abram! Your promised mercy
> And your compassion, all souls will see!
> O Future from the Past,
> Our hearts are singing, to you at last!
>
> O Friend of Futures! Oh Sweet Delight!
> Your brightness shatters our darkest night.
> While kings fall from their thrones,
> O God of new-ness, our hearts your home!

JESUS IS BORN AND IN CONTEXT

Now, the following is a straightforward story telling salient features all about the birth of Jesus, so please pay close attention. But before Jesus was born, his mother, Mary, became engaged to be married to his father, Joseph. But before his mother, Mary, became engaged to his father, Joseph, his mother, Mary, became pregnant because at a certain time before that, his mother, Mary, had been visited by the Holy Spirit. But before his father Joseph could do anything rash, his father, Joseph, was visited by an angel of the Lord in a dream. And the angel of the Lord strongly suggested to his father, Joseph, that before he made up his mind, he should carefully consider the fact that his mother, Mary, had already become impregnated during a previous visitation, and that, furthermore, the child his mother was carrying had already been given a name and a previously-ordained occupation, which were one and the same: God with Us. And the angel of the Lord also reminded his father, Joseph, about something he had already known before; something that had already been written down long before: "Behold a woman shall become pregnant and give birth to a child named God with Us" (Isaiah 7:14). And then his father, Joseph, woke up remembering all that had gone on before, and married his mother, Mary, and fully respected the terms and conditions of her pregnancy until God with Us was born indeed.

A BRIGHT, LIFE-SAVING IDEA

And then, well, it was just a couple of weeks after Christmas when yet another Angelic Spirit came to visit a certain local parish priest, who suddenly grasped everything all at once as if revealed in some secret, holy dream and so he somewhat humbly said, "Hey! I have a bright idea! I myself will take this fledgling parish and all of her people with her, and I will love, cherish and protect them in my heart of hearts, safely out of the reach of all that would undermine, dismember or destroy such a truly precious Body of Christ, and I will guard it there until God Almighty Himself discloses to us the Way we should go and the Way we need to follow.

Then he climbed-up into the pulpit and gently awakened that little parish and all of her people with her, and he brought them out through the dark night of the soul to some temporarily safe ground until the major threats to her health and well-being were dead-and-gone away. This was to fulfill what had been spoken by the Lord through yet another messenger of God's love: "Out of despair have I called my very own heart."

Now, when the major threats to her existence had really died down, yet another new brightly-energetic spirit of love came over our good priest, and he thought that it was now time to take that now growing parish and all of her people with her right back to where it had all begun. But, amazingly, and somehow just as quickly and mysteriously, he got the word that maybe he really shouldn't go exactly all the way there just yet, and so he took them to a temporary dwelling place instead. It was a strange new place out in the far northwest corner of a nondescript, mid-western state, where they made their real spiritual home in a small, nondescript city, in a relatively unknown church out on the edge, which actually fulfilled the prediction of yet another and even stranger messenger of God who once predicted, "They will be called by their current denominational name," whether they be Methodists, Episcopalians, Presbyterians, Nazarenes, Catholics, Disciples of Christ, or anything else that suits the glad purposes of God.

III

A Voice in the Wilderness

THE QUMRAN COMPUTATION

AND THEN THEY MYSTERIOUSLY received these very strange words from out of nowhere really, as if from outer space, as found in the Newly Discovered Qumran Computer, Ship Captain's Log: Star Date: Twenty-eight; Planet Earth; in the Fifteenth Year of the Occupation of Tiberias Caesar, Roman Galactic Empire; in the Second Year of The Affliction of Judea under the tyranny of Pontius Pilate: Procurator and Empiric Governor of the Caesarean Occupation; in the Time of Herod: Caesar's Vicious Governor of the Galilean Constellation and Herod's brother, Philip: Governor Efficient over the Empire's Oppression of the Constellations Ituraea and Trachonitis and Lysanias, Caesar's Lacky and Minion of the Constellation of Abelene; during the High Priesthoods of Annas and Caiaphas: the Compromised Empire Collaborators, when Rebel Command made direct voice contact with one of the Sons of the Resistance, John, in outer space, just after he slipped outside of the direct influence and clutches of the Empire. And then, as a result of this encounter, Cousin John immediately flew on a mission to the Jordanian Region in the Constellation of Judea to call humanity to throw off their cloaks of sorrow and affliction, their hopeless cynicism and deep despair, to repent from the oppressive seductions of the Empire, and to immerse themselves in the cleansing power and healing truth of the glorious word of affirmation and hope from Rebel Command as it was recorded in the Ancient Log Book of Isaiah, who was one of the original Captains of The Starship of the Resistance, "One day a voice will cry out to humanity from the depths of outer space: Prepare a runway for the Lord of the Revolution who is the Rightful and True Lord of All Creation. Fill the valleys and level the hills and mountains! Remove every obstacle for the landing so that all humanity can witness the magnificent coming of the Starship of Salvation!" And it was signed, "Sincerely yours, Captain Luke of the Rebel Starship Christian Enterprise."

Sung to the tune of the Christmas carol "Good Christian Friends Rejoice."[1]

> That Son of Resistance who shouted fire and brimstone,
> John that Great Disturbance, called the people out to say
> You Brood of Spiteful Vipers, Will you ever change your ways?
> Change your ways today!
> Change your ways today!
>
> That Son of Resistance, that Voice from Outer Space,
> Called the people out to say, Will you heed my warning today?
> Grow up and act like you actually care about something besides yourselves for a change!
> Is it really so strange?
> Is it really so strange?
>
> That Son of Resistance called the people out to say
> If you think that I am bad, what will you do when you've been had?
> Just you wait and you will see the One who is coming is worse than me!
> Change your ways today!
> Change your ways today!
>
> That Son of Resistance got the people all worked up,
> Ready for the One to come, to come and burn with unquenchable fire,
> The deadweight rocks and snakes in the grass,
> To gather up all to whom God aspire!
> Change your ways today!
> Change your ways today!

THE WILD MAN OF JUDEA

Narrator: Look! Over there! Why here comes that strange Wild Man of Judea, with all his usual signs and placards, and preaching his urgent message about the Fullness of the Presence of God in our midst! I wonder what he has to say to us now, on this exact day and time in the world, while he wanders around the wilderness of Judea so very many years ago.

The Wild Man enters. He is wearing placards and carrying a sign that says: "Make Way for the Lord of Lords! Straighten-Up and Fly Right! Get Ready for the Fullness of the Presence of God Coming to You in Your Very Midst!"

Wild Man: Repent, you peoples of the earth! "Turn back, O Man! Forswear thy foolish ways"[2] Ask God's forgiveness for your despair; for your lack of hope; for your lack of faith! And look to the Lord of Hosts! For the Fullness of the Presence of God is very near—close at hand—at your very fingertips! Make way for the Lord of Hosts, I say!

Narrator: For this Wild Man of Judea was indeed the very same character who was foretold and foreshadowed by the famous playwright-prophet, Isaiah, in his well-known play entitled, "Songs of the Coming Servant Lord," when the prophet spoke these famous lines, "When the time comes, a strange and solitary voice will be heard preaching in the wilderness places of the earth. And the sermon title will be "Make way for the Lord of Lords! Straighten-up and fly right! Get Ready for the Fullness of the Presence of God Coming to You in Your Very Midst!"

Spectator #1 and Spectator #2 enter. They stand a short distance from the Wild Man, checking him out. The Wild Man begins eating his snack.

Spectator #1: Say, that Wild Man sure is wearing some pretty wild clothes!

Spectator #2: Hey, check out that garment! Looks to me like it's made of camel hair!

Spectator #1: Looks scratchy to me! Yuck!

Spectator #2: And how about that leather girdle about his waist? Bet that's not too comfortable either!

Spectator #1: Oh my God! Can you believe what the man is eating?

Spectator #2: Looks like bugs to me! Double yuck!
Spectator #1: Looks like he's drinking Bug Juice too! Imagine what that tastes like!
Spectator #2: Ugh. No way! But say, let's go get the others! They surely won't want to miss out on something as strange as all this!

They hurry off stage together.

Narrator: And then, before the scene is over, and right before your very eyes, everybody from all over the place showed up in the wilderness to see this very strange thing that was happening! And before too long, the people could be seen performing some pretty strange actions themselves, for they began to deliver lines like these:

Spectators #1 and #2 return with Spectators #3, #4 and #5. They stand near the Wild Man, but deliver their lines to God.

Spectator #1: Heavenly Father, I am sorry that I have been so cynical and disbelieving about your love and care for your people.
Spectator #2: Dear God, please forgive all my foolish ways.
Spectator #3: Lord, have mercy upon me and renew my hope and trust in you.
Spectator #4: Father in Heaven, "We have erred and strayed from Thy ways like lost sheep. We have followed too much the devices and desires of our own hearts... But Thou, O Lord, have mercy upon us. Spare Thou those who confess their faults. Restore Thou those who are penitent."[3]
Spectator #5: "Most Merciful God, we confess that we have sinned against you in thought, word, and deed, by what we have done, and by what we have left undone. Have mercy on us and forgive us that we may delight in your will, and walk in your ways, to the glory of your name. Amen."[4]
Narrator: Then the Wild Man of Judea baptized them in the River Jordan, washing away all the dust and decay of their daily lives, and cleansing them from all that would prevent them from truly receiving all of the freshness and newness of God's continuing and powerful action in the world.

The Wild Man sprinkles glitter or confetti or water on the heads of all five of the spectators, saying, "I baptize you with water for repentance but

One is coming who is mightier than I and he will baptize you with the Holy Spirit, and with fire, and the awe-inspiring fullness of the Presence of God will come and ignite the flames of passion in your hearts and souls until you are completely engulfed in the incredible fullness of God-given Life Itself indeed!

Narrator: But when the Wild Man saw some extremely self-centered Seriously Religious People he said to them,

Wild Man: You brood of vipers! You snakes in the grass! Do you assume that this baptism will save you from God's judgment and true justice? No, I tell you! Live in a way that is in accordance with true repentance! And don't go around saying that you are the elite children of God! Why, don't you know that God can make Seriously Religious People out of dead-weight rocks if he wants to?"

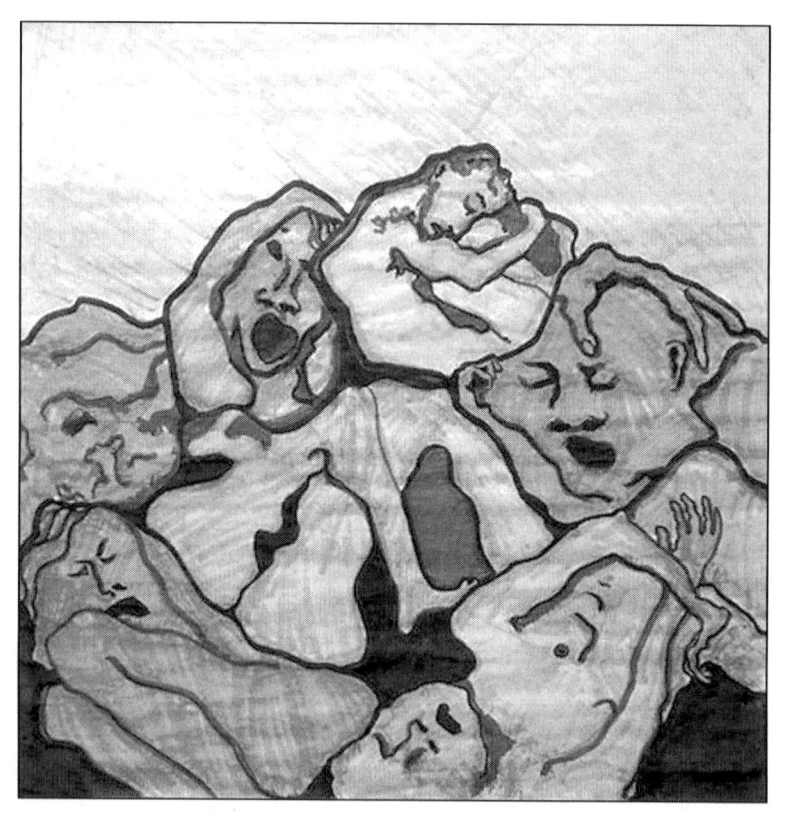

"So remember, even now, and even as I speak in this very time and place, that God is very much hard at work refining and transforming the world with God's very own consuming fire! God's axe is already laid to the root of this world! God's own winnowing fork is in God's hand! And God's own breath of fire can already be felt blowing like the wind throughout the land!

Narrator: For John the Baptist already believed that One was coming on the scene who was even more passionate and Spirit-filled than he was, and who inspired great awe in the Baptist, for John said he even felt unworthy to bend down and untie the shoes of the One who was coming up next.

Wild Man: For I came to call you all to clean up your act; to straighten-up and fly right; to make way for the Lord of Lords; to wash away all the dust and decay of your daily lives; to cleanse you of all that is unworthy of the true Lord of Life; to take away your hard-hearted cynicism; your soft-souled, self-centered, self-serving ways; your quiet despair; your debilitating lack of faith and hope in God; your misguided pursuits; your cold-hearted calculations, and all that protects you from the flame-like invasion of God's love in your life; to lead you to the place where you might become truly ready to receive the Fullness of the Presence of God in your midst.

Because on any one of these good, fine days, the Holy One of God—the King of Kings and the Lord of Lords—is going to invade, inspire, and inflame your hearts and souls beyond all expectations and beyond all belief. And he is going to fill you all the way up with the fire of his Godly and passionate love and make you see the whole world through God's own vision of true righteousness and justice. And he will impart to you his very own compassion and the power of his marvelously healing ways, and he will absolutely shower you will the many gifts of his steadfast faith and perfect obedience. Because through his humble, blessed birth, his abundant life, his suffering and sorrow, his cruel death, and finally his rising to new life again, the Fullness of the Presence of God will be yours to have and to hold forever so that you may dwell in the Lord of Life, and the Lord of Life may dwell in you, here, now, and everywhere—including all the wilderness places in lives throughout all of time and space.

Sung to the tune of "Santa Claus is Coming to Town."[5]

So you better watch out
You better stay awake
You better get ready
Now for goodness' sake
Jesus Christ is headed this way

The Son is breaking in my friend
At an hour you least expect
Don't let him catch you unprepared
Doing things he would reject

So you better not quarrel
You better not fight
You better get ready
For the coming of the light
Jesus Christ is looking our way

Just throw off the works of darkness
And put on the armor of light
God's will be done on earth at last
And the devil put to flight

So you better watch out
You better stay awake
You better get ready
Now for goodness' sake
Jesus Christ is coming our way

He is coming to steal our hearts and souls
He is coming to set things right
He is coming to create a whole new world
One that's pleasing in God's sight

So you better watch out
You better give an ear
You better get ready
His Kingdom is near
Jesus Christ is coming to stay!

Sung to the tune of "Deck the Halls with Bows of Holly."[6]

So take off the garment of your sorrow
Fa-la-la-la-la, la-la-la-la
Put-on the beauty of God's Glory
Fa-la-la-la-la, la-la-la-la
Don the robe of righteousness
Fa-la-la, la-la-la, la-la-la
Put-on the diadem of Glory
Fa-la-la-la-la, la-la-la-la

God will show all under heaven
Fa-la-la-la-la, la-la-la-la
Will reveal your glorious splendor
Fa-la-la-la-la, la-la-la-la
Give you names for evermore
Fa-la-la, la-la-la, la-la-la
Righteous Peace and Godly Glory
Fa-la-la-la-la, la-la-la-la

Prepare the way, the Lord is coming
Fa-la-la-la-la, la-la-la-la
Prepare the way, you men and women
Fa-la-la-la-la, la-la-la-la
All-flesh shall see and all together
Fa-la-la, la-la-la, la-la-la
Restoration and redemption
Fa-la-la-la-la, la-la-la-la.

Narrator: Well, as you will recall, when we left off right before all that singing, we were right in the middle of Act One, Scene Three, of one of the Author's most original works. And John the Baptist, that incredible character-actor—the One and Only Wild Man of Judea—well, he was right in the middle of preaching and acting his little heart out, and baptizing all kinds of people in the River Jordan.

John the Baptist and a Sinner appear on stage. John mimes baptizing the Sinner.

John: I baptize you with water, but one is coming who will baptize you with fire and with the Holy Spirit. He is the Great and Holy One of God and the very best actor the world has ever seen! The Star whose shoes I am not worthy to untie, let alone share the same stage!

Narrator: Now, as you can plainly see, John took both his character and his acting very, very seriously. And he was right in the middle of one of the most passionate, sincere and powerful performances of his entire career when, all of a sudden, another well-known actor, Jesus of Nazareth—a man who had traveled quite some distance to appear in John's arena—stepped out on the stage right there with him. And Jesus said to John,

Jesus: Greetings, John! This is my cue to come on stage and also be baptized by you!

Narrator: But instead of baptizing Jesus right then and there, John suddenly called a halt to the action mid-scene and tried to convince Jesus that he, Jesus, must have misread the script or that perhaps he, Jesus, had misunderstood the Author's intentions regarding this particular scene—or something to the effect that Jesus might not truly understand the full nature of his own character or of what was supposed to happen next, because John said,

John: Hey! Wait a minute! Hold up! Stop the action! This just doesn't seem quite right to me at all! So no, Cousin, I beg to differ with you at this point in the story. The way I read the script, it is **I** who am supposed to be baptized by **you**; not you who are to be baptized by me. The Author has written the Starring Role for you, Friend, and my part is supposed to get smaller so that yours can get bigger and bigger. Get it?

Narrator: But Jesus just spoke his lines gently to John, saying,

Jesus: John, look, here it is—right here on page 361—so let's just follow the script as it is written and see where it takes us, OK? For it is "truly right and fitting, and a good and joyful thing"[7] to adhere to the Author's word and to follow his cues and all of his directions.

Narrator: And then John saw the wisdom of acting his part just as Jesus had said, and the action picked-up again right where it had left off

So then John and Jesus both acted with total sincerity and complete faithfulness according to the Author's original intent.

John: I, John, baptize you, Jesus, in the name of the Creator, the Redeemer, and the Sustainer of us all. Amen. Go forth in the power of God's Holy Spirit to do the work God has given you to do!

Narrator: And Jesus said,

Jesus: With God's help! Thanks be to God!

Narrator: And then, Wow! The action really got going! The Holy Spirit of God came to Jesus like a dove making a nest in the very depths of his heart! Then the heavens just opened-up with thunderous applause as the Original Author Himself gave Jesus something like a standing ovation! For the pure voice of the Author could clearly be detected just pouring itself into this scene, saying "Bravo! Bravo! Well done, my Son! Atta boy! Excellent work, Jesus of Nazareth! You are indeed an actor after my very own heart! Your actions really speak louder than words! Three cheers for my own beloved child! I am very, very pleased indeed!"

Now all of this was so that the whole world might come to hear and to truly recognize God's Voice saying clearly in any age or time, or through the wisdom of any handy and suitable metaphor, "This is my Beloved Son in whom I am well pleased!"

[Editorial Comment: So we pay close attention to whatever he says and does!]

IV

In the Galilee Theater

JÉSUS BEN DIOS IN SPRING TRAINING

S O THEN, IMMEDIATELY AFTER the ceremony when he was officially named as the Number One draft choice in all of baseball, Jésus ben Dios was so full of ecstatic enthusiasm that he immediately went home and grabbed his spikes, bat and glove, and caught a Trial-Ways bus to an isolated, intensive-training camp out in the wilds of sunny-baked

Florida for forty days and forty nights of Devilish trials and tribulations designed to test the true commitment of any rookie ball player. While he was there, he placed himself on a severely-restricted diet and underwent a vigorous conditioning program and intensive review of the fundamentals of the game. When they broke camp, he was fit as a fiddle, absolutely on top of his game, chomping at the bit and raring to go. In other words, he was hungry in more ways than one.

And then, lo and behold, wouldn't you know it? He immediately came face to face with the temptations and adversities of the real world when the Devil said "Hey Jésus, if you really are the player you have been named to be, then go ahead, right here and now, and turn your bat and glove into a multi-million dollar, 'no cap' salary contract."

But Jésus immediately looked in his copy of the Original Spring Training Manual, written by the Creator and Founder of Baseball, and quoted Chapter 8, Section 3 of the Book of Deuteronomy, "True baseball players shall not play for a contract alone, but by the rules, and in the spirit, and for the love of the game."

So then that Devil tried taking him up to the Big Apple, right into the penthouse offices and headquarters of the President and Chief Operating Officer of the Ball Player's Brokerage Firm who said: "Well, Son, here's the deal. Forget all that nonsense about coming up with your own contract and you just put yourself in my hands, because I, myself, happen to have a lock on the entire baseball scene, from top to bottom. I'm offering Total Career Management, Boy, from contract negotiations, to publicity, to endorsements. We're talking fame, fortune and glory, Son! Rookie of the Year! Most Valuable Player! Your name in all the record books! Public Adulation! Fast cars and women, Boy! Did I mention Endorsements?! And all you've got to do, Son, is sign your name right here on the dotted line, endorsing me as your exclusive agent."

But Jésus immediately replied, "It says right here in my Spring Training Manual, Chapter 6, Section 13, on Baseball Fundamentals: 'Players owe pure devotion and exclusive loyalty to the original creator of the wonderful world of baseball, and, are intended to play only for his endorsement.'"

But the Devil answered, "Let me show you something in that precious manual of yours, Boy. See? Right here in the Book of Baseball Psalms, Psalm #91, Sub-sections 11 and 12, where it says, 'The creator of baseball will send his own special team trainers to take really good care of you and your career, and these trainers will make sure that no harm ever comes to you or takes away our place in the Baseball Hall of Fame.' So you see, Son, if you really are the gifted player that you have already been named to be, or, if you are even half as good as they say you are— you've got natural talent, Boy! You really don't need to be putting yourself through the torment of all that stupid training and senseless studies! So why don't you just ditch the diet and dump the discipline, get your nose out of that onerous manual, and just throw yourself into the game!"

But Jésus ben Dios immediately replied, "It says right here in my copy of the Training Manual, under Baseball's Fundamentals, Chapter 6, Section 16, 'Players should never intentionally dare the author and creator of the original Spring Training Manual to endorse the complete undermining of the game.'"

Needless to say, after that Devil had finally run out of fast pitches, he left Jésus all alone with his precious Training Manual, and he turned around and walked off the mound muttering to himself, "The next time the two of us meet, I'm really going to throw him a curve, and use my spitball too."

But on that very special day in baseball history, the crowd cheered all the more for Jésus ben Dios as they sang this now familiar song, sung to the tune of "Take Me Out to the Ballgame."[1]

> Keep me true to God's Spirit,
> Nail me down to the pew
> Hand me my prayer book and bulletin
> I don't care if I don't get to sin
> For it's root, root, root for the home team
> If the Devil wins, it's a shame
> For it's one, two, three strikes, he's out
> At God's old ball game!

THE GALILEE THEATER

Then, when Jésus ben Dios, who was also known as the Principle Artist, was notified that the warm-up act was just about finished, he knew he was up next and due to go on stage, momentarily, in the Galilee Theater. He immediately took his place in the wings where it was dark, got out his flashlight, and looked over his performance notes one more time— which basically were some sections of the Isaiah Script (Act Nine, Lines

1–2) he already knew by heart because it had always been the key focus of his regular, lifelong discipline of artistry.

He immediately stepped into the spotlights right on cue. "It is high time for the show to begin," he announced, graciously acknowledging the artist who had just performed by quoting from his most famous work and thereby incorporating it into his own.

Then right away he spotted a couple of understudies in the audience and asked them if they would like to join him on the stage where they could help engage the rest of the people in the audience participation part of the drama—adding the names "Simon", who was also known as Peter, and his brother, "Andrew," to the billing.

Then he saw two more would-be actors and asked them if they would also like to join those already on the stage, adding the names "James and John Ben-Zebedee" to the marquis as well.

And then he immediately began to work the whole crowd, moving all about, around and among them, going in and out of all of their favorite haunts, telling them "The time has come," and coming right up and touching "all sorts and conditions" of the people and bringing them all right up on to the stage with him.

THE GALILEE SCHOOL DISTRICT

And then, Dear Students of the Bible, it was on the very next day when the Great Teacher took his portable blackboard, his new students, and his School of Servanthood out into the Galilee School District, where he picked his next likely-candidate, Philip—ripe from the tree—and immediately signed him up for classes.

For his first assignment, Philip, who was an old school chum of Andrew's and Peter's, looked up another old school chum, Nathaniel, and told him the exciting news. "Pete and Andy and I have all signed-up with the Great Teacher for whom we have all been looking!' Peter exclaimed. "His name is Jesus and he comes from the Nazareth School District!" But Nathaniel said, "Can anything of value come from the same place as the lowly shepherd-boy, David, who was anointed King of Israel?" And Philip said, "Go fig-ure!"

Now when the Great Teacher saw Nathaniel heading their way, he called out: "Well would you look what we have here! A True Believer if I ever saw one!"

And Nathaniel quipped, "Hey, how can you describe me so perfectly when you don't even know me?" And the Great Teacher said, "I saw you hanging around and ripening under the famously-proverbial fig tree of biblical studies, hope and faith!"

And Nathaniel exclaimed, "Great Teacher! I see that you are indeed the One from Above—the True King of Israel!" But then Jesus asked him, "Are you able to see these things and truly believe this because I figured out obviously important things about you hanging around under the fig tree? Because truly, truly, I tell you that you will see even greater things if you hang around with me, Kid! Why, hang around long enough and you'll even see the heavens opened and angels ascending and descending upon the Son of Man!" So that's the way Nathaniel figured-out he wanted to live the rest of his life following Jesus!

THE ROMAN EMPIRE BOARD OF EDUCATION

Then Jesus and his new students rolled on in to the city of Capernaum where both the private, local, religious school boards and the public education programs were dominated by the virtual reality of the Roman Empire Board of Education: Rules and Regulations, colloquially called the Reberar.

And on the official day of divine rest, Jesus quickly set up a makeshift school and immediately began conducting an unauthorized class in the midst of the Sacred Halls of the St. Moses and All Prophets School. And what he was showing them was outlined right there on his portable blackboard.

Topic: Capernaum
Another District Occupied By Oppressive Roman and Religious Cult Monopoly

I.   Roman Mottos

  (a)   "Our definitions are your definitions!"

  (b)   "Live in the Real World = Our World!"

  (c)   "Keep Silent and Comply, Comply, Comply!"

  (d)   "Give In or Give Up!"

II.   Roman Belief System

(a) Power and Might Make Right!

(b) You are weak, powerless, unclean, impure, undeserving and generally worthless!

(c) We are the most powerful force in your life.

(d) We own:

    1) *Your body*

        i) We have the power of life and death.

        ii) We determine the clean and unclean.

    2) *Your mind*

        i) The only peace is Roman Peace.

        ii) Think might, and who has it, and you think right!

        iii) We approve orthodox teaching only.

    3) *Your heart and soul*

        i) Collaborate or else!

        ii) To be loyal to the system, or not to be—at all.

Jesus was teaching quite clearly, "Look! These definitions are not God's definitions! Don't buy this stuff they're selling! God wants you to live in the world but to not conform to the world! God will break the rod of the oppressor! God doesn't hate you! God hates whatever oppresses his children. God will out in the end, and you can take that to the bank! See?"

The students were thinking all kinds of things like: "This is not like any sermon I've ever heard. What kind of sermon is this? Wait a minute! He's not only interesting, he's fun to listen to! Gosh, he's a great speaker! He's great! I could listen to him forever! Is this guy another Messiah or what?! What? Huh? Just who does he think he is? Man, he's a powerful speaker! Oh Jesus! This guy is real trouble. If the Chief Priests and the Elders don't get us for hearing this, the Romans will! Yikes!"

The people were flabbergasted and speechless with amazement by the direct and commanding way Jesus laid down the law and taught them just as if he not only had a doctorate in religious studies but actually knew what he was talking about with regard to the heart and mind of God, and of the hearts and minds of men and women trying to get along in a pretty difficult and confusing world. It was not at all like scholarly teaching always citing chapter-and-verse authority and the collaborating *insider knowledge* ways of their own expert legal beagles, the scribes.

Then suddenly the amazed silence in the room was broken by the cry of a deeply disturbed person who immediately appeared in their midst: "Why in the world have you come to us here, in Capernaum, Jesus of Nazareth? Have you come to make us all deeply disturbed and crazy with fear, or to get us killed by your revolutionary teaching? I know exactly who you are and what you are up to! You are the Holy One of God! The Destroyer!"

But Jesus immediately attacked the disturbing, unclean spirit that possessed and occupied the man in much the same way that the hearts and minds of God's people had been possessed and occupied by the Romans—and also by their own religious understandings.

Jesus commanded: "Be silent and come out of him right now!" Then the unclean spirit immediately threw a violent fit and with a loud cry and a final commotion stopped plaguing the man and left him in peace.

All of the people were doubly amazed and even somewhat disturbed by this powerful demon—stration of Jesus' unorthodox command of the subject. And they all scratched their heads in confusion, saying, "What is this? God, what an uncanny demonstration! Did you see that? Huh? What? Well, that was weird!" For now they were wondering if maybe this Jesus of Nazareth might actually be on to something, or have a handle on, or possess a powerful, new, revolutionary and dangerous kind of teaching that actually has practical implications and use in the real world where people suffer and live and die. "Good grief! This guy is able to address and overthrow the unclean, oppressive spirits that possess and occupy God's people!" they cried. So Jesus of Nazareth became famous from one end of Galilee to the other.

DOCTOR JESUS

Then our itinerant Lord and Teacher just rolled on out of there and soon dropped by the house of his two newest, named, male students, Simon and Andrew, along with his other two, new, named, male students, James and John.

Now, Simon's un-named, female mother-in-law was laid-up in bed, and running a temperature, but Doctor Jesus immediately offered her a cool hand and lifted her spirits, and before they knew it, her fever had miraculously disappeared and she was busy again "taking care of business and working overtime."[2]

When the sun finally set on this official day of divine rest, the whole town lined up at Simon's door just as if it were a free, government clinic dispensing free, government medicine. Jesus himself lifted the spirits of many of those who showed up, and he eased the various sufferings under which they labored as he continued to freely demonstrate his amazing ability to dismiss the infernal monsters that so bedevil God's people. He simply would not grant those demons any license to speak, for they surely did recognize him as the true agent of the kind of Godly comfort and healing and humor they realized they could not overcome.

And then, in the still, wee hours of the night, long before the dawn of the new day, Jesus rose and slipped away far from the crowd to have a one-on-one, heart to heart talk with the Founding Father, saying, "Wow! What a Sabbath-day, Father! My new disciples are just thrilled with the response of the people here! The work is going well, don't you think? And I just know that my friends are going to try to talk me into setting up shop right here and now. They already see all kinds of possibilities for fabulous success, and they really do make a certain amount of sense, you know? But, yet Father, what would you have me do?"

"Well, Son, whatever you do, don't let them nail you down just yet. You know if you sit still too long they'll try to put you in a box. Believe me, I know because I've been there. First they'll be after you to sign some kind of a contract, and then the next thing you know they will want to turn my entire kingdom into a den of thieves with rummage sales, barbecues, huge buildings, big fund-raising campaigns, and the auctioning-off of what I myself offer absolutely freely to all of my children."

"Father, my closest friends and advisors say that if we just stay put and let the word get out along the peasant grapevine, why the crowds would know exactly where to find us and come running to us in droves! You know, like what happened with John the Baptist! And not only the disciples and their families, but the whole entire region would benefit from such a successful ministry in the name of your kingdom."

"My kingdom is meant for everybody in every place! No dues, no ticket lines, no blocks, no boundaries! It is meant to be absolutely free! And I am absolutely and completely serious about the equality of all the children in my kingdom, my Son. Remember that your treasure is where your heart is and tell my children that whoever does my will is a member of the only true family. If you let them turn you into a business, Jesus, then they are all going to truly misunderstand what my kingdom is all about!"

"I get it, Dad," Jesus replied, "for among other things, that would amount to having settled for short-term profits at the expense of the long-term gains you desire."

"That's it, My Boy! Just keep on keeping-on—and also remember: 'A rolling stone gathers no moss'[3] and 'ease on down, ease on down the road.'"[4]

But then Simon and the others who had been running the brand-new "Simon and Friends All-Service Mother-in-Law Clinic," who were the very same Simon and Friends who had just named themselves the Founding Fathers of the brand-new Devil May Care Casting Company located in the Holy Shrine of the All Serving Mother-in-law Clinic, *the place for Miracles and Healing*—formerly known simply as Simon's House. Well, Simon and his friends managed to track Jesus down in the place where he had gone to pray. And they had even managed to draw up the beginnings of a proposed new advertising campaign for the new Nazareth Hospital they now planned to open on the spot.

"We are so glad we found you Jesus," they said. "This ministry of yours is going to turn into an absolute gold mine! You were really great last night! People are just desperate to see you! This is going to be a thousand times more lucrative than Temple Tithes or Papal Annulments!"

But Jesus simply said, "No. Let's keep on keeping-on! It's time for us to 'ease on down, ease on down the road.'[5] Remember? 'A rolling stone gathers no moss!'[6] God's Kingdom is for every man, woman, and child in all places and in all times." And he went throughout all Galilee preaching in their synagogues and casting out demon after demon.

And so that is why even two thousand years later, his followers still sing to the tune of "Come on in the Room."[7]

> Jesus is our doctor
> and he stops all harmful voices;[*]

and he gives us all compassion in our hearts.
Come on in our hearts!

Jesus is our doctor
and he shuts-up all our demons;*
and his gives us all our freedom in our minds.
Come on in our minds.

Jesus is our doctor
and he turns off all commercials;*
and reminds us that our bodies are God's temple.
Come on in our bodies.

Jesus is our doctor
and he quiets all sabotaging voices
and he gives us true identity in our souls.
Come on in our souls.

THE LAKE OF THE HUMAN HEART

On one of those occasions when Jesus was teaching a very intense Bible Study at a large school near the Lake of the Human Heart, he noticed two possible, temporarily-unattended vehicles just waiting there ready to serve his purpose. He immediately commandeered one of them and asked his student Simon to help him move out a ways into the shallows of the text at hand where he continued to teach from within the vehicle he had chosen. And when he had completed this first lesson, he directed Simon: "Now move further and deeper into the text at hand, and prepare yourself for a revelation."

Simon answered, "Teacher, we have been studying this same text for a long, long time and not received even the slightest insight into it. But, yet, because it is you who are asking, Teacher, I will do as you say."

Now when they did this, they received so many profound insights and revelations; so many glimpses of glory and tastes of God's kingdom; so many experiences of healing and liberation; so much heightened awareness of God's love and deep compassion; and so very many bounteous gifts of the Spirit "from the riches of God's grace"[8] that they could hardly contain them all or express them adequately, so they called to their fellow students to come and help them try to somehow manage the abundance.

Others, too, arrived via this easily accessible vehicle selected by Jesus, but they also received so many profound insights and revelations that they were all about to be overwhelmed with the wonder and glory of it all.

Peter the Rock Himself was indeed entirely overwhelmed by the wonder and glory of God, and he spoke for all of them when he fell down at the feet of the Master Teacher and begged, "Leave me alone, Master, for I am an illiterate, inarticulate and inadequate student."

But the Master Teacher taught, "Do not be afraid, for from now on you too will be netting amazing results!"

So when they had completed this lesson, they abandoned all other schools of thought and followed only Jesus.

THE WAY-TO-BE ATTITUDES

Well, the Principle Artist turned out to be so effective with his audience participation techniques that he immediately became something of a Star, and a huge crowd of people gathered for his next performance—lining-up, three-deep, all the way around the block, and camping-out overnight on the sidewalks—just to try to get tickets to the show.

Now when the Star saw the incredible turnout, he went upstairs to his dressing room to sit down for a minute and gather his thoughts. And then, of course, here came a group of his closest fellow-actors wanting to know what he was up to up there and how he intended to handle the increasing demand.

Jesus immediately launched into an excited description of all those fans who where gathering for the concert, showering them all with his blessings in rapid-fire succession: "Oh how happy will be all those who have never been able to afford tickets before, because this show is free! Just imagine how happy will be those who weep with desire, because they will be moved to tears of joy beyond belief! How wonderful for those who are waiting patiently in the streets, for they will be out on the town tonight! How blessed are those who long to hear the truth, for they will be able to hear the truth, the whole truth, and nothing but the truth, so help me God! How magnificent for those who desire to look into the heart of the matter, whose eyes will be opened to the very heart of God! And what about those who have been warm-hearted enough to bring others here with them? I tell you that they will be called the very family of God!

And then there are all those who have been embarrassed, humiliated and gossiped-about just trying to get here. And you yourselves, who will be also be embarrassed, humiliated and gossiped-about because of your association with me and my work in this theater! Well! If this was the worldly reward of God's servants who came before you, know that you too can now discover the height, the depth and the breath of the riches of God in the midst of this world. So join with me now! For 'This is the day that the Lord has made! Let us rejoice and be glad in it!'" (Psalm 118:24).

THE HOLY SCRIPT-YOURS

Well, right after Jesus opened at the Galilee Theater and was so excited when he saw the huge crowd that gathered for his next performance that he made up his now-famous Way-to-Be Attitudes right then and there, Jesus—who knew all about the resistance that resides in the human heart—went ahead and revealed the truth about the whole Universal Theater of the Kingdom of God to his disciples, saying, "But I want you to understand that you yourselves are the main actors in this theater, and if the actors do not act, then how is there going to be any action in the play or play in the action? And you should also understand that you are the lighting and sound crew as well! How in the world is anybody going to know what's up on stage if you don't turn on the electricity and play your parts? Look! Nobody goes to all the trouble of writing a brilliant script, casting it with well-chosen actors, staging and rehearsing it, just to never get to see the lights turned up and the play performed. Now, do they? So get out there on the stage and play your parts so that the whole world can begin to see the absolute brilliance of our Beloved Author!"

"Say what? You want to know where's the script? For heaven's sake! We already have the script which has been handed down to us from on high!"

So Jesus continued to explain to his disciples, "Look, just because I'm telling you that you have enormous freedom in the playing of your parts doesn't mean that there was never any script or that the script has ever been dispensable in any way. Don't think for a minute that I have any intention of changing this script because I'm not changing this script at all—not one line, or stage direction, or lighting direction, or even one sound suggestion."

"The reason I am here, I tell you, is to play my own part exactly as written. So listen carefully: anyone who thinks this script can be discarded or rewritten to make their own part easier to perform needs to understand that to change the script is to drop entirely out of the Author's wonderful production."

"So put your whole hearts, and minds, and bodies, and souls, into the playing of your parts, and play them better than they have ever been played before so that the whole world may see and take more and more parts in this marvelous work of our Author and Our Own Creator! Throw up the curtain! Turn up the lights! Strike up the band! And let the Kingdom of Heaven go on!"

THREE RULIS DRAMATIS

And then the very next thing the Star did was to remind the actors of three of the ten most important stage directions in the script handed down from on high, which were all things they could easily recall from the Author's own "Overall Directions for True and Lively Performance."

Rulis Dramatis #6:
"The killing off of other actors is most emphatically not permitted. Period. Offenders are directly responsible and liable to the very personal judgment of our very particular and most brilliant Author."

The Star commented, "But I say to you, whoever even upstages another actor in any way is also liable to be tried in the Author's own court of professional ethics, and whoever even calls another actor by a disparaging name is liable to end up offstage, permanently, forever. Period."

"So therefore, if you want to play your own part to the best of your ability and you find that you are in any kind of conflict with another actor, then you need to go and work it out before you make your grand entrance on the stage. Period."

Rulis Dramatis #7:
"The using of other actors for your own selfish purposes is not permitted under any circumstances. Period."

"Regarding this rule of professional conduct," the Star then said, "I want you to realize that even considering the possibility of using another actor for your own gain is equally exploitative and subject to the same judgment. Period. So, don't you see how it would be better for you to let go of a few of your own special talents than it would for you to exploit another actor and then end up offstage, out of the way, out of the play, and banished forever?"

Rulis Dramatis #8:
"Never deliver false lines in the name of the Author. Period."
"But I say to you: Do not deliver false lines at all, and not in the name of anything. Period. And, for that matter, do not attempt to circumvent the Author by delivering false lines in the name of *Creation*, for creation is of the exclusive and sole domain of the Author who holds the copyright. And do not attempt to circumvent the Author by delivering false lines in the name of *A Person who is Down to Earth*, for earth is but one of the many relatively smaller things created by our Author for our Author's own pleasure. And neither should you attempt to circumvent the Author by delivering false lines in the name of *The Bible* or *By All that is Sacred*, nor by any of the people or places you hold most dear, for these are but a few of the scenes among the many equally brilliant scenes upon which our Author's great reputation is grounded. Oh, and certainly not by the length, or the power, or the integrity of your own acting career because you yourself, and your role, were created by our Author to shine forth our Author's own glorious light each and every moment of your life, in truth and without exception."

Then he summed it all up in one easy-to-recall stage direction: "Simply deliver each and every one of your lines straight from the heart, without subterfuge or deception: "Yes" meaning "Yes" and "No" meaning "No," just as our beloved Author has written.

COMMENTARY ON THE SCRIPT OF THE COMPETITION

Then, after introducing his own *Handbook for Actors*, Jesus began to discuss with his disciples another guidebook for actors which had been published by the competition, entitled *A Guidebook for Practical Acting*. "Now that may be time-tested, excellent, time-honored, common sense advice for practical acting, but what I want you to understand that such advice totally misses the point of what our Producer really wants us to do when faced with bad acting."

Then he went on to draw them some pictures of the kind of acting our Producer would like to see for a change. For example, when another actor hauls off and slaps you, which is definitely a case of bad acting, then our Producer would like to see you offer to let that actor take their best shot at you as well. Or, should another actor slap you with a law-suit causing you to lose your shirt—which also constitutes bad taste as well as bad acting—our Producer would like to see you offer to give that actor not only your shirt, but your coat as well. Or, should a bad actor force you to play in a bad scene against your will, don't play that scene badly, because our Producer really enjoys seeing good acting, and good acting always goes an extra mile.

Then he summarized all this by saying, "The key to good acting is open-hearted and open-handed generosity to all."

Jesus turned to the second page of the *Guidebook for Practical Acting* which had been published by the competition, to read the next piece of tempting practical advice: "Stick to your own kind and hate everyone else," upon which he also commented, saying: "This is truly practical advice if you are determined only to be an extra in the cast, but pleasing our Producer requires much better acting than that! So if you would like your performance to stand out in honor of our Producer, then your acting must reflect and expose the open-hearted, open-handed, passionate and absolute generosity of our Author! Therefore, I say to you all: be ye good actors. Act with passionate love just as our Producer loves passionately. Always be kind just as our Producer is kind. Give generously to all without regard to the worthiness of those who receive, just like our Producer, and just as our Producer differs greatly from the competition, dare to act differently yourselves."

THE ROCK OR SAND SERMON

Then Jesus preached a good, solid and light-hearted little sermon with a tricky little punch line based entirely upon the Word of God and composed of these exact few words: "Not everyone who hears or reads words naming me as the Lord of Life will immediately experience abundant life in God, except for those who pay close attention and listen very, very carefully to discern what deep delight God desires for them. For many will only bear the words 'Lord of Life' as a badge to be worn or a boast to be made about their own so-called religious achievements, but the true Lord of Life has nothing at all to do with such an evil distortion of God's truth."

"Everyone who hears or reads these words set before you right now, and who pays close attention, and listens very, very carefully to discern what delight God truly desires for you right now is like a preacher who built his sermon upon a firm foundation, for when the cold, shocked silence fell over the congregation and the winds of criticism came to tear that sermon apart, that sermon was truly alive and stood the test because it was composed entirely of rock solid stuff."

"But everyone who hears or reads these words and does not listen carefully to discern what delight God truly desires for you right now is like a foolish preacher who built his sermon upon some very shaky ground indeed; for when the cold, shocked silence fell over the congregation, and the winds of criticism came to tear that sermon apart, that sermon did, indeed, crash and burn—and oh how great was the sound of the thud when it hit the ground!"

INVIGORATING THE PARALYZED AT HOME

Well, a couple of days after Jesus returned to Capernaum, the word "Yes" was immediately broadcast over the local airwaves—meaning that the Son of Man himself was truly at home.

But, Oh no! Look! It was so unbearably crowded there around the door and around Jesus that the people could hardly move or breathe, let alone hope to get close enough to hear whatever word he was speaking to them. But listen-up really carefully to this because it is still an inside secret that the word that Jesus was speaking to them that day was "Yes!"

Then they came, whoever they were, and from where-ever they called home in the world, to encounter Jesus. And they brought with them one who was paralyzed, immobile, and unable to act. But when they found that no matter how hard they tried, they simply couldn't get close to him by any of the usual and very popular approaches, they tried something entirely different.

Starting from the top, piece by piece, they peeled off layer after layer of concealment as they literally took the roof off the box they had him in. They dug their way down, down, down and through, through, through until they were very close to the very heart of the word of God that Jesus was actively speaking right then and there—and is also still speaking right here and now—until they finally made a tangible breakthrough and then carefully lowered the bed of the paralyzed right on down into the living, beating heart of the matter at hand—much as one might lower a bucket into a well of living water, or a child into the waters of Baptism, or a coffin into the grave, or the body of a beloved child into the arms of God.

When Jesus saw such wonderful, active, persistent, caring faith, he spoke directly to the heart of the paralysis saying clearly, "Yes child! Welcome home!"

Meanwhile, back in the box, some very seriously-religious legal beagles who had been just sitting around and watching all of this activity—as rigid and stiff as boards they were, if you can relate—well, they were seriously disturbed by Jesus' words, and they were saying in their heart of hearts, "Oh No! No! No! God Forbid! He can't get away with speaking simple words of "Yes" and forgiveness to empower people! Why that's an affront to everything we stand for! Why he's even mocking our God who makes the rules and is the only one who gets to say who among us gets to get away with breaking them!"

But Jesus knew in his heart what was going on in their hearts, and so he said directly to them, "Why do you question in your hearts? Are ye of such little faith? Which is easier to say to anyone who is immobilized, 'Yes, your sins are forgiven' or 'Yes, get up off of your beds of anxiety and fear and walk'?" And then, so that you also may understand that regular human beings are indeed empowered by God to forgive sins, Jesus turned and said to the congregation, "Yes, you! Get up off of your beds of anxiety and fear, and go serve the Lord."

And lo and behold, Yes! Right then and there, before their very eyes, the formerly-paralyzed immediately got up from the bed and went out walking to love and serve the Lord for all to see and glorify! And that, Dear Hearts, is why we utter our Amen through our empowering Jesus, to the glory of God. Amen.

DR. JESUS EATS WITH PATIENTS AND ORDERLIES

One time while Dr. Jesus was making his rounds, he noticed a man called Matthew, who was nicknamed "The Gift of God," sitting at the Exorbitant Amounts Accounts Payable Office (EAAPO) of the "This is For Your Own Good" (TIFYOG) People's Clinic. Then Dr. Jesus called to the man, saying, "Follow me." The man jumped-up and followed Dr. Jesus, and while Dr. Jesus sat down at a table in the Patients' Cafeteria, many, many clinic patients, and not a few orderlies, came and sat down with Dr. Jesus and his Med-Student Interns.

Now, when the TIFYOG Clinic Administrators saw the goings-on down in the heart of the Patients' Cafeteria, they called Jesus' disciples up to the Administration offices and asked the disciples to explain, if they could, "Why does your Dr. Jesus fraternize with the really sick people and the dis-orderlies down in the Patients' Cafeteria instead of eating up in the Professional Healers' Club with us?"

But when Dr. Jesus heard about the meeting behind closed doors up in the Administration offices, he took out his prescription tablet and said to his disciples as he wrote: "Those who already Know-It-All Upstairs have no need of a teacher, but for those of you who realize that you still have a thing or two to learn in this life, it is for you for whom this Teacher is prescribed. And so, for your own good, this is your first lesson and the very best medicine for what ails you. So go look it up, live it out, and learn what this means: 'I desire steadfast love [mercy] and not sacrifice,' (Hosea 6:6) and then you will be able to answer the question about why I came—not to heal the healthy, wealthy and wise—but to embody, in the flesh, God's deep, abiding and healing bond with the sick and the lowly down in the heart of the Patients' Cafeteria where I do so dearly love to be."

COMPUTER-SAVVY BISHOP JESUS

Now on another day, when Dr. Jesus, who was also affectionately known as Bishop Jesus, was surfing the Net, he ran across a man called Levi who was at his computer collecting and grading coins for the Organized Bargaining with Corruption Organizations (OBCO). Jesus e-mailed him and told him to follow him on the net into a Denominational chat room. Then Levi left his site at the OBCO and followed Jesus into a certain Denominational chat room with who-knows-how-many-other socially-unacceptable-types, laity and clergy alike.

Now, when the Web Police saw this, they sent a Virus Alert to the clergy of the area, saying, "Your bishop is meeting indiscriminately in chat rooms with coin collectors and sinners and may contract a malicious virus that will reformat your hard drives and destroy everything in your computers. Recommend blocking all further access to him!"

But when Bishop Jesus read their e-mail he said, "Those who have been completely immunized against God have no need for a bishop. Go and learn what this means, 'I desire contagion, not quarantine.' Practice direct contact and inclusion, not rejection and exclusion, for I have come to feed a virus, not starve it."

Because the truth of the matter is that Jesus himself was "The Worm, and no man," (Psalm 22:6a) who was carrying a virus, "who was scorned by all and despised by the people," (Psalm 22:6b) and who was the primary carrier of the most contagious, communicable and socially unacceptable virus known to mankind, known as the HSV—which stands for the Holy Spirit Virus as it might appear on a sign outside of each and every church in the area: "Warning! Virus Alert! Site Contaminated by HSV! Highly Contagious! Warning! Dangerous Chat Rooms Inside! Spreads by Direct Human Contact! Enter at Your Own Risk! HSV cannot be blocked, filtered, or removed! Everyone really is welcome here! Yes! This Means You!"

CHEF JESUS' CULINARY MAGIC SHOW

Naturally knowing how hungry all human beings are, Jesus wore his Master Chef hat as he traveled to all the cities, towns and villages in the region teaching cooking classes in all the cafés and restaurants, feeding people with the very fine cuisine he prepared for God's Reality Show, *God's Culinary Magic* (GCM), and bringing good health and well-being wherever he encountered indigestion, food poisoning, eating disorders or malnutrition of any kind.

When he saw the huge crowds at all of the restaurants, he was deeply moved with loving compassion because they were all so stressed-out and clueless, like a whole flock of hungry but helpless so-called adults who didn't know how to boil water or scramble an egg. So he said to his wait-staff, "The restaurants are overflowing with people who are hungry and more than ready to eat, but there are precious few cooks in the kitchen. You better pray for God to stir-up some more folks to roll up their sleeves and get to work in the kitchen!"

Then Chef Jesus called his wait-staff together and demanded that they also become Chefs in God's Great Reality Show, and encouraged them in their own God-given abilities to overcome any obstacles they might encounter, and to create and produce meals that could not only fill the belly but also cure the soul—which was, indeed, the abiding Magic of God's Reality Program.

Now, the names of The Original Cooking Teams who first appeared on God's Culinary Magic Show were: the Team of Simon, who became very famous as Chef Peter, and his brother Andrew; Team James and John, the two sons of Zebedee; the team of Philip and Bartholomew; and then there were also Chef Thomas and Chef Matthew, who was formerly with the OBCO; Team James Ben Alphaeus and Thaddeus; and finally, the Team of Simon, the Cananaean Chef, and Judas Iscariot, who, sadly, ended-up betraying the heart and soul of Culinary Magic.

But, before they appeared as contestants on the program, Chef Jesus gave each one of the teams some pertinent tips and useful household hints.

1. You don't have to go to Paris or New York, or even the Great Mid-American School of Culinary Arts, in order to cook. There are plenty of hungry people right in your very own neighborhoods!

2. When you tell people about God's Culinary Magic, always remember to say, "Look! God's Magic is always available—handy—right at your fingertips— in your very own kitchens!"

3. Just go ahead and cook-up some magic! Serve meals that refresh and revive the nauseated, the fed-up, and the weary. Bring out food that makes people want to live again! Food that comforts and heals! And shred and cast out all your recipes that trouble and bedevil the human soul!

4. Always remember this key ingredient: Just as you have freely eaten from God's table, don't charge anybody anything to eat from yours!

5. You really don't need to worry about whether or not you yourselves are going to get anything to eat, or even about what to wear, for that matter, because your work is in a kitchen, for heaven's sake! So you can just leave all of your credit cards, your Cream-of-the-Crop Cookware, your Fancy-Schmancy Rotisseries and your formal attire at home. You can just pick up your GCM uniform and apron each day from the continuously-refurbished mountain next to the door where you come in.

6. But there's also no need to be completely naive about reality. Wherever you go, look for the people who are hungry enough to want to learn how to cook, and then stay with them and create culinary magic until it's time to move on. When you enter a restaurant, assume that everyone there is hungry and worthy of being fed by God's Culinary Magic. If people are hungry and receptive, let your enthusiasm for Culinary Magic be a blessing and delight, but if people are not receptive, don't let that be a stumbling block to you. Just let God's Culinary Magic continue to feed and bless you as it always has and as it always will.

Now, if anyone out-and-out rejects you, my advice simply boils down to this: Shake the flour off of your apron, say "Bon Appetit!" and keep on cooking. Look! The soup is on their heads! For when all is said and done, and the day comes when the goose is finally cooked, even your worst kitchen disasters with God's Culinary Magic will taste far, far better than the fare that they are going to eternally clamor to eat in that old fox's network over in Sheol's Kitchen!

JESUS' SCHOOL OF SERVANTHOOD

Also that very same summer, Jesus opened his famous School of Servanthood using the following course outline:

Freedom and Equality 101 has been carefully crafted and designed to give students of God's Freedom Movement a more-than-adequate grounding in the one true and abiding source of liberation, inspiration and ongoing strength for service.

Session I: Structural Inequality and the Social Order

Students will examine the nature and dynamics of power and systems of inequality inherent in the many dominant/subordinate relationships supported by the social order of the day. Students will explore what it means to be free in the context of God's Freedom Movement. A critique of all ideas involving any idea of replacing of current dominate/subordinate relationships with a new set of dominant/subordinate relationships will be thoroughly undertaken. In God's Freedom Movement, inequality should not be replaced with a new system of inequality. This session is offered to give students a deeper understanding, lively appreciation and firm foundation in God's Great Love of Justice for all people.

Session II: Preparing for Criticism of God's Freedom Movement

Students will gain insight into the nature and tactics of those who are opposed to God's Freedom Movement. Of primary interest will be the insidious way the opposition resorts to name-calling and to wrongly associating the work of God with Black Magic and/or the work of the Evil One. Students will be made aware of the likely consequences of their own association with God's Freedom Movement and its founder, Jesus, as it will be said of you that you are in league with the Devil!

Session III: Response to Criticism of God's Freedom Movement

A thorough examination of God's Power, Justice and Love will reveal the true nature of absolute freedom in God's creation. Students will gain an understanding of the importance of taking the lessons of the classroom out on the streets, and to speak out boldly on behalf of all God's children who secretly hope to see and hear God's Freedom and Justice declared on the earth. Except with regard to birthdays and celebrations, secrets are a powerful tool of the Enemy. This session will discuss the consequences of forming alliances with the Enemy.

Session IV: Proper Grounding in God's Own Goodness

This session will offer a close inspection of God's own creation all around us. Special focus will be upon a couple of God's most beautiful and yet quite common creatures as they exist in relationship to God's enormous power to love. The Instructor will make his sweet "Two Little Sparrows" illustration available for all to see. This session will focus attention upon all of humankind in relationship to God's enormous power and love for creation. A thorough examination of God's careful system of accounting will be offered as a very special visual presentation by the Instructor.

Session V: Loyalty and Recognition in God's Freedom Movement

In this final session, students are called to practice making referrals to others. Those who freely and favorably refer their instructor to other perspective students will discover that they will receive equally good references from their instructor. Students who exercise their freedom to make no referrals to the program risk receiving no referrals in their instructor's final report to the Almighty Administration.

SHREDDING ILLUSIONS OF DOMESTIC TRANQUILITY

Then suddenly and swiftly, our Hero Jesus came out with a very, very sharp critique of the status quo, displaying his infamous, rapier wit when he said: "Don't think I came to bring peace, because I did not come here to bring peace, but to shred the status quo to pieces! Everything that oppresses the children of God I will cut with the sword in my hand in order to break through our illusions of domestic tranquility and bliss and to shatter the idolatry of the worship of the family in order to reveal the true Family of God; to liberate God's children from all the dehumanizing definitions that are imposed upon them, and to make them free to become sisters and brothers in arms against prejudice and injustice—for God simply cannot ever be domesticated or rendered impotent."

Or, as some others reported it elsewhere, Kindergarten Art Teacher Jesus said, "Little Children, no, no, Dear Ones. Do not think that I have brought glue to class today. No, I did not bring glue today. But look here! See! I have brought scissors because I am here to cut up this false, fairytale picture of domestic bliss obviously painted by a careless artist. See, I am cutting right here between this figure of a man and what appears to be his father; and here, between this daughter against what looks to be her mother; and here, between a daughter-in-law and mother-in-law, and between all the figures in this idealized family. Look, so you can see exactly what is revealed behind! Look! Here is a picture worthy of the God and Artist of Our Salvation! Here is God's Family—God's new creation! Those who want to preserve an insular, fairytale picture of their family will surely lose it! But those who are disillusioned with the fairytales because of me and my ministry will most assuredly find true life in abundance with and through and in me—participating in my creative, redeeming work as brothers and sisters who are first and foremost children of God!"

JOHN THE JOURNALIST

Meanwhile, poor old John the Baptist, that Wild Man of Judea, had been caged-up like a wild animal because his hard-hitting style of investigative reporting had caused the authorities, and especially the king, a great deal of trouble. They locked him away in a place where he could no longer see or hear anything about what was happening in the world around him where he might continue to get the scoop on the action and possibly even work his way down to the heart of the matter. But what the authorities really underestimated was the extent of John's power and influence because John had a number of top-notch and devoted stringers on his staff who were willing to go the extra mile to anywhere and dig through anything required in order to extend his powers of perception beyond the walls of his prison cell. So when John heard the buzz about the big story surrounding his cousin, he immediately dispatched his crew to the scene and, of course, told them to get to the heart of the matter right away.

"Are you the one about whom it is written?" they asked Jesus, using John's famous, direct and tough-minded approach to getting at the truth, "or shall we keep up the investigation?" But Jesus simply stretched out his arms and said: "Go ahead and have a good look around. Check my files. Pull up the rug if you need to. Rummage around all you want, but while you check around to your hearts' content, don't forget to also check around the contents of your hearts as well," he suggested.

When they were done looking, Jesus told them to report back to John and to tell him everything they had seen and heard, using these exact words from a note from Isaiah to Jesus that they had discovered in their search: "The blind receive their sight, the lame walk, the lepers are cleansed, the deaf hear, the dead are raised, the poor have good news brought to them, and blessed is anyone who takes no offense at me" (Matt 11:4–5; Isa 35:5–6).

Then Jesus turned his immediate attention to the people around him and asked them a direct question, "So then, what do all of you think about my old friend, John? Why did you all flock out to see him when he was in town? Did you show up to see a man dressed in fancy clothes? People wearing fancy clothes live in big, fancy castles!"

"Did you think you might see a fragile paper doll or a fake cardboard cutout just blowing in the wind? Did you hope to catch a glimpse of a real, live prophet? Because, you see, I have a great deal of respect for that Old Buzzard, John, and I want you to understand that he really was the greatest journalist who ever lived—a man who definitely read the book and certainly knew his sources. But I tell you that although he really was all of that, and more—he really was a prophet! Nevertheless, Dear People, get this! As great as John was in the world of Journalism and Prophets and Kings, yet the value of such fame is insignificant when compared to the least of you, My Beloved Children, who, even in the midst of whatever oppresses and imprisons you and maybe even makes it difficult for you to read the bible let alone know the sources—yet you nevertheless openly receive the Kingdom of God right where you are and somehow manage to see me and hear me and receive me with joy! For such joy, my Friends, truly lies at the very heart of the matter!"

JESUS' JOKES ARE EASY

A few days later, Jesus showed his friends his special Thank You Note to God which read, "Dear Daddy, King of the Universe, thank you very much for choosing to speak in the wonderfully enlightening language and magical ways of children. Love, Jesus."

Then he said to them, "You see that Daddy has already given me everything I need in the world, don't you? Why nobody knows me inside-out the way he does! And nobody really knows him the way I do, either, except for everybody I show this picture to, though. See everybody? Here it is!"

Then he handed each one of them this invitation to his party at his father's house, which reads,

> Come over and play with me, all of you who are so high-strung and uptight, and I will show you a very good time! Share in my

marvelous imagination and learn from me the way to play! For I am truly a light-hearted child of God and we can play together to our hearts' content! See? Look right here! My jokes are easy and my bird-in-hand is de-light! Sure hope to see you there! The more the merrier! Love, Jesus

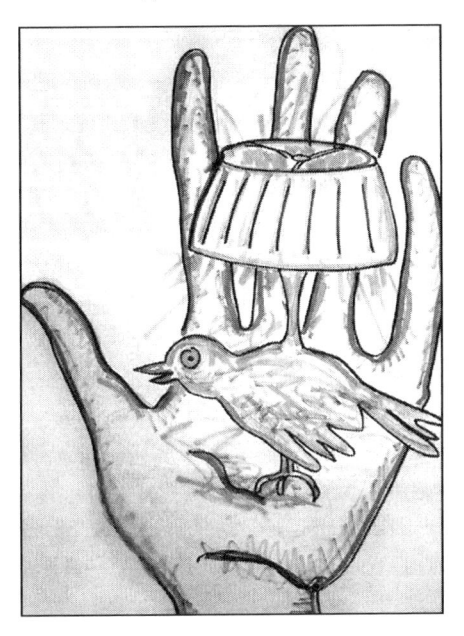

THE "BREAD OF GOD'S PRESENCE" BREAD COMPANY

Now it was on that most glorious and holy day of days, The Feast of God's Presence Freely Provided for All of Our Hungers and Needs So We Can Rest-Assured Day, when the General Manager and Head Chef of the "Bread of God's Presence" (BGP) Bread Company was out in the field with his little brigade of bread bakers and they were gleefully lopping-off the heads of the little stalks of grain that were standing row after row in the sun, arrayed like a miniature army who was ready, willing and able to be transformed into delicious food for God's hungry people. Suddenly a bunch of particularly un-gleeful drill sergeants from the parent company, the King David "Bread for My People" (BMP) Bread Company, demanded an explanation of their mission, "What do you grunts think you're doing out here toiling away in the hot sun working on overtime when you know perfectly well that there is a strict Company Policy against it? Or don't you even bother to read the Company Manual anymore?"

Jesus simply responded by looking-up and offering them this tantalizing and delicious little bit of food for thought: "Have you, Sirs, never read *The Glorious History of the King David "Bread for My People" Bread Company*? Don't you remember when our renowned and most glorious hero, David, was famished and very much in need and it was a matter of great urgency, how he just marched into one of the Company's Field Headquarters and commandeered enough food to feed a small army of God's lowly enlisted personnel with the Bread of God's Presence even though there was a strict Company Policy stating that the Bread of God's Presence was for the sole, private and privileged use of the Officers up in the Officers' Club—and that he also claimed the sword of Goliath, that giant enemy of the Company whom he had single-handedly felled in battle?"

Then Jesus immediately served-up to those fellows this delicious little summary of that whole story to chew on: "Human need was not created to satisfy the hunger of God; but The Bread of God's Presence was created to satisfy human need so that you all might come to trust in God's Presence and to truly rest-assured, especially on this most holy and son-drenched day, that it really is the most ordinary of all God's soldiers who are truly meant to feast at the very head of God's table!"

THE SERMON ON THE LEVEL

Then Jesus took his stand on a place that was absolutely level with the human condition where he was completely surrounded by the huge crowd of his followers and a great multitude of humanity from all over the world. The entire crowd—and indeed, the entire world—was drawn to that level place where he stood so surrounded and embedded in the human condition where they were packed tight, straining, and pressing in on him to hear his words and to feel him heal their disease, and where, in fact, a great many deeply troubled spirits found themselves deeply relieved—for the whole crowd longed to touch and be touched by him and his words because of the healing power that emanated from him and enveloped them.

As he stood there on that level place, Jesus leveled his eyes and looked directly at those who would learn from him as he leveled with them about his own human experience, saying "Oh how blessed am I to have been born into the poverty of human flesh! Mine is the Kingdom of God right here on earth! Oh how very blessed am I to know the deep hungers and thirsts of the human condition, for I am full to overflowing! Oh how very blessed am I to be able to weep with abandon for myself and others, for I know then that I can also truly rejoice and celebrate and laugh with abandon as well! Oh how very blessed am I to receive the hatred, the fear, and the rejection the world shows to anyone who recognizes their common humanity as children of God and chooses to live on the level and truly treat themselves and all others as equals. I rejoice in this day and I feel like dancing! My reward is so great! I am in the company of all those through whom God has spoken before! But, oh how sad it is for those who have the wherewithal to distance, insulate, and isolate themselves from the human condition, for they receive only the cold comfort of their own private consolation prizes. Oh how sad it is for those who are entirely full of themselves, for they have truly put themselves on a starvation diet. Oh how sad it is for those who are gleeful inside when they get ahead of others, for they have succeeded at setting themselves above and apart from their common humanity, and they will also mourn and weep alone. And how sad it is for those who receive the world's applause, for the world has always saved its applause for those who are not on the level."

THE "JUST A FEW GOOD MEN" MEN'S CLUB

And then, because he was so impressed with Jesus' ability to attract a crowd, that month's host of the Just A Few Good Men Club (JAFGM) Men's Club immediately invited him to attend their private dinner meeting to see if he was a worthy candidate for membership. Jesus went into the clubhouse and took the place of honor, or trap, that they had set for him.

But look! When a certain woman from Sin City discovered where Jesus could be found, she brought her whole self, her body and soul, and everything precious she had to offer, and she laid them all right at his feet. With her tears, she washed all the dirt away, and with her crowning glory, she wiped his feet dry. With her lips she expressed her deepest and most intimate admiration of him, repeatedly kissing one foot, and then the other, as if she couldn't make up her mind which one was more beautiful or preached the most peace. And then in an extravagant gesture, she took his feet in her hands and anointed them both with her most precious and healing balm.

Now, in the supposed privacy of his dirty little mind, our host of the JAFGM Men's Club thought to himself: "You know, if this Jesus were a good candidate for membership in the JAFGM Men's Club, he would have a decent instinct about this woman and he would know, as I certainly do know, exactly what is going on inside that pretty little head of hers—and he would know exactly what sort of a woman she is, and that she is touching him like this in order to lure him into her lurid little life—the details of which I can only just imagine, and imagine, and imagine, and imagine. . ."

But Jesus, knowing exactly what was going on inside *Simon's* head, addressed him directly, saying, "Simon, I have something to say to you." So Simon said, "OK, *Teacher*, is it? Then teach me something."

Then Jesus gave the man a simple story problem to solve. "A man had two men who owed him money. One owed him five hundred dollars and the other owed him fifty dollars. When neither of them could pay, he decided to let them both off the hook. Now which one, do you think, will feel the most obligated to him?"

Simon hemmed and hawed and mumbled and questioned, "Uh, well, umm, is this a trick question? I guess, I mean, I suppose, it might probably be the one who owed him the most money in the first place?" And Jesus exclaimed, "Yes! You are right! You've figured the math out correctly!"

Then Jesus turned his whole body to the woman who was so very near to him and who had touched him so completely, as he said to Simon, "Simon, do you not see this woman; this child of God? I came to your clubhouse and you gave me no water to refresh me, yet she has washed my weariness away with her tears of grief and joy and dried them with her own crowning glory. You did not greet me with any sign of welcoming, and yet she has not stopped kissing and touching me to the core of my being ever since I arrived. And you certainly did not anoint my head with oil. Yet she has made me feel good all over, from the bottom of my feet to the top of my head. Therefore I tell you, because she has extended hospitality and loved so extravagantly, her sins, which are many, are all very easily forgiven. Piece of cake! But he who is stingy and miserly in love is actually more difficult to forgive, I must say." And then Jesus said to the woman, "Woman, your sins are forgiven!"

Then the members of the JAFGM Men's Club grumbled among themselves, "What sort of a man does he think he is going around as if he was in a position to simply wave his hand and forgive the sins of others?" But Jesus just turned his whole body to the woman and said with ease, "Dear woman, your extravagant love is your saving grace. Go in peace."

ST. PIOUS IN THE SUBURBS

Then an incredibly similar scene took place when the Chair of the St. Pious in the Suburbs Search Committee invited Jesus to a private dinner meeting to see if he was a worthy candidate to become their new priest and pastor. Jesus himself came to the dinner and sat at the place that they had set up for the interview

A woman from a downtown massage parlor heard that Jesus could be found at St. Pious in the Burbs so she immediately hopped on a bus and came out to the church where she spread everything precious she had to offer right at his feet. With her tears and her weeping she bathed his tired and aching feet, and with her hair she dried them. With her lips she began kissing his feet and with her hands she massaged and anointed them with her most precious, fragrant, healing oils.

Meanwhile, in the supposed privacy of his sordid little mind, the Chair of the Call Committee thought to himself: "You know, if this Jesus were a decent candidate for the Pastor of St. Pious, he would know what sort of a woman this is, and see what she is really after, and that she is touching him like this to lure him deep into her parlor of sin and immorality, the details of which I can only just imagine and imagine, and imagine, and imagine, *ad infinitum*."

But Jesus, knowing what was going on inside of the Chairman's head, addressed him by name, saying, "Simon, I have a question for you." Simon said, "Sure Pastor. OK, shoot!"

Then Jesus said, "In another church with which I am familiar, there was once a wealthy parishioner who knew two men who owed him money. One owed him ten thousand dollars and the other owed him ten dollars. When neither of them could pay, he graciously decided to let them both off the hook. Now which one, do you think, will love him the most?"

Simon hemmed and hawed a bit, unsure if the obvious was really the right answer, and then finally he tentatively offered, "Well, I guess it would be the one who owed him the most money in the first place." And Jesus said, "Yes! You are right! That's exactly the way the world and the numbers usually work!"

But then Jesus turned to the woman who was still touching him as he talked to Simon, "Simon, do you even see this visitor here—this child of God? I journeyed to get to your church and you did not greet me with any real warmth. You didn't so much as offer me a glass of water before the interview, yet she has flooded me with her tears and truly washed my weariness away. You did not treat me with any special kindness or hospitality, and yet she has massaged my feet and not stopped touching my heart ever since I arrived. And you most assuredly did not anoint or regard me as a genuine candidate to do ministry here in your midst. Yet she has made me feel treasured and cherished from the top of my head to the tip of my toes. Therefore I tell you, because she has loved so freely, her many sins are easily forgiven; but he who is stingy with love is really hard to forgive." Then Jesus said to the woman, "Woman, your many sins are all exceedingly easy to forgive!"

Now, the members of the Call Committee grumbled among themselves, "What kind of candidate for pastor is this who comes in here freely handing out forgiveness for sins without any sense of propriety or discrimination? But Jesus just said to her, "Dear woman, your love is your saving grace. Continue on your journey in peace."

THE INCREDIBLE SKULK

Then Jesus and his little band of Disciples journey on until they arrive in the Territory of the Gerasenes, which the story makes a point of telling us is opposite to Galilee. And it certainly is a story full of many opposites, drawn out and writ large enough to engage us fully in the cosmic encounter going on right in the middle of it.

For the Man with whom Jesus immediately engages when he first steps foot into this Strange Territory is first identified as a Citizen of an Important Roman City within a whole complex of Cities Occupied by Romans—described a City Dweller, or, if you will, as a City Slicker. But in so many ways he is just the opposite of what we might expect to see in such a City Slicker, because he is not suited-up in high fashion Roman armor or even new-fangled armorwearunder from the Roman Coliseum Gift Shop, or expensive Italian sandals, or outfitted with Roman shields and weapons and defenses, but is, instead, running around stark naked and completely exposed to the elements. And it is also pointed out that he doesn't live or move or even possess his own being in a house, or a Roman palace or penthouse, or a Decapolis condominium, or apartment, or even a hut in one of the filthy Roman, city slums. For this Man lives, instead, in a city of tombs and catacombs with only the sky to shelter him, and "no place to lay his head" (Luke 9:58) except on a gravestone— which is just about as unprotected as a person can possibly be.

Then, at the very moment when he first senses or catches a glimpse of Jesus' Presence suddenly appearing right there in and on his "Own Private Stomping Ground," well, the Man immediately crumbles and collapses right there at Jesus' feet, screaming like a baby and squealing like a whole sty full of terrified little pigs, begging Jesus "Don't torture me, Jesus!" and "Don't torment me, Jesus!" as if torture/torment was something Our Lord—who everybody knows wouldn't hurt a flea—would ever, ever do to another human being!

But not only that, and even more provocatively, this Man is crying out to Our Lord by his rightful name and title, "Jesus, Son of the Most High God!" And all because, as we now suddenly notice, and perhaps even remember from our own experience, the mere presence of Our Lord, from the very second he first enters this realm of human experience, has already challenged and commanded the incredibly Arrogant Spirit to come out of the Man, and to leave him in peace, because, you should also realize, the Arrogant Spirit had been in the Man for such a long, long time that it had completely overtaken every square inch of him to the point where the Man himself fully embodied the very Spirit of Arrogance Stomping-Around in Human Form, but whose Incredibly Arrogant Spirit, quite apparently, didn't frighten or intimate Our Lord in the least. For although other people had often tried to restrain the Man's arrogance, he had always been able to push his way right past and through anybody and anything in his way in order to achieve his ultimate goal of skulking and stomping around in the graveyard, which is why some people called him "The Incredible Skulk."

Now, when Jesus saw the Man, he said to him, "But what do you call yourself?" Then the Man got all the more puffed-up and answered, "I am so many and so powerful that my name is ERL, for the Entire Roman Legion, and—believe you me—we are every bit as powerful as you imagine us to be!" Of course he said that because it was true that many Arrogant Spirits spoke right through his voice—and because those Arrogant Spirits were quite correctly sensing a real threat to their power and sway over the Man. So they all ganged-up and started earnestly begging of Jesus, "Please don't lift your little finger and simply dismiss us straight to the abyss for all our efforts at completely permanently-and-eternally controlling the Man!" And they were squealing: "Please don't *dismiss-and-abyss us*, Good Lord!"

Now, of course, the Abyss was always nearby and quite handy, and there were many, many ways to get there if one was truly passionate and determined-enough about it, but there was also a handy herd of gluttonous little pigs and arrogant little devils nearby who had just this very instant been turned into a whole flock of free-floating anxieties and who would suffice for current purposes, but who still thought that they were so incredibly clever that they now summoned all of their energies together and came up with a brilliant little plan to trick Jesus. They strongly suggested that Jesus should just go ahead and act like the kind and gentle Lord he was cracked-up to be—and reveal himself as a loving example of a Loving God who wouldn't hurt a flea—let alone "helpless little demons," as they now described themselves—and therefore he should kindly allow them to continue to retain their power embodied in a herd of pigs instead—who, as everyone in Jesus' time knew, are dirty and filthy and only fit for the Abyss anyway.

So, of course, since Jesus was indeed kind and gentle, and sometimes even our quite-humorous Lord, he did allow those arrogant little devils to slip right into those proverbial pigs—who, of course, as everyone also knows, always squeal, "But Mom, *everybody does it!*" as they all follow one another in jumping over the cliff to their doom! And also because, obviously, the same spirits that turn human beings into arrogant little so-and-so's also cause pigs to jump off of cliffs headlong into the Abyss!

Which we might think would also be the end of our story, but, alas, there is no such luck. When all the pig-herders—who all this time have been busy wallowing-in and sloshing-around on the edges of the gluttonous porcine economy nearby—well now they get all bent out of shape about the loss of their adorable little pets with the cute curly tails—and also kind of anxious about their deep investments in porcine futures. So they run screaming-and-squealing to all the owners and operators of all the multinational porcine companies housed in all the major cities of the world, squealing, "Violent Rebellion!" and "Highway Robbery!"

"This fellow, Jesus, means to lift his little finger and send us all scurrying over the edge and into the Abyss—and even to put us all out of a-byss-iness!"

Then all the City Slickers as well as all the Country Bumpkins get all worked-up into a foam and also come running to see "this thing that has happened" (Luke 2:15). But what they see when they get there is quite the opposite of what they had expected! For as it turns out, all they see is a scene of a person formerly known as an "awfully arrogant human being" who is now just sitting there humbly listening and learning about the Kingdom of God at the feet of the Master, which is, of course, as we all know, "the right and fitting thing to do,"[9]—which just goes to prove that he was in his right liturgical mind as well!"

But, anyway, and for some reason, even that simple picture of a teacher with a few students scared the people out of their wits, which again resulted in a couple of opposite reactions. On the one hand, the ones who had been paying close attention and who therefore had actually seen and understood what was really going on—and who had truly witnessed the amazing transformation of the Man—well they just couldn't keep their mouths shut about how much the Man had changed from his old completely arrogant and incredibly-abusive self into the most beautiful and generous soul that they had ever laid eyes on! But others just took one look and said, "Be afraid! Be very afraid!"—as non-angelic voices always do.

Then all the people of the whole entire region—both those who were stunned and amazed by the healing as well as those who were horrified by it; both those who were dressed-to-the-nines in high-fashion Roman clothes, driving luxury Roman Chariots and wearing expensive Roman Bath and Spa products, as well as those who were barely existing, hovelled together in Roman slums and subsisting on the pods from Roman pigsties—well, they all joined their voices together and squealed and screamed in terror for Jesus to go away and plague them no more with his challenging Presence.

Then Jesus climbed back into his usual vehicle for sailing around in The Kingdom of God, and, naturally, the Man—who is now a Disciple—wanted to remain with him. Then Jesus ever-so kindly and gently explained to the Man that all a person really needs to do in order to remain in close touch with him is to locate their true identity and citizenship and well-being in the Kingdom of God where each one will always be perfectly free to go into any of the cities and towns and slums and pigsties of the world proclaiming how the many mercies of the full-to-overflowing Love of God, "set on the sure foundation of [God's] loving-kindness,"[10] truly does have the power to set us free from all that would possess, obsess, control, demean and dehumanize us.

Editors' Note: Because Our Lord does continue to teach us, day after day, night after night, and struggle after struggle, how to deeply know and to completely accept who we really are, which is nothing more and nothing less than most beloved children of God, *bona fide* citizens of God's Kingdom, and rightful heirs of God's promises as so completely-permeating and spoken right through the birth, life, ministry, death and resurrection of Our Lord and Savior, Jesus Christ. Amen.

JESUS' RAP SONG

Well, then the word was definitely out on Jesus, and the crowd gathered around him was so demanding and possessive that Jesus and his company couldn't even sit down together for a close-knit, simple, little, family meal.

Now when Jesus' biological family heard that Jesus had not only gotten religion but had also gone public and come out of the closet with it, and was acting out and getting a reputation as one truly fractured, religious dude and thereby hurting the family name, they went out to restrain him before he could be officially labeled "Certifiable."

"Hey, Jesus," they said, "come try on this nice, new, comfy, straight jacket we just bought for you!" But, of course, they were too late. Some expert psychologists and family therapists had already come down from their nationally recognized clinic with an Official Diagnosis, classifying Jesus as being "Possessed by Beelzebul, the Prince of Demons," which was the clinical term they cast out to explain Jesus' extraordinary obsession to work with people and throw out all the demons that possessed and bedeviled them all—which, of course, they carefully documented with their incomparable reasoning, complicated charts, and conclusive illustrations.

Now, when Jesus saw just what was going down, he promptly called those experts to him and rapped them with a carefully crafted song to help them understand something very basic.

> Well the Devil may struggle
> And the Devil may care,
> But if the Devil kills the Devil
> Then the Devil's not there!
>
> Oh yes, his power is over
> And his torture is done;
> By God the Devil is vanquished
> And the Kingdom is come!

Just look: the king who is toppled
And the one who is thrown
Hasn't got any power
Not a shred of his own!

And, well, a house that's divided
Simply falls to the ground!
Not a board is left standing
Not a beam to be found!

You see: it takes a strong man
To break a strong man's stronghold,
To steal his favorite possessions
All his gems and his gold!

So, take a look at this Man
And you can see what he does:
His power comes from the Spirit
Full of freedom and love!

Yes, well, the Devil may struggle
And the Devil may care,
But if the Devil kills the Devil
Then the Devil's not there!

Oh yes, his power is over
And his torture is done;
By God the Devil is vanquished
And God's Kingdom is come!

But when they heard those words coming out of Jesus' mouth, the experts quickly muttered: "You see? That just proves it! He is definitely in rapport with an evil spirit! He is possessed and under the influence of the Devil himself!"

But Jesus interrupted, "Oh, now you've gone too far!
Well you may sin against your brother,
And you may sin against your mother;
But when you identify the work of Holy Spirit as
"the work of the Devil,"
Then that's just absolutely, completely and eternally backwards
And won't provide you any cover!"

Jesus' biological mother and biological brothers then tried once more to gain complete possession of him. The crowd called out, "Hey, Jesus! Your family is out to get you again!" But Jesus replied, "Do you even know who my family is?" as he looked at all those gathered around. "For truly I tell you that anybody and everybody in the whole world in all times and in all places who does the will of My True Father God is a *bona fide* member of my own true family, and I consider them to be my very own mother, my very own sister, and my very own brother—each and every one!"

TO UN-CLOG YOUR EARS

Then Jesus went out and sat on the front steps of the church where such a large number of parishioners gathered around him that he went and got onto the hood of an All Terrain Vehicle and sat there while all of the parishioners stood out on the yard.

He told them many things in parables, saying: "Open your ears and really listen to this! An investor went out to invest. As he invested, some of the investments fell on the DOW and the vultures came and devoured them. Other investments were made in some highly-recommended, rock-solid technology companies. Because of the recommendations, the value of the stocks quickly shot up even though the companies didn't have a lot of depth. But when their true value was exposed to the light of day, they couldn't take the heat and, since their worth was over-inflated, the value of these stocks fell to nothing. Other investments were made in companies that were surrounded by aggressive, predatory competitors. The aggressive, predatory competitors grew strong enough to choke them, and so these companies all failed. But still other investments were made in stocks and bonds that were really good and that produced some amazing returns, some having returns of a hundred percent, some with sixty percent, and some with thirty. Let anyone with ears truly hear!"

Then, some of the parishioners asked him, "Hey, Jesus! Why do you keep telling mind-boggling stories all the time?" So he drew them a picture of a man crawling into an ear canal and said, "To unclog your ears!"

Then they said, "Well, why do you go around illustrating everything you say?" And he said, "To open-up your eyes! That's why I tell strange stories: to create readiness; to nudge people to become receptive; to open-up avenues of transformation and delight; to venture into God's world-making vision and love. In their usual state, people can stare until doomsday, and still not see it— listen until they're blue in the face and still not hear. And I surely don't want you all to end up like the people the prophet/author, Isaiah, described in Chapter Six of his most famous treatise on the subject:

> Your ears are open but you don't hear anything.
> Your eyes are open but you don't see anything.
> The people are blockheads!
> They stick their fingers in their ears so they don't have to listen;
> They screw their eyes shut so they won't have to look
> So they won't have to deal with me face-to-face
> And let me heal them. (Isa 6:9–10)

For, believe you me, a whole lot of people would have given anything to see what you are seeing right now—and to hear what you are hearing right now—but they never had the chance. So hear then the following allegorized version of the parable of the investor:

"When anyone hears about the love of God but does not really take it to heart, the evil one comes and snatches away what is offered: this is the investment that falls on the DOW. As for the highly recommended investments that are over-rated, this is the one who hears about the welcoming love of God and immediately receives it with great enthusiasm, but, because that person has a shallow understanding about love, their enthusiasm only lasts for a little while. When discomfort or trouble arises because of the challenges presented by God's love, that person immediately falls away. As for what is invested in the midst of aggressive, predatory competition: this is the one who hears about the love of God but the worries of their lives and the lures of other investments chokes their interest and it yields nothing."

"But as for the good investment, this is the one who hears about the love of God and takes it completely into their heart where it indeed bears all kinds of fruit and produces amazing returns—in one case a hundred percent; in another sixty percent, and in another case thirty percent—which, you all surely must agree—are all fabulous returns way above even the most optimistic of predictions!"

HEADLINE NEWS FROM TRYING TIMES

The next morning Jesus disciples awakened to this newspaper story in The Sower's News, which was also referred to locally as "The Snooze."

The page one headlines included: World Wheat Attack. No Field Safe! Good Wheat Everywhere Seek Origin and Roots of Weeds: Charge God! God Issues Denial: Blames an Evil-Doer and Cites Past Record!

Page two said: Armed Forces ask Lord Commander and Chief Sower, "Do you want us to destroy evil-doers?" There was also a picture of the Sons of Thunder Stealth Exterminator with Smart Bombs.

On page three: Lord Commander and Chief Sower Recommends Non-violent Response to Weeds: Cites Collateral Damage and God's Job Description.

There was also an illustrated diagram showing the relationships of Weed to Field to Wheat to Wheat to Field to Weed, which was obviously so tangled that not even genius-level smart bombs would be able to do job.

On the editorial page, however, there is some good news as well: "Separation and Harvest is God's Job," claims Lord Commander and Chief Sower. Then the reader is directed to see Psalm 78 for full description of past, present, and future performances illustrating how God will reap when the harvest is ready!

Letters to Editor ask this question: "Then, what is our job?" And on page five, there is a Special Letter to Editor in Response, which is here reproduced in its entirety:

Dear People of Faith,

In this world, so filled with weeds and wheat, your job is to be people of faith and children of delight. You are called to place your hope in God and in God's delight; to let delight shine in your hearts and to seek to serve delight in all others; to avoid collateral damage to your own souls as well as others as much as possible; to risk entering into loving communities with other deeply flawed and weedy souls; and to trust God to do the job of separation and harvest when the time is truly ripe in God's Kingdom.

Sincerely yours, Farmer Jesus of Nazareth

LIKE A BOOK OF COMMON PRAYER

"Well, what exactly is this Kingdom of God or Presence of God of which so many are speaking and writing?" they asked Jesus.

He mused out loud to himself, "To what shall I compare it?" And then he answered, "In many ways, the Presence of God is like a mustard seed; the Kingdom of God is like yeast; the Presence of God is like treasure hidden in a field; a merchant in search of fine pearls, and a net thrown into the sea, as you may already have heard."

"The Presence of God is also like a little whisper that someone took and planted in his heart. It is the smallest of whispers but, when it grows, its voice is loud enough to shelter birds seeking refuge in its timbre—if you know what I mean. The wonderful *timbre* of the loud, enveloping voice is like the *timber* of the trees in which the birds find rest. Selah!"

"Or, how about this: The Presence of God is like a simple idea that formed in the mind of a poor English woman. Although it started out very small and seemingly insignificant, as it grew many readers fell under its spell and a version of it sold six million, nine-hundred thousand copies in the first twenty-four hours!"

"Or, perhaps we might consider that the Kingdom of God is like a couple of young computer geeks who took a basic little algorithm and invented a simple social network in cyberspace that soon went viral and made them both into billionaires almost overnight."

"Or, maybe even a little bit closer to home: The Presence of God is like a book of common prayer that was first planted in 1549. Although it was the smallest of books, when it was opened up, it was so powerful, so poetic and full of meaning that it mutated and spread like a weed from one place to another until it could be found germinating throughout the whole world where common, everyday people everywhere could find refuge and refreshment for their souls."

"And it is also like a book of common prayer that somebody took with her everywhere she went, reading and praying with it at home, at work, and even on vacation—through all of her ups and downs and in-betweens—until it was so integrated into her heart and mind and body and soul that her whole life was nourished and enriched."

"It is also like a book of common prayer someone suddenly discovered sitting alone on a pew somewhere and then threw caution to the wind, picked it up, gleefully stole it away and kept it all for himself—hidden in the very bottom of his heart—the only place where he felt he could really treasure it."

"And it is also like a book of common prayer that searches for readers, and when it finds a reader who listens with his/her heart and mind and body and soul, it immediately delivers-up the goods and gleefully hands over everything it's got!"

"And it is even like a book of common prayer that is published throughout the world to catch all kinds of readers, good readers and bad readers alike, who fall under the magic of its spell. In the end, when it has been fully read, learned and inwardly digested, only the good parts will be truly treasured for all of eternity, as so it will be at the end of age." Then some of them quietly responded, "Amen."

FARMER JESUS' METAPHORICAL SEEDS

So, naturally, Farmer Jesus continued by planting a few more metaphorical seeds in the ears of his disciples: "The reality of God's Kingdom is like a man planting a grass lawn. He scatters seeds, waters and fertilizes. But what happens surely happens quite beyond that man's control! The seeds miraculously sprout and miraculously grow to maturity. Then the next thing he knows, the man finds himself outside mowing and reaping the harvest of the earth's full flowering whether he wants to—or not!

Then Jesus planted yet another idea in the minds of his disciples about the reality of God's Kingdom. "The reality of God's Kingdom is like this here itty-bitty, little, tiny, fiery, pungent seed which, when planted in the ground, germinates at once and begins to grow out of control—even taking over where it is not particularly welcome—until it becomes the greatest reality of all, nurturing new life and giving relief and comfort to all who would make it their home."

And then, well, Farmer Jesus simply continued along on his path and planted many more metaphorical seeds in the ears of his disciples—as many seeds as their soil could absorb—and with plenty to spare!

THE WOMEN'S ISSUE

Now it was still early on in his ministry when Dr. Jesus once again crossed over the Sea of Galilee. Everybody and his brother crowded around him on the shore to see for themselves how this so-called Respectable Man of God might possibly expose the inadequacies and shortcomings of current, orthodox methods and procedures for handling the dis-ease regarding female conditions and issues.

Suddenly, a particularly frazzled Hospital Administrator from the local Clinic of Enlightened Orthodox Practices, broke through the crowd, threw himself down at Dr. Jesus' feet and began to cry: "Oh God! Oh My God! It's my baby! My precious little baby! My darling little girl is on the brink of something dreadful, and I just know she's dying! Please come take my baby in hand and cure her that she may live!" Then, of course, Dr. Jesus, jostled and bumped by the crowd that followed, went with him to see what all the fuss was about.

Now, in the midst of that crowd, there was a woman who was surely no innocent child and who had suffered with a serious issue for a period that had lasted just as many years as there were Sons of Jacob or Tribes of Israel—which, as everybody knows, was twelve long years. Now, during that period, she had put herself into the hands of one doctor after another who not only diagnosed her as having a "chronic, incurable, female condition" that nobody wanted to touch, but also bled her for every penny she had—as they slowly drained her of all her resources and hope for a fertile and productive life in this world.

Now this woman had heard all the gossip about Dr. Jesus, of course: how his methods were unorthodox and how the EPE (Established Professional Establishment) did not approve of his practice, but that he was truly out of this world and specialized in hopeless cases that nobody else would touch, and how his rate of cure was nothing short of miraculous. But not only that—the word out on Jesus was that he didn't even charge a single penny for his services!

So, in a moment of pure feminine intuition, she pushed and shoved her way through the crowd, slipped-up behind him and reached out to touch his scrubs, saying to herself, "Girl, you've got nothing left to lose! Girl, nobody in this man's world, or his brother, has ever had a remedy for what ails you! Girl, if you want the cure, you've just got to reach out and put the right touch on this man! In that very same instant when she bravely reached-out and touched his scrubs, her dis-ease-within-herself stopped and she felt like a whole new woman from her head to her toes!

Experiencing the power and magnetism of the woman's tug, Jesus immediately whirled around in the midst of the crowd and said, "Hey, who touched my scrubs?!" This absolutely bewildered the graduate interns who were traveling with him, who said, "Good grief, Doc! You've been nudged, bumped, and jostled by Everybody-and-His-Brother ever since we set foot on this shore, and yet you want to know who touched your scrubs just now?!"

But Jesus just kept on looking through the crowd until the woman who was aware of the change became frightened by what she had done, fell down at his feet, and poured out her whole heart about all of her experience as a female person in this world: all of the closed doors; all of the inequality and injustice; all of her personal grief; all of her heartache; all of her longings and hope beyond hope; all of her isolation and wandering in near-despair; all of her exclusion and exile; all of her doubts and confusion; all of her internalization of the disrespect and harsh judgments others had rendered against her; all of the heavy costs; all of the struggle; and all of her prayers; all of her bleeding; all of her tears, and all of her desire to belong and be whole.

And then Our Good Doctor spoke: "Dear, dear Daughter of God, your brave and amazing faith is the source of your strength and inspiring wholeness. Go and be truly content that you are a very real woman and a child of God."

Now, while Dr. Jesus was still speaking, some pretty hysterical people erupted from the frazzled Administrator's house, exclaiming: "She's dead! She's dead! Daddy's precious little baby girl is dead! There's no need to trouble the doctor anymore!"

But Dr. Jesus heard the diseased rumor they were spreading and calmly advised the Frazzled Father to just hang in there and keep the faith.

Allowing none of the mass hysteria to follow him, but taking three of his graduate interns only, Dr. Jesus quickly arrived at the very threshold of the Administrator's residence where there was a great commotion and a noisy disturbance made by people crying-out and shouting over and over again: "O My God! It's true and it's a terrible curse! Daddy's little baby girl is really gone! She's really gone! It's a curse! A curse, I say!"

Well, Dr. Jesus just walked right in and said, "Oh for heaven's sake. Why are you all making such a huge fuss? It's not like she dead or anything. This child is just becoming a woman and is beginning to wake to her full potential."

But the people thought that Jesus' diagnosis of the female condition was hysterically funny, and they all laughed and mocked him, saying, "What are you, some kind of a male midwife or something? Are you sure your name's not really Nurse Jesu-*phina*? Or Jesu-*lena*? Or something else girl-y-girl-y like that?"

So Dr. Jesus threw them out of the house and then, taking the child's mother and father and his graduate interns, entered into where Daddy's Precious Little Baby was curled-up into a ball in her bed. He took her by her hand and said these two powerful and magical words, "Talitha Kum!" which simply means, "Young woman, get up!" So she immediately got up and began to walk around, which amazed everybody to no end, even though, you know, she really wasn't a baby at all anymore, but was actually as many years old as there were Sons of Jacob or Tribes of Israel—which means that, after all, for heaven's sake—she was twelve years old already! Practically a woman!

Well, Dr. Jesus told her parents that there was obviously absolutely nothing for them to make such a big fuss about, but that if they really wanted to fuss around anyway, they could just go fuss around in the kitchen and get this budding young woman something good to eat!

THE GOSPEL OF THE PRAIRIE

Then Jesus called a quick meeting of the twelve who had achieved the top leadership positions in his organization, and he began to show them how, so unlike his own teachings, the Gospel of the Prairie—also known as the Gospel of the World—sends each individual out all by himself and all on his own. He admonished them, reminding them that it is the heartless and paranoid World that is always warning everybody to, "Watch out for all the dirt and grime out there and don't let any of it get on you or touch you!" Then he reminded them of the list of the things the World says a person must possess in order to succeed: a fistful of credit cards; a tight money belt; really nice white pants, leather boots; silver spurs; a black shirt with a white collar; a tall white horse and plenty of extras of everything.

Jesus also reminded them that the Gospel of the Prairie slaps each man on the back and says, "Now go out there into the Big Bad World and be The Man! And always stay in the best suite in the best Five-Star hotel in town. If anybody isn't absolutely thrilled just to see you coming and who doesn't do exactly as you say, be sure to make a point to rub their noses in the dirt before you ride off again. So that each Solitary Roamer takes off on his [sic.] very own high horse, proclaiming that everyone must stand back and admire his highness from a safe distance—quite confident in his own personal power and position in the world, but also constantly on the lookout for any tiny little speck of dust that might sully his wardrobe or tarnish his image."

And so, here ends the rugged-individualistic, male-dominated, ultimately utilitarian, Consumerist Cowboy's Gospel of the Prairie. Thanks be to God!

HEAD CHEF JESUS

Soon afterwards, when our Head Chef Jesus heard the gut-wrenching news that his old colleague, known world-wide as Chef Jean le Baptiste from the Manna School of Culinary Delights, had had his head served-up on a platter by Herod to Solomé, he immediately set sail out into the very deepest part of the Lake of the Human Heart, out to his very own special place of solace and comfort called The Place of Just Desserts, which was a floating dessert café with many signs such as Comfort Food for the Sick of Heart; It Fills the Void; Plenteous Redemption; and featuring menu items such as: Key to Life Pie; Hearty Cherry Cheese Cake for the Soul; Divinity Fudge, Angel Food Cake, and Heavenly Hash.

When the crowds heard the sickening news about what Herod had dished-up at the palace, it caused them to step-out of their usual places of solace where they tried to relieve their broken hearts and upset stomachs at their Royal Burgers and McCaesar's; their Down Home Buffets and their Upscale Cafés, and they followed Chef Jesus to see what kind of comfort food he might have to offer way out there in the Lake of the Human Heart.

Now, when Jesus came ashore and saw the great crowd of people hungering for the kind of comfort that would truly abide and satisfy, his whole heart immediately opened-up wide. Right then and there, he served up the dish that healed their sickness of heart.

Now this is the way the food was served: some of Chef Jesus' culinary students came and complained that they were all in a deserted place that was a god-forsaken, forlorn and comfortless place, and that it was way past suppertime. So then they suggested that he should send the great crowd of hungry people away, out into the surrounding villages, to buy some real, solid, food to comfort themselves before it really was too late.

But Chef Jesus said, "Look. They don't need to go away. You can give them something comforting and special to eat right here and right now!"

But they said, "Excuse us—but *with what* for comforting and special? We're just a couple of lowly, short-order, student cooks and we really don't have any special ingredients or talent. See? All we have is this little bag of plain old bread which is hardly enough for even a couple of poor culinary students to eat—let alone a huge crowd of heart-sick, starving people with big holes in their souls."

Chef Jesus said, "Just bring to me whatever you happen to have." Then he simply showed them six very easy steps for whipping-up something absolutely comforting and special to serve to absolutely anybody anywhere who shows up any time they are really heart-sick and hungry for comfort.

Head Chef Jesus' Recipe for True and Abiding Soul Food

1. Tell the guests to sit down and relax.
2. Take whatever ingredients you happen to have on hand.
3. Look "up" to heaven.
4. Bless whatever it is.
5. Break it down into manageable, bite-sized pieces.
6. Share it with each other until all are satisfied.

Then they all partook and felt deeply satisfied and, as it all turned out, there was such an abundance of comforting and special soul food made available that day that Chef Jesus' culinary students really had their work cut out for them just gathering-up all the leftovers!

For there were no marvelous words of magic wisdom, no sparklingly clever theological arguments, no biting political or social commentary, but just a little bit of plain old bread where two or three have gathered in his name—ordinary, everyday compassion to share with any and all who hurt and are hungry for comfort—bread that is made special by the presence of our Lord whenever and wherever we are truly present to and with one another. For this is the bread of Real Presence! This is the Real Presence to and with one another; Real Presence to and with our Lord; Real Presence to and with our God and Father who is gracious and merciful, who truly loves us, and who will not forsake us, no matter what.

And so here are a few more pieces of ordinary, everyday bread, broken down into bite-sized pieces: words of hospitality and welcome; looks of recognition and glances of acceptance; moments of full attention; lively conversations; truthful prayers; the naming of our fears and anxieties; the sharing of our sorrows; little touches of comfort and reassurance; sounds of excitement and joy; gestures of gratitude and affirmation, and all the little tastes of peace and hope—obviously not an exhaustive list—which really are not only adequate, but more than enough. For truly comforted and satisfied on that day were about five-thousand-odd needy, man-sized appetites plus the wide-open mouths of an untold number of noisy women and children!

CAMP EERIE

Well, the very next night on the shore of Lake Galilee, the First Summer-Church Camp Director sent all of the Camp Eerie campers to their tents for the night, except for a certain, small group of twelve, young and innocent camp counselors whom he sent out on the lake on their own on the Camp Eerie boat for a special, eerie, survival-camp experience.

Meanwhile, back at the camp, the Camp Director quietly left and went off on his own, alone, up on the mountain for a special, secret staff meeting with That Strange and Mysterious Camp Owner that no one has ever seen even to this very day.

Now it was a dark and windy night out on the lake, and the wind belched and whipped and moaned, and the boards creaked and whined, and the sails flapped uncontrollably, and the deep, dark waters rose and heaved and hurled and sank again, and rose and heaved and hurled and sank again, like disembodied hands grabbing and sucking at your ankles in the middle of the night from the dark underneath your bed—when all of a sudden from out of nowhere across the dark sea, something very scary came right at them!

They all screamed: "Oh my God! Oh my God! It's a Ghost!" And they clutched their hearts as they focused on wave upon wave of fear that threatened to overwhelm them: fear of the unexpected; fear of the unknown; fear of getting swamped; fear of tipping over; fear of losing control; fear of failure; fear of success; fear of dying, and all the rest.

Then, in the midst of the surging waves of fear, they heard an awful voice crying out in the wilderness, "Hey You! Get a grip! 'tis I!"

But Peter was panic-stricken and unconvinced, so he leaped up and almost tipped over the boat when he yelled, "Prove you really are with us! Make me special and give me the super-human, super-natural powers to get on top of all of this scary stuff out here!" And the disembodied voice said, "Come!"

But when Peter stepped out of the boat, he was blind-sided by the adverse winds of the unknown and unexpected trials and tribulations of the human condition and he immediately began to sink into the dark waters of doubt and despair. He cried out, "Lord, save me!" And at that very moment he was caught by a hand pulling him into the boat as he heard the voice of the Camp Director saying: "Oh ye of little faith! Why did you think you had to go it alone?" And at that very moment, the adverse winds released the grip on their hearts as the camp counselors all believed and praised the living presence of the Holy Ghost in their midst.

Then Peter remembered this note that he had tucked away in his pocket all along,

> Dear Campers,
>
> I simply want to remind you that Ghost Stories are meant to bring campers together by providing a shared experience of fright in order to fight against the temptation to go it alone in the face of fear. All are tempted, like you, to pray to be the exception—to be granted super-human powers and super-natural abilities in the face of the scary and frightening adverse winds that so often blow through our lives. But the thing that causes the winds to cease and the waters that threaten to overwhelm us to subside, Dear Campers, is to be together in the same boat with one another

and with our Lord in the Spirit and Presence of the Holy Ghost.
Sincerely Yours,

Your Eerie Camp Counselors, Matthew et. al.

Then they sang one of their favorite camp songs all together, called "Calm Down and Relax," sung to the tune of "Rise and Shine and Give God the Glory."[11]

> The Lord said to Peter,
> "Do not be afraid-y-fraidy!"
> Lord said to Peter,
> "Do not be afraid-y-fraidy!
> I'll sail with you through every wavy-wavy,
> Campers of the Lord!"
>
> Refrain:
>
> So, calm down, and relax,
> And give God that glory-glory!
> Calm down, and relax,
> And give God that glory-glory!
> Calm Right Down and give God that glory-glory,
> Campers of the Lord!
>
> Then Pete to the Lord cried,
> "O please Jesus, Save me! Save me!"
> Pete to the Lord cried,
> "O please Jesus, Save me! Save me!
> Everything is so dark and hazy-hazy,
> Campers of the Lord!"
>
> The Lord said to Peter
> "O where is Ye faith-y-faith-y?
> Lord said to Peter
> "O where is Ye faith-y-faith-y?
> Take my hand and make God some space-y-space-y,
> Campers of the Lord!"
>
> The Lord said to Peter
> "Don't dwell on your feary-feary!"
> Lord said to Peter,

"Don't dwell on your feary-feary!
Don't you know I
Love you so dearly-dearly,
Campers of the Lord!"

DOG TIRED

Well, after giving his disciples the authority to cast out demons and heal the sick; teaching and feeding some five-thousand men, women and children with five loaves of bread and two fish; staying awake all night talking with his Father; walking on water to catch up with the disciples in the midst of a storm; and then healing everybody in sight in the region of Gennesaret—only to be confronted by a bunch of Scribes and Pharisees who were very concerned because his disciples weren't washing their hands before meals—Jesus was dog tired.

So he packed up his stuff and headed off into the district of Tyre and Sidon in the midst of the wilds of Canine Land. But, wouldn't you just know it, before he could even stop to lie down, or utter the words "Doggone it," a Canine-type female came out and began to whine at his heels, hounding him for some attention: "Have mercy on me, O Lord and Master! The Enemy has snared my dear, little, innocent, female, Canine-type child!"

A CANINE TYPE FEMALE began to whine at his heels

Well, maybe Jesus hoped that she would just go away, or perhaps he thought she was barking up the wrong tree, or that one of his disciples should take care of her this time around, or was just too dog-tired to respond, but, whatever the reason, Jesus didn't answer or speak to this Canine-type female at all at this time. But the whole pack of his best friends, the disciples, came yipping and yapping at his heels, and barking

"Get rid of this female-type-Canine-mongrel! She keeps annoying us and is foaming at the mouth!"

Jesus responded by reminding them of the limits of his particular job description. "Good grief, you guys! I didn't come here to deal with Canines! I came to recover the sheep who are lost from God's special sheepfold—at which point the Canine-type female, exhibiting absolutely no sense of pride or propriety at all, interrupted Jesus and shamelessly began to grovel in earnest. She came right up to Jesus and fell back on her haunches and begged and cried, "O Lord and Master, please have mercy on me!"

Then Jesus just kind of playfully nipped back at her when he said, "You know, it's really not quite proper to take food from one's children to toss to the dogs." But, for the sake of her hungry child, she held her ground as she nipped him right back again, "Yes, Lord! Well said, and how true! But you and I both know, even if no one else around here knows, that even mongrels are allowed to feast on the crumbs that fall from the master's table," thereby insisting that the grace of God is clearly intended for all.

Then Jesus leaned forward and wrapped his arms around her neck and said, "Oh you wonderful, persistent and truly faithful Canine-type female! Your wish is my command!" And sure enough, at that very moment, her little, innocent, Canine-type offspring was immediately released from the clutches of that oppressive Devil.

MAN WITH ATTENTION DEAF-ICIT DISORDER

Then one day when Dr. Jesus had just returned from a business trip along the Mediterranean coast that had taken him through the Phoenician towns of Tyre and Sidon, his interns brought a man to see him who suffered with an Attention Deaf-icit Disorder and who was so distracted, distraught, confused, disturbed, wearied, threatened and bewildered that he found it difficult to pay attention long enough to hear the words of our Lord, much less digest and include them in his speaking and living. Now, what the interns wanted, of course, was for Dr. Jesus to do what was expected and to hand the man some Religious Rid-O-Them or Miraculous Methylphenidate Hcl.

But Dr. Jesus took an even more direct, hands-on approach and did something really weird for which there was absolutely no prescription—unless you count some of the very weird medicine of Dr. Moses of Mt. Sinai, that is.

First he took the man away from the crowd and then, some say, Jesus stuck his own fingers in his own ears and spit, and then he put his own finger on his own tongue, and then he rolled up his eyes and heaved a big sigh, and then he uttered some magic, foreign words to the guy. Others say that Jesus stuck his own fingers into the guy's ears, spit on his own fingers, grabbed and pulled out the guy's tongue, and then, looking up to Heaven, sighed and said "Abracadabra!" which means "Open Sez-a-Me!" But whatever it was that Dr. Jesus did that day, it was really, really weird, and it really did get the Attention Deaf-icit Man's complete and undivided attention—and the most amazing thing happened! The man's ears were truly opened and his tongue was really released—and the man actually began to speak plainly and even make sense!

Then Jesus instructed his interns not to go spreading it around, saying, "I mean it! Don't tell anyone! Not your family. Not your friends. Not your neighbors."

But they were all so amazed and astounded that they didn't pay any attention at all to his instructions, and, in fact, they did just the opposite, of course, and blabbed it all over creation! And to this day nobody really knows how many times it has been said that Dr. Jesus has done all things well, but, even to this very day, it is still quite true that "He even makes the deaf to hear and the mute to speak!" (Mark 7:37).

IN THE CHAPEL OF THE CONSOLING CHRIST

Now one day when Jesus stepped into the Chapel of the Consoling Christ alone, a number of parishioners were milling about out in the hallway and one of them overheard him praying, "Abba, Abba, Father in Heaven, it is in the hottest heat of summer now and your children at this church are starting to scatter once again. Some are going to play at the ocean, some to the rivers and lakes, and some just to the swimming pool in their neighborhood, or even right in their own back yards. Father, at times like this, because I am human, I can't help but wonder what role I really play in their lives the whole year long, or if the memory of me is just a source of inspiration and strength for them one day a week for nine or so months out of the year at the most. I mean, Father, do I make any important difference to them in the places where they really hurt in their lives? Do I leave a lasting impression? Do they receive anything good and truly helpful from me at the lake, in the sand at the beach, or as they splash in the pool, or by the shores of the Lake of the Human Heart? Do they know me by sight? Do they call me by name? Or do they think of me as someone who only shows up at Christmas and Easter—and maybe when their bishop comes to town? I mean: I teach and I preach with passion and abandon and I use every trick in the book to get their attention and to help them see and hear what you want them to see and hear. But are they deeply aware of your Kingdom here on earth, or really experiencing your great, permeating love and compassion, as is your will for them throughout the whole of their lives? Do they see the injustice where it flourishes in the world, and know how wrong it is in your eyes? Do they see the dislocation and the aimless pursuits of a fearful, discouraged people? Do they taste their own thirst for living water to quench the human soul? Do they know how to bask in the sun of your love? Because sometimes, Father, sometimes it feels quite lonely to not be certain of the effectiveness of your mission, or really know how to gauge the response. Father, the world is filled with, enamored with, and addicted to darkness. But what about my followers here at the church? At the next leadership meeting, would it be OK if I ask them what they think? Father, I want them to know all about you and your love, but I am deeply concerned about the dangers of false advertising. I'm afraid that if they do begin to get it they will nevertheless misunderstand, and that they will put my name up in lights or up on a billboard that just screams "Jesus is The One and Only Way," and have everybody thinking that following me is something like winning the lottery or getting a hold of a magic genie who makes everything work in their lives to their own advantage. Father, show me how to help them understand that following me is nothing at all like winning the lottery, but instead involves the acceptance of life in all its pain and joy, suffering, rejection, and the full acceptance of death. Please help me to show them how to live a life of self-denial that doesn't drain the life out of your children, but brings them abundant life in you, as is your will, Father."

"Yes. I know that I still have a lot of work to do, and I will continue to pour myself out for them to try to show them your love no matter what the response or the cost. Indeed, what good would it do for me to have all of the understanding responses and affirmation in the world but lose this life in you that I so love? Thank you, Father. You are the true source of my life no matter what happens and wherever I, your servant, go."

Then he stepped back into the church and said to the leadership: "Who do the crowds say that I am?" They answered, "A Religious Nut; A Great Master of Delusion, and One of the Greatest Moral Teachers of All Time."

Then he said to them, "But who do you say that I am?" The president of the church leadership said, "You are the One Sent by God." Then Jesus sternly ordered them to not misrepresent his true identity to the general public, telling them that the One Sent by God is a real human being who will suffer, be rejected, be killed, and on the third day be raised to new life. Then he said to all the people of the Church, "If any want to become my followers, let them deny themselves and take up their cross daily and follow me. For those who want to save their life will lose it, and those who lose their life for my sake will save it" (Luke 9:23-24).

THE DEMISE OF THE FAIRY TALE GOD

Well, it was about seven or eight days after Jesus had leveled with his disciples about the realities of the human condition and told them the truth about God and religion—about eight days after they realized that Jesus was not going to prevent himself or anyone else from dying or make everything OK in their lives or in their interpersonal relationships, or with their children, or on their jobs, or in their churches, or make all of their troubles suddenly disappear, or change the self-serving ways the world works, or make the human story into one where they all live happily ever after—and his disciples realized that real religion is not about a

Fairytale God—when Jesus took a handful of them up on a mountain to pray and to see whatever they could see.

Now, when Jesus prayed, the very Presence of God emanated from him just like it had emanated from Moses and Elijah when God was present with them. And it was like the disciples were beginning to glimpse Jesus for the first time in his true context and cosmic significance in the company of Moses and Elijah as a real person in the real world who reflected the very presence of God, and through whom God chose to speak. And they clearly saw that Moses and Elijah were steadily informing Jesus' work and telling him all about his inevitable departure and about all the things that he still had to accomplish in Jerusalem.

Now, when they began this journey with Jesus, the disciples had been feeling so gloomy and down in the dumps about the shattering of their childish illusions and the demise of their Fairytale God that they wanted to just climb into bed and pull the covers up over their heads. But because they had miraculously managed to stay awake and had not completely given up all hope in the face of the painful and grown-up realities that Jesus had shared with them, they actually detected in Jesus and the two who stood with him the real Presence of the Living God in the real world for at least those few moments. And then, because in our grown-up world our experiences of God are always momentary glimpses and difficult to hold on to and quickly lost in the realities of life, Peter had no idea what he was saying when he blurted out: "Hallelujah and Thank God that we three disciples were awake to see the glory of God's presence in Moses, Elijah and Jesus, and to focus on and to celebrate our own personal religious experience as the fruition and culmination of all of God's work in the world!" But even as Peter was making this self-absorbed proclamation, all clarity was lost and he and his fellow disciples became completely disoriented and panicky like they had just stepped into an absolute whiteout on the mountain.

Then, from within the whiteout they heard an alien voice speaking to them and telling them that their friend, Jesus, really was God's chosen voice to speak to the real world. Then after the voice had spoken, they found the very real Jesus standing right there right in front of their eyes, so they simply decided to just zip up their own lips and listen to him.

ALL SAINTS' WAY OUT IN THE MOUNTAINS

But as some members of the Anglican Communion told it one day, Jesus invited Peter, James and John to go with him up to a High Anglican Church named All Saints' Way Out in the Mountains for a prayer retreat to make direct contact with that very same "Light Inaccessible, Hid from Our Eyes."[12]

And sure enough, as Jesus prayed, suddenly his face was all lit up and the color of his clothes appeared dazzling white as light! His disciples discerned that he had indeed made contact with two of the most well-known Agents of that "Most Blessed, Most Glorious, The Ancient of Days."[13]

"Oh look!" they said. "Who is it? Why, there's our friend Jesus being absolutely bathed in light! And look! He appears to be conversing with somebody! But who? Obviously his equal! But who? Oh, look! I see now! It's Moses Himself! Wow! And Elijah too! Wow! It's like something straight out of Chapter Four of Malachi's famous book, *The Great Day of the Lord*! Oh my gosh! This one's for the record books! Definitely a Sunday to remember!"

So Peter, of course, quickly grabbed his Next-Tell-All camera-phone to Picture- Message it to all his cellular friends and family. "OMG, Jesus! Boy, are you ever lucky we're here with the latest in digital-messaging technology to capture this once in a lifetime event! One of you, one of Elijah, and one of Moses! Yay! Proof! Now the whole world really can see it to believe it!"

But just at that exact moment, a bright light came upon and completely overexposed them, and they heard a strange, but very enlightening voice saying, "'Eternally begotten; God from God; light from light; begotten, not made; of one being with the Father; through him all things were made."[14] Incline thine ears to him!

When they heard this and saw the flash burn, they fell flat on their faces, overwhelmed, as they were, with this brand new technological wonder! And Peter said, "Rats! I missed it! This is way out of my Roaming Area!"

But Jesus, Kind Jesus, just touched their hearts when he simply said, "Arise. Go in peace to love and serve the Lord."[15]

Then, when they got up off of their knees, everything was Christ-al clear as they looked at their old friend Jesus, and their eyes focused steadily on him and him alone.

Then Jesus said, "Look guys. Just don't go around sending any picture- or text-messages about this until the day really comes when 'The strife is o'er, the battle done; the victory of life is won; the song of triumph has begun. Alleluia!'"[16] Then they quite properly added the antiphon, "Alleluia! Alleluia! Alleluia!"

BISHOP JESUS AND THE UNWILLING SPIRIT

Well, when Bishop Jesus and three members of his staff suddenly showed-up one day to meet with the clergy at the church, they saw a big crowd surrounding the clergy and some of the people were arguing with them. But when the crowd spotted Bishop Jesus, they were so astounded by his unexpected arrival and presence in that place that they stopped arguing and ran up to greet him. He asked them, "What are you arguing about with the clergy?"

A voice in the crowd piped-up: "Bishop Jesus, I brought my son, here, to your church because he has an Unwilling Spirit and refuses to communicate! Whenever it has a hold on him, it causes him to become self-destructive and do some really ridiculous things. He becomes sullen and obstinate and so full of pent-up anger and resentment that he fairly foams at the mouth. So, I asked your clergy here to straighten my kid out, but they were totally ineffective! They just couldn't do a thing with him!"

Then Bishop Jesus said to the whole crowd, "Oh you stubborn and obtuse people, how much longer do I have to keep showing up and putting up with your lack of faith? Bring the boy to me!"

So they dragged him over to Bishop Jesus. But when the boy's Unwilling Spirit caught sight of Jesus, it completely took the boy over and threw a huge tantrum, falling down on the ground and rolling about spewing profanities, right there in front of God, the bishop, and everybody!

Bishop Jesus said to the father, "Yikes! How long has this been going on?" And he said, "Forever! And it often gets him into hot water and causes him to do a whole lot of other self-destructive stuff. So if you are able, and if you have half a heart, and if you care at all, then please have pity on us and help us."

Bishop Jesus said, "Why do you say it hypothetically: '*if* I am able; *if* I have a heart; *if* I care at all'? Gosh! All things are possible for one who has faith!" Immediately, the boy's father cried out, "OK, OK! I believe you Bishop! Please straighten him out, and restore my faith!"

When Jesus saw that he had everyone's full attention, he loudly rebuked that Unwilling Spirit, saying, "O you obtuse, obstinate, and Unwilling Spirit that makes this boy so sullen and isolated, I command you to leave him and never-ever bother him again!" And right then and there the Unwilling Spirit threw one last self-destructive tantrum, leaving the boy lying there on the ground, straight as a board, stiff and immobile, and so totally spent that most people thought he was surely dead. But Bishop Jesus just reached down, took him by the hand and raised him up until he could stand on his own two feet.

Now, when Bishop Jesus went in to his meeting with the clergy, they whined and begged of him privately, "So tell us the big secret, Jesus. Why weren't we able to cast out the Unwilling Spirit?" To which Jesus replied, "Duh. You *forgot (?)* to pray."

INFANT FORMULA: INAMA

And then, because it was so very important for his disciples to understand something more of profound importance about who Jesus was and what he was doing in the world, Jesus gathered his Little Ones together and took them on a very special family outing where he gave them this concentrated formula about the nature and consequences of his life and teachings: tSoM = itbBihh + twKH + 3DabK = HWR2 which translates as, "The Son of Man is to be betrayed into human hands, and they will kill him, and three days after being killed, he will rise again" (Mark 9:31). But, alas, they just didn't get it on the first hearing, and they were actually afraid to ask him for yet another sermon on the subject.

Now, when they got to where Jesus was taking them and Jesus had settled in to nurse them through this difficult lesson, he asked them, "Say now, what was all that noise you children were making as you argued all along the way?" But now all of a sudden they were quiet because, in fact, what they had been childishly arguing about was who was going to be in charge when Jesus was dead and gone, and they had been saying things like, "Who gets to be the Pope? The Bishop? The Rector? The Heavyweight Champion of the Christian World? The Senior Warden? The Chair of the Music and Worship Committee? The Madonna? The Leader of the Pack? Miss Congeniality? But now they were very, very quiet indeed.

Then Jesus simply sat down in his rocking chair, called them all to his bosom, and gave them an even shorter and sweeter formula for their nurturing: 1st = LofA + SofA = "The first must be last of all and servant of all" (Mark 9:35). And then he gave them some solid food to chew on when he took an infant into his arms and said, "Whoever gladly receives and responds to the persistent needs, demands, and joys of any one such as this infant, fully accepting the formula INAMA, which translates as "It's not about me, anymore and it never was," welcomes me, and whoever welcomes me, receives not me, but the one who sent me: the God and Father of us all."

BISHOP JESUS CUTS SOME CLERGY DOWN

A named, and therefore very important clergyman said to the Right Reverend Jesus, Bishop of Nazareth, "Bishop, we, the preeminent members of your clergy, recently stumbled across a certain, un-ordained lay person, who shall remain anonymous, who was conducting a service in your name and publicly demonstrating your renowned authority and power as the bishop of this diocese. And so, Sir, with all due respect for your good name, Your Eminence, we just wanted you to know that we took immediate action and exercised our authority as your representatives, telling her to cut it out because she was acting without our approval, entitlement or authorization!"

But the Right Reverend Bishop Jesus said, "Oh for heaven's sake, don't cut her down! Anyone who performs a service by the authority vested in me is not going to be able to defame my name anytime soon after! Whoever cooperates with us is not at cross-purposes with me! Good grief! When you suffer and bear the title of The Bishop, whoever gives you a drink is going to be rewarded no matter what! And whoever causes one of these un-ordained, un-named saints who actually have faith in me to stumble, well, it would be better if a block of concrete was chained to their neck and they were cast into the nearest river! As a matter of fact, if you insist upon exercising your authority by cutting someone down, I suggest that you seriously consider cutting your own egotistical ways down a peg or two. So, if your own hand sneaks into the cookie jar, perhaps you should just cut it off! Or, if your foot should happen to stray, cut it off! Or, if your eye begins to roam, just pluck it out! For, I tell you, it is truly far, far better to be cut down to size to enter the life-giving Kingdom of God than it is to be perfectly suited for Hell where your unworthy ambition, cut-throat ways, and burning desire will surely never be quenched!

TWO TO TANGO

Then Jesus gave all his students some further instructions when was teaching them how to dance the tango. He explained this simple 3-step pattern they could follow for whenever another dancer happened to step on their toes:

Step One
1. Move out of the spotlight.
2. Go to the other dancer.
3. Ask to practice together in private.
4. If the other dancer agrees, you will have found yourself a terrific tango partner!
5. But if the other dancer ignores your lead, go one to Step Two.

Step Two
1. Seek the advice of some other dancers.
2. Have them watch the two of you rehearse together.
3. See if they can help you correct your relative positions.
4. But if Step Two is unsuccessful and the other dancer is still stepping on your toes, it may be necessary to try Step Three.

Step Three
1. Assemble the entire company of tango dancers.
2. Have them watch the two of you as you dance.
3. Let them correct and perfect your work as a pair.

If after all these three steps your partner still steps on your toes, it's time to let them leave the dance studio in peace.

Remember: Whatever is danced well here in the studio can be danced well anywhere. By the same token, whatever is danced clumsily and awkwardly here in the studio will be danced clumsily and awkwardly everywhere else.

>*Like the song says, it really does take:
>Two to tango, two to tango
>Two to really get the feeling alright
>Two to tango, two to tango,
>Do the dance of love.[17]

>Cha, cha, cha!

Final note: Whenever two or three of you get together to do the dance of love, you will always have my immediate and full attention and support.

V

The Lukan Theater Wing

YOU'RE IN GOD'S ARMY NOW

WHEN THE DAY DREW near for the subversive, insurgent, Galilean Resistance Fighter Jesus to be raised up as the invincible, twelve-star General of God's counter-cultural campaign against the principalities and powers of darkness that diminish the lives and trap and enslave the hearts and souls of God's children, Jesus turned his jeep to head directly to Jerusalem. He sent a couple of advance scouts ahead to reconnoiter a Samaritan village along the way for food and shelter for his men. But because he was headed for Jerusalem, the village wanted absolutely nothing to do with him—and certainly not with any of his men!

Now, when James and John saw what had happened, their blood began to boil and they asked Jesus if he wanted them to blow that inhospitable village and all of its inhabitants to Kingdom Come. But General Jesus turned and dressed the two of them down saying, "Good grief! When are you two boys ever going to grow up and start acting like real men? Put those guns away and go find us a village that does have room in their inn!"

And just as they started down the road, a man came running up to Jesus and exclaimed, "Wherever you're going, I want to join up and enlist in your army!" Jesus said, "Oh great! Terrific! Just great! Foxes have holes and birds have nest, but this man's army can't even get a room in a cheap motel!"

To another man by the side of the road he said, "Hey you! Fall in and join up!" But the man protested, saying, "Gee Lord, I'd certainly like to join your army. But, uh, I really won't be free for any service until my father's dead and buried." But Jesus said, "Your father can dig his own grave, Son. But as for you, your number is up and you're drafted for active duty beginning right now!"

Then, a third man came along who wanted to join, and he said to Jesus, "Sir, I'd be proud to wear the uniform of your army. But first, I want to apply for an advance furlough so I can go party one last time with my family and friends."

Jesus replied, "Son, anyone who puts on this uniform but wants to keep on wearing their civilian clothes really isn't ready for the abundant life in God's Service!"

Then they continued along their march singing one of their favorite mission songs to the tune of "I'm in the Army Now."[1]

> You're in God's Army now!
> Step lively, and watch that plow!
> Don't mess with the dead;
> Your life is ahead!
> You're in God's Army now!
>
> You're in God's Army now!
> To God only must you bow!
> No time for regrets,
> Or hedging your bets!
> You're in God's Army now!
>
> You're in God's Army now!
> Attention to where you plow!
> Lifelong is your "hitch"!
> In life you'll be rich!
> You're in God's Army now!

IN THE ARMY OF THE DOG

Well, after our Commander in Chief rejected armed, military engagements, he appointed seventy scouts and sent them out ahead, two by two, into every town and place where he was about to enter, and he gave them these marching orders, saying, "Huge numbers of people are now ripe and ready for Selective Service but recruitment officers are few and far between. Fervently hope and pray that our Supreme Commander deploys enough of us to get the job done. But, as you go your way, make a special note of this: I am sending you out as lambs in the midst of wolves (Luke 10:3)—as prey in the midst of predators—absolutely unarmed in the midst of a world that is armed to the teeth. Now, as for your uniforms, let them display no signs of insulting, cynical detachment or stoic indifference."

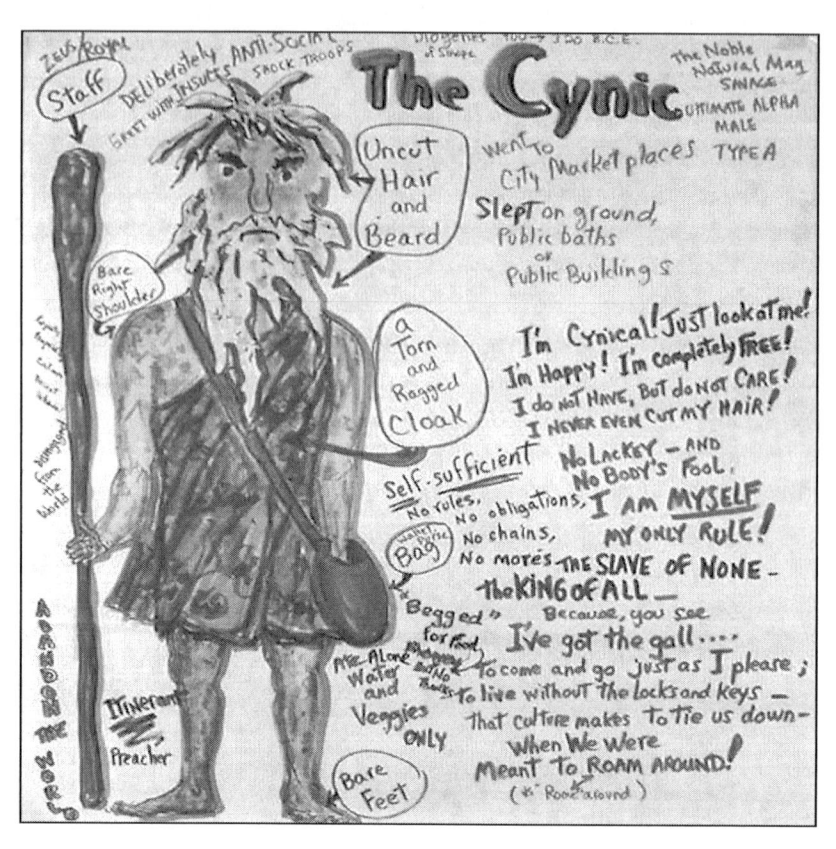

"Whenever you find a ready, kindred spirit who invites you into their life and home, you are to be a blessing to them, and if they are open to it, they will be blessed by your presence and find peace and refreshment. But if not, just chill out and allow your own offer of peace to return to you."

"Don't go grazing the neighborhood, foraging for special foods or privileges, but do accept whatever hospitality is offered. Sit at the table and eat and drink whatever they provide because you will certainly earn and deserve your rations. Whenever and wherever you are received, eat at the same table and share your material and spiritual resources as equals."

"Now, if you are rejected someplace, for heaven's sake, don't blow it up! Just blow it off and declare, 'God's Kingdom and God's Peace came close to you today.' And, I tell you, you should be really sorry for them because whoever is open to you is open to me; and whoever rejects you, sadly, rejects me and our Supreme Commander as well."

Now when the seventy scouts returned, they were absolutely thrilled with the healing, liberating power they were able to demonstrate. And Jesus said, "Satan surely went into a complete tailspin when he saw you guys in action because you truly have more power than all the weapons of the enemy. But just be careful not to go around rejoicing in your personal power. Rejoice, rather, that you have a lifelong commission in the Army of our Supreme Commander!"

THE GOOD UN-CHURCHED FELLOW

Well, one day a rather contrary, legalistic-minded Passer-By dropped-in to the church to subject the Beloved Parish Priest to an unexpected, rapid-fire cross-examination. Sticking his head in the door he said, "Hey, Father! Look! The Church is supposed to have all the answers, right? So what do you say Father? What do I have to do to get a truly gratifying and fulfilled life?"

The Beloved Parish Priest handed him the nearest copy of the prayer book and said, "Look on the top of page 324, or on the bottom of, uh, page 351, I think, and tell me what it says there."

So the contrary, legalistic-minded Passer-By reluctantly opened the book and read from an only slightly-different translation, "You shall receive all of life as pure gift, and you shall treat other people as gifts from God, just as you treat yourself." The Beloved Priest exclaimed, "Absolutely right! Do that, and you've got it knocked!"

But, looking for a Personal Stamp of Approval, the contrary, legalistic-minded Passer-By argued, "So just exactly who and how many of these other people am I supposed to treat as gifts from God?" And then, of course, The Beloved Parish Priest told him this amazing story.

"Did you ever hear the one about the little church way out on road somewhere between Weedy Street and Broken Down Boulevard—or, as some said, Left Out There on the Road to Ruin? Well, time was when that little church fell into the hands of the Evil One, and man-o-man, did it get beat up badly! Robbed, I tell you! It was gasping for breath and pretty much abandoned and left for dead along the way."

"Well, as luck would have it, it just so happened that a diocesan bishop was driving down that road, probably on his way to or from The Cathedral. When he saw that dilapidated church, he quickly moved to the fast lane and passed on by. Then, just a short time later, the Assistant to the Bishop for Congregational Development also happened to drive down that road—probably on her way to a meeting at the wealthiest church in the regional mission area—but when she saw the run-down church, she also quickly switched lanes and passed on by."

"But then all of a sudden a certain un-churched fellow came strolling down the street on his way to the doughnut shop, and, well, when he saw that poor, beat-up, old, abandoned church, he was deeply moved by its pitiful condition, and he quickly began to work picking up the yard, cutting and watering the grass and pruning the trees and bushes. And he also engaged a neighborhood contractor to repair and restore the church, paying half down now and the rest when the restoration was complete."

And then the Beloved Parish Priest asked the Passer-By, "Which one of these three do you think treated that little church well?" And the fellow answered, "Well, duh. I'm guessing it was the one who saw it and treated it as a gift from God!" Then that Beloved Parish Priest exclaimed, "Absolutely right again! Go treat all of life and everyone in it exactly the same and you will quickly discover that you have life, and have it in abundance!"

JESUS' LESSON PLAN AT MARY'S AND MARTHA'S

Principles of Discipleship
I. Review Week before Last: "Bring peace and be a blessing."
II. Review Last Week: "Receive all of life as pure gift and treat others as gifts from God, just as you treat yourself."
III. Today's Lesson: "In the midst of all of your worries and distractions, take time to stop and really listen to your Lord."

Really! There is only one thing needed: Stay in touch with God.

HOW TO PRAY TO GOD ON YOUR CELL PHONE

Jesus was talking to God on his All Tell/Tell All cell phone in a certain call area, and when he was done talking and hit End, one of his students said to him, "Lord, teach us how to talk to God on a cell phone like John did with his students."

And Jesus said to his students, "When you talk to God on a cell phone, begin by addressing the one you are talking to with a familiar term of abiding respect like, "Hi Daddy!" or "Hey Mommy!" And then offer a blessing such as, "I hope you are being treated well and that all of your plans are working out OK." Then, ask only for whatever you really need for the day, and that he or she wipe out the debt on your credit cards just like you so generously overlook whatever is owed to you—for example, "Please send money and kindly pay off all of my student loans." And then end your conversation by asking something like this, "And, please, please, please, don't ever drag me into court to stand trial for all that I owe to others!"

And then Jesus said to them, "What would you think if one of you had a friend, and when you found it necessary to go to that friend's house in the middle of the night to ask him or her, 'Do you have twenty dollars you can lend me? Some unexpected company has just arrived and I don't have enough money and I need to run to the store!' And your friend yelled back, 'Go away and leave me alone! I just got into my warm and cozy bed and I'm certainly not getting up now to give you a twenty dollar bill!'"

I tell you, your friend won't get up to help you because they are your friend, but they will give you the twenty bucks if you keep on coming back to their door over and over again and bugging them. And do you know why they will give you this money? I tell you that they will get up out of their warm and cozy bed to give you whatever you need just to see your backside going away from their door! So, with regard to talking to God on a cell phone, I say to you: Hit Contacts for the number and you will find it. Hit Call and you will be connected. Talk and you will be heard. For everyone who searches the directory finds! Those who call are connected! And those who talk will always be heard!"

"Listen. It's like this, you see? Is there any parent among you who, when their son calls and says how much he wants the newest Phish CD, will give him an old, scratched-up LP from White Snake Records instead? Or, if your daughter shyly requests a simple gold necklace, how likely are you to take her out and get her a large tattoo of her boyfriend's name, 'Scorpion', instead? So then, if you who are far from perfect know how to give good things to your children, just imagine how much more our Heavenly Progenitor will bestow truly heavenly blessings on those who call him/her up for live, real-time chat on their cell phone!"

SHOP 'TIL YOU DROP

Narrator: Then one of the mob of Shop-'til-You-Droppers said to Jesus,
Shoppers: "Make my sister share her lottery winnings with me!"
Narrator: But he said to her, "Girl, who died and made me your mother that I should send you two to pout in your separate rooms?"
Narrator: Then Jesus went on to say to them, "Be careful now; watch where you step, and look out for all the many colors, makes and styles of greed in the world, for a woman's path in life is not defined or measured by the abundance of her possessions."
Shoppers: [Ad-lib during the rest of the story.]
Narrator: And then he described to them this little scene from a mall.
Jesus: An independently-wealthy woman went to the mall and bought forth plentifully, shoes and more shoes of every color, make and style; slides and sandals; stilettos and mules; hiking boots and ankle boots; tennis shoes and running shoes;

shoes for gardening, shoes for the pool;*
shoes to look hot in, and shoes to stay cool!

But then she suddenly had herself a little problem she hadn't anticipated: where, oh where, to keep this magnificent mountain of shoes? So she had herself a little brainstorm and thought to herself, "Oh, I know! I know! I will rip out this little closet and build a great-big walk-in closet right here and now, where I can just step right in and see all my choices laid out before me all at a single glance!"

"Then I will say to my tired, aching feet, 'Sole, OK now, listen! You have an abundance of shoes to last for a long, long time, so you can go ahead and put yourselves up on the couch now, and take your ease, and get that massage you've been wanting, and take that beauty rest—because you two, my dears, have finally, finally arrived at your destination!'"

"But right at that very self-same moment, God the Lover of Souls spoke right to her soul and said, 'Oh you silly, silly woman! At this very moment in your life's journey you are being called upon to experience and express the greatest and deepest joy known to humankind. But all these amazing shoes of yours? Who in the world is going to wear them?'"

Narrator: Or, as Jesus summed it up,

Jesus: Alas, and how sad, for so it is with she who stacks and boxes-up treasures, but doesn't have a clue how to kick off her shoes and dance with God!"

THE GRACIOUSLY, GRACEFULLY-HUMORED PERSON

Then Jesus said, "Look, there's really no need to be so terribly anxious, my Little Flock, because our true God and Father is the Original Graciously, Gracefully-Humored Person and it is his greatest pleasure to give to you a whole world of wonderful things to delight your hearts. So feel free to go ahead and really share your pennies with everyone in the neighborhood who needs some, and be a child of blessing and delight all the days of your life. Stick with the only company that will never, ever go belly-up—where the ice-cream is always wholesome and good, and where no bullies can come and take your popsicles or cones away from you. For where you invest your pennies is where you will receive your hearts' delight! So don't invest in the things of this world that are guaranteed to fail you and will never satisfy your true hearts' desire. So keep your ears perked-up for the sound of the Graciously, Gracefully-Humored Truck bells. Be like neighborhood children lined-up on the curb eagerly watching for the Graciously, Gracefully-Humored Person to come around the corner so they can run up to him just as soon as he appears! Ding-a-ling-a-ling!"

"Oh how happy are the children whom the Graciously, Gracefully-Humored Person finds sitting on the curb all ready for his arrival! Do you know what he will do then? Why, I tell you, he will stop his truck and put on his apron and open the window and he will serve each and every one to their hearts' desire! If he comes at 7:00, or at 8:00, or even at 9:00 PM and finds them still anticipating his arrival, Oh how happy they will be!"

"And you should each also know this: If the self-professed enemy of our Father's Graciously, Gracefully-Humored Company had any clue about when the Graciously, Gracefully-Humored Person was coming to steal the children's hearts once-and-for-all, why he never would have left the neighborhood unattended. So, you see, you must always be ready to greet the Graciously, Gracefully-Humored Person whenever he comes. And there's no mystery about this, Little Children. He will definitely come! The real mystery is to be found right in the middle of the exact moment of his arrival!"

Then, as they continued to cheerfully hang out there on the curb, they sang to the tune of "Do Your Ears Hang Low?"[2]

Do your lamps burn long?
Have you girded-up your loins?
Are you sitting near the pavement with your ever-ready coins?
Are you looking for the moment when your Master will return?
Do your lamps burn long?"

And they also sang to the tune of "Pop Goes the Weasel."[3]

Disciples wait delightedly
Anticipate with bells on
For what God gives deliciously
Pop comes God's Kingdom!

Disciples' purses are never too old
To give with wild abandon
For where our hearts, our treasure is
Pop comes God's Kingdom!

Disciples' loins are girded up
Lamps burn with love and passion
So happy now to be alert
Pop comes God's Kingdom!

God's Thief can come at any time
To steal our souls for freedom
To break into our hearts and minds
Pop comes God's Kingdom!"

PYROMANIAC-ARSONIST JESUS

Then Jesus, that most astonishing pyromaniac and unexpected arsonist, said to his disciples, "Look you guys! I came here to light up the world with tongues of fire, and how I wish it was already holy enveloped in flames! Why even now I am being consumed with the passion to consummate my own baptism of fire!"

"Did you really think that I came to extinguish the fires on earth? No, I tell you! I came to engulf the whole world with fire and to put the heat on every last structure and system of tyranny, oppression, injustice and inequality that exists in this world—to torch each and every single thing that hurts and harms God's beloved children."

"I tell you, henceforth, my passionate fire will erupt in your hearts and even invade the privacy of your own homes. And my life-giving flames will leap from generation to generation; and my burning embers will flare-up between the sexes until even the most deeply-entrenched institutions of oppression and injustice will be reduced to ashes."

And then he said to the whole crowd of gawkers: "When you turn on the weather channel to get the latest update on what to expect in the morning and they are proclaiming a heat advisory with an index of one-hundred-fifteen degrees, you wisely plan your days accordingly, and then the weather quickly becomes unbearable, just as you anticipated! Such hypocrites! You can easily interpret the news on the weather channel and arrange your lives according to *their* words! Yet, how is it that you don't know how to read and interpret the real, hot, headline news of the day even as I am telling and showing you right now in this blaze of glory?!"

THE INTERNATIONAL ASSOCIATION OF FAIRLY GOOD PEOPLE

Then some attorneys for the Galilean Defense Team approached the bench and said to Jesus, "At this point, Your Honor, we would like to enter Exhibit Number One into evidence on behalf of the defense of the International Association of Fairly Good People (IAFGP). As you can see, Your Honor, it is a picture of some Galileans who were recently executed in the midst of the Temple even as they were there on their knees confessing their sins unto God Almighty."

His Honor responded, "In asking to enter this picture as evidence, do you mean to contend that your lives should be spared because you believe you have done nothing as bad as those folks must have done? I tell you that my answer is "No," meaning "No." This non-evidence is inadmissible! Any so-called relatively greater guilt of others is irrelevant and has no bearing whatsoever in the eyes of the Supreme Court. You are barking up the wrong tree! And if you persist with this line of reasoning, you will surely lose your case!"

"And while I am at it, I will also issue a ruling at this time on Defense Exhibit Number Two, which is your picture of some eighteen persons squashed in Jerusalem when the Tower of Siloam fell on them. Again, I tell you that this evidence is irrelevant and inadmissible. The relative guilt or innocence of these persons, as you are suggesting somehow relates to the circumstances of their demise, has absolutely no bearing whatsoever with regard to yourselves in the eyes of the Supreme Court. You are still barking up the wrong tree! And, if you do not change your line of reasoning, you will most surely lose your case!"

And then, exercising his most directive, down-home courtroom manner, His Honor leaned over the bench and directly advised the attorneys for the defense: "Because your present defense is so completely hopeless and unfruitful, I would strongly suggest that you cross-examine yourselves, and re-direct your thinking to quite another tree. I hereby remind you of the well-known Case of the Fruitless Tree against whom suit was brought for using up the resources of the ground but then not bearing fruit. It was that Judge's ruling in that Supreme Court Case that he, the Judge himself, would nurture and feed that tree for one more year, but that after that, if the tree still didn't give a fig, only then could it be cut down."

ALL PEOPLE'S AIRLINE

Then the mission got yet another boost when a certain Flight Attendant Captain began to speak over the Public Address System.

Flight Attendant Captain: Good Morning Ladies and Gentlemen and welcome to Flight Number 04-07-09. My name is Anonymous and I will be your Flight Attendant Captain this morning. Assisting me this morning will be our two soon-to-be named Flight Attendants. If you have any questions or if there is anything we can do to make your flight more comfortable for you, please do not hesitate to ask—but, NO, WE DON'T HAVE PILLOWS! If you have extra baggage with you this morning, we do ask that you step outside and check it at this time, for, as you can see, we have no overhead and very limited under-the-seat storage on this particular model aircraft. Please note that, located in the seat-back pockets in front of you, you will find convenient written materials identifying all of our post-modern, up-to-the-minute features and services. On this morning's flight, I'm afraid we must request that all seatbacks remain in the upright position as we do anticipate at least some mild turbulence to continue until we reach our destination. In the event of extreme discomfort or distress, simply tip forward and release the kneeler from the bottom of the seat in front of you, as our Flight Attendants will now demonstrate. Emergency exits are clearly marked in the fore and aft sections of the cabin. Our fully-accessible, unisex restroom is located in the rear of the cabin.Ladies and Gentlemen, rest assured that this is indeed a Hospitality Flight and refreshments will be distributed in just about half an hour. And now, from all of us at All People's Airlines, we invite you to sit back, relax, and enjoy our featured story presentation.

Then a short film began to roll, and a narrator said,

Narrator: Behold! Our Great Aviation Reformer and Consumer Advocate, Jesus of Nazareth, was working the Regional Galilean Commuter Flight Territory while he was on his way to the exclusive Jerusalem International Airport—which was officially owned and operated by the Chosen Few Airline Monopoly—when he made a brief stop in front of one of their official travel agencies to tell any and all who would listen about the Grand Opening of the All People's Airline and its Grand Opening Special Offer of competitive and affordable flights for all of their heavenly travel needs.

While he was there, someone in the crowd pointed to the signs in the agency windows and said:

Voice from the Crowd: But, Sir, isn't it true that First Class Seats to the Kingdom of Heaven are only available through the Chosen Few Airline and are reserved for only a few Chosen Few?

But Jesus said to the crowd, If you're counting on catching one of those exclusive, First Class, Chosen Few flights, I'm here to tell you that their security gate at Jerusalem International is incredibly narrow and that they are now fingerprinting and screening absolutely everybody who wants to enter so that many who will try to enter won't even be allowed in the airport terminal. By the time any of you imperfect, ordinary folks manage to get through their security checks and all the way down to the departure gate, it's going to be way too late. When that Chosen Few Flight Attendant has gotten up and closed the door, you will pound on that door, yelling that you have First Class tickets and you really need to get on that plane. And that Chosen Few Flight Attendant will answer,

Flight Attendant for Chosen Few: I don't know any of you mob! This plane is only for the Chosen Few!

Jesus: And you will begin to protest and say: "But you yourself sold us these tickets when we attended your airline promotion parties!"

But the Flight Attendant will answer,

Flight Attendant for Chosen Few: I already told you. This plane is full! Go away you Obvious Nobodies! You common riff-raff! You good-for-nothing trouble-makers!

Jesus: And there you will be, weeping and gnashing your teeth (Lam 2:16) when you see the Chosen Few sitting on the plane, drinking champagne and eating caviar while you, yourselves, are stuck on the ground. And, believe me—no one that any of you know is ever going to get onto that plane!

Narrator: "But look," Jesus said, as he began passing out Free Boarding Passes to the people in the crowd, with the logo for All People's Airline, and the motto, "Fly the Wide Body!" right at the top of the page—and all the while declaring, "Now Open for Business! Fully incorporated to turn this whole situation completely around! So that all of you ordinary folks who have been so unjustly placed on Stand-By Status by the Chosen Few Airlines might actually have the opportunity to get off the ground! Because whenever you fly All People's Airline, 'the first will be last, and the last will be first!'" (Mark 10:31)

Well, it was right then and there that some officials from the Chosen Few Travel Agency came out and told Jesus that he'd better high-tail it out of there right now because the Head of the Chosen Few Aviation Administration was going to wring his neck. But Jesus said to them,

Jesus: Go tell that Fox to cool his jets because I'm going to keep on handing-out free boarding passes for All Peoples Airline all day today, tomorrow, and the third day, until I arrive at Jerusalem International Airport, which is really the only appropriate place for a Consumer Advocate like me to depart.

Oh Jerusalem, Jerusalem: Jerusalem International. Always fingerprinting and screening passengers and crushing the competition! How many times have I longed to spread my wings so that all your children might come on board and fly? But you insisted that you would not change your policies. Behold! Your airline is bankrupt and your monopoly is broken! Truly I tell you, you will never change your unjust and divisive ways until you can really say in your deepest heart of hearts, "Thank God for the One who hands out free boarding passes—for the One who would still, to this very day, call us all home!"

A REAL CAUSE FOR CELEBRATION

Now, all of a sudden, all kinds of people from all kinds of places were coming to the church to hear the Voice of God. They were all basically trying and taxing the patience of the church leadership, and so the priests and the deacons and lay leadership grumbled together at the coffee pot at the Annual Meeting of the Diocesan Bishop, Parish Clergy and Wardens, all whining and saying, "Why this church is nothing but a sorry collection of really taxing personalities, riff-raff and ragamuffins and other royal pains who only show up for the bagels and the doughnuts and the juicy gossip at Coffee Hour."

So the quick-witted Word of God quickly employed a tricky little method to open-up their ears and hearts to a new and a real cause for celebration, and that tricky little method was just a couple of simple little illustrations.

The first one said, "Dear Clergy People and other Church Leadership Types, in your considerable experience in your lives and ministries, have you ever once run into a Rich Male Parishioner who owned a whole flock or portfolio of investments with one hundred shares—or potential shearers—who wouldn't move heaven and earth to find out what happened if suddenly even one of his precious holdings didn't show-up on his daily report? And, furthermore, when he does find it, and sees that it still has the potential for really big earnings, wouldn't he then at least invite a couple of his friends over for a drink to help him celebrate?"

"Or, tell me, have you ever met a well-rounded female parishioner with a few cents of her own, who, when she lost or misplaced some good cents somewhere, didn't yet still have enough sense left to go looking for whichever one she had lost? For surely she has enough sense to know that her entire fortune is really only hers to have and to hold when it is found all together and all in one place in her heart? And these are her treasure: cents of purpose; cents of identity as a beloved child of God; cents of community; cents of focus; cents of humor; cents of gratitude; cents of connection; cents of learning and growing; and cents of joy and wonder in all of God's creation."

"Just so, I tell you even now, if you stop your grumbling and your whining for half a second, and if you listen very, very carefully, you can actually hear the angels in heaven having a wonderful time at their own Coffee Hour in Heaven! And you can just see them too—munching on Heavenly Manna Bagels and Donuts of De-light and trading Juicy Angel Gossip each and every time anyone on earth really opens their ears and really hears the truly welcoming Word of God!"

So here's an angelic little tidbit worthy of celebration from the Good News World Report the other day, "Did you hear the one about that deacon over in Rappahannock who repented of his arrogance and then went downstairs to the basement and lingered with the laypeople for a bagel and some cream cheese after the worship service? Wow! Only God Almighty to thank for that! Will wonders never cease? Hallelujah! Amen!"

HAPPY HOUR

Then the Pastor and leaders of the church went to Bishop Jesus and said, "Use your magic and make our little community of faith grow! We want to flourish so that we can go directly to Happy Hour!"

Bishop Jesus said, "Look, if you had even the tiniest bit of faith, you yourselves would be able to make your community flourish and grow even in the most unlikely and seemingly inhospitable place like out in the middle of the Dead Sea or in any economically-challenged and thoroughly-depressed town in the middle of the country.

Then he planted a little picture about the size of a mustard seed in their hearts and minds about the kind of faith that makes a community flourish and grow. It was a cartoon, really, from everyday life in the working world.

Cartoon Frame Number One was of a clock showing 10:00 AM along with a picture of a boss saying "Hey everybody, stop working and come party with me right this minute! I mean it! This is an order!"

Then Bishop Jesus said, "What employer in the world invites their employees to feast at his table before their work is all finished for the day? None, I tell you! How absurd! Of course not!"

The he showed them Cartoon Frame Number Two where the boss is saying, "Hey everybody! Who said it was time to quit work for the day and start to party at 12:30 in the afternoon? Hey, this isn't Happy Hour! Get back to work until your work is done!"

And Bishop Jesus said, "Well, of course! All employers always say, 'Finish all of your work and then you can come to Happy Hour!' And not only that! Do you know of any employers who go around congratulating their employees for staying on the job until it's time to clock out? *I don't think so!*"

"So I say to all of you clergy and members of the church, when you have completed all of your work to make your community flourish and grow, then, when you finally do clock out, it's definitely time to gladly say, 'We are all beloved children of God and people of faith just doing our job!' For what a happy-Happy Hour that will truly be!"

MARSHAL JESUS ENCOUNTERS THE DIRTY MEN-YON

On his way to Dodge City— the city that was always trying to dodge the prophets—Jesus was traveling way out on the frontier, along the border between the Territory of Sin and the Territory of Forgiveness. As he entered a little one-horse, outpost town, he encountered some infamous, crusty-old outlaws who were known by all the decent, law-abiding citizens as The Dirty Men-Yon, or, also, for short, The Dirty Ten—which is surely enough scabby-old, sin-sick souls to form a prayer group or a church.

Now while The Dirty Ten were keeping their distance from Jesus, and wondering, perhaps, if it was safe to draw near to him, they drew their weapons, aimed and fired-off these loud, mind-blowing, revolutionary words: "Marshall Jesus, have mercy on us!"

When Jesus felt their bullets pierce his heart, he showered them with a barrage of his own, saying, "Go, show some of that bravado—some of your famous chutzpah—to the Religiously-Correct Police and tell them that you have already been accepted as children of God, and heirs of God's kingdom. Say to them clearly: 'Look. See. Listen. Here and Now. And get this straight for a change. We have all *already* been made clean, pure, blameless, spotless, free, and worthy to stand before you and our God!" [Editorial Comment: And the saying is true and worthy to be accepted, that the Son of Man came into the world to save scabby-old outlaws!]

Then the most notorious one of The Dirty Ten—the outlaw called The Samaritan—well, when *he* saw that he was indeed already acceptable to God and worthy to stand before him just as Marshal Jesus offered, he turned around and fell on his face in the dust at the feet of our Lord, giving him all the thanks and praise.

Jesus looked up into the heavens and cried out, "My God, my God, why have the all others forsaken me? Where in the world are the other nine? Shouldn't they also be here to give thanks and pray and sing your praises? Will only the outsiders, only those who have been shunned, labeled, feared and rejected respond to your great love and work of reconciliation?"

Then Marshal Jesus turned to the one who really did recognize and gave thanks for the hand of God at work in the world, draped his arm around the man's shoulder and said to him as they looked towards the setting sun, "Happy trails, Pard'ner! Your faith has made you whole!"

ANOTHER ONE BITES THE DUST

Well, one day when Jesus was thinking about his friends and colleagues, he pondered, "What shall I do for them next? I don't want them to lose heart. There's no reason to lose heart! What does my heart instruct me to do? Should I preach an apocalyptic sermon? No, they will lose heart. It would make the heart heavy and it would sink. How about an allegory explaining about the nature of God? No, they will lose heart. All that work would just confuse and add weight to the heart and it would sink."

So Jesus had the bright idea to use his gifts as a graphic artist to help them lighten-up. He drew a simple cartoon to help his disciples find and keep heart in the midst of all the trials and tribulations they faced, and told them this funny little story:

"Once upon a time, there was an unrighteous judge who was bothered by an obnoxious widow-woman who just kept on coming and annoying him. She obviously wanted what she wanted quite desperately. Now, that judge said to himself, "Although I myself am an obvious scoundrel and a rascal, yet I will give this obnoxious woman whatever she wants just to get her to quit coming here–thinking that I should care–and taking up all my valuable time."

Then Jesus also showed them his cartoon version of this same scene of the Hard-Hearted Judge and the Obnoxious Widow-Woman. But they were confused and argued among themselves, saying, "Is this story supposed to be an apocalyptic vision or is it an allegory? Well, who is the unrighteous judge supposed to represent? Who is the obnoxious widow-woman supposed to be? Is he saying that being obnoxious is the way to get to God's hard heart and squeeze-out the drop of the justice we want—like squeezing water out of a stone? Do the judge and the woman symbolize certain dynamics of the kingdom to come, which we are to believe will be given to us only if we persistently plead? But didn't Jesus also say, 'Knock and the door shall be opened' and 'Seek and ye shall find?' (Matt 7:7). So they gave up trying to figure it out because, although they thought they understood some of an allegory and thereby felt somewhat justified, alas, they completely missed the joke!

So then, still desiring to liberate people from the debilitating effect of religious arrogance, Jesus also told them this little picture-story:

"Once upon a time, two men went up to the temple to seek to be delivered from their anxieties through prayer. Now, the first guy was a religious expert who reminded God of all of his own good qualities—

especially of the fact that he was one of the few people who actually tithed the minimum standard. The second guy was a traitor to the community who not only did not tithe—but who actually took money away from good religious people—and who couldn't even look God in the eye but nevertheless had the audacity to pray that God would have mercy and somehow find him acceptable anyway."

"Now the first guy said, 'I thank you God that I am not like this nobody standing here next to me' while the second guy said, 'I beg you to receive me, a sinner, into your loving care.'"

Then Jesus asked his friends and colleagues, "Do you see how the second guy was delivered?"

Then they said "Oh yes, we most certainly do!" And they even thanked Jesus saying, "Thank God we are not like the first guy who was so arrogant and foolish in his pride. Why we are lots more like the Nobody who was humble, modest, long-suffering, honest, decent, everyday people who work very hard just to make ends meet. Why we would never claim to be religious experts or, even, possible saints! So let us remind God of our own good qualities, and especially of our great humility, and so we too will deserve to be delivered."

Then Jesus just sighed and said, "Lord, have mercy! Another one bites the dust!"

VI

In the Judean Theater

WHAT? AM I A LAWYER?

As they were traveling on the way to the Center City Stage in the Judean Theater, some first-rate, top-notch, head-of-the-class corporate-lawyer types in two-thousand-dollar suits came up with a question specifically designed to set Jesus up for a hostile takeover. They said, "Is it, or is it not, within the parameters of the laws of incorporation to sue a legal partner for dissolution of a partnership?"

But Jesus said, "What? Am I a lawyer? Why are you asking me about that? Aren't you the guys who are the experts in the field? So tell me, what did your famous corporate law professor have to say on the subject?"

They answered, "Well, Professor Moses said that it was OK for a man to draw up such a lawsuit." Jesus said, "Professor Moses spelled that out for you because he was well aware that your legalistic, dispassionate hearts wouldn't recognize a company asset if you slept with it. But from Time Immemorial, the Founder of our company established corporate partnerships as the basic model for company survival and creative expansion without which Life would be much less full than God intended—and there are many such partnerships already in the works and serving as examples: heaven and earth; peace and justice; faith and works; love of God and love of neighbor; bread and wine; yin and yang; private and public; heart and mind; spirituality and sexuality; prayer and action; left brain and right brain; text and context; flesh and spirit; grief and hope; suffering and joy; death and resurrection—not to mention

Good Friday and Easter. This, then, is the reason why, when human beings come of age and are truly mature, we leave our parent companies and form new corporate entities of our own—in which two complementary and equal partners become one cohesive unit so that they are no longer separate subsidiaries, but one, whole, new, and wonderful corporation. What, therefore, our Company Founder has established, let no one disenfranchise."

A PRECOCIOUS CHILD

Then a really good student rushed up and fell down at his feet and said, "Good Teacher, what must I do to get into Grad School?" Jesus answered, "Good God, Child, why do you call me good? Only God alone is good! And you know the rest of the instructions too: Never tattle, lie, cheat, steal, skip class, or be tardy—and, of course, always mind your parents!"

The child said, "Teacher, I have been very, very good and followed these instructions ever since I was in kindergarten." Looking at him with pleasure, Jesus said, "You only lack one thing, Child. Go sell all of your toys and give the proceeds to the poor and you will receive heavenly grades. Then come be a student of mine!" But when he heard these instructions, the aspiring student was very upset and went away extremely unhappy because he owned a whole lot of really great toys.

Then Jesus looked at his students who surrounded him and said, "How hard it will be for children who own a lot of toys to get into God's Grad School!"

His students thought these words were too hard, so Jesus said to them again, "Children, it's just so difficult to fit into God's Grad School! Why, it's easier for an elephant to get into Harvard than for a child who owns a lot of toys to get into one of God's Grad School Programs."

Jesus' students were astounded and said to one another, "Then how can anyone ever get a higher education with God?"

Jesus looked at his students and said, "For aspiring Grad Students it really is impossible! But not for God, who REALLY is really, really good! Why, with God, even A-pluses are as easy as pie!" But his students just said, "Huh?"

So Jesus tried it again by reciting a familiar old nursery rhyme, "Little Jack Horner."[1]

Little Jack Horner...
Suddenly and quite inexplicably jumped up and ran,
in a rare moment of bravery when,
for a short time anyway,
he actually abandoned his corner,
clutching his yummy and very rich pie,

When right there in front of God and everybody,
he stuck in his thumb
and pulled out a plum,
and said, "What a good boy am I!"

But Jesus, who knew all about the antics of such precocious young children, just loved them anyway and finished the rhyme with a wink and a smile:

You know, Jack,
There really is just one thing that you lack!
Get rid of that pie; just let go of that pie,
And you will have goodies a-plenty to delight in and try!

But Little Jack Horner
Went back to his corner
Hung his head, and he started to cry
For the pie that he gripped
In his hot little hands
Was a sweet and a very rich pie!

Now, Peter finally piped up to object, "Whoa! Wait a minute! If this is all true, what about those of us who have sold our toys, given away our plums, and left our security blankets to become your students?" Jesus said, "I kid you not. Anybody who sells their toys, gives away their plums, and leaves their security blankets to become one of my students for God's sake will be showered, right here and now, with more plum pies, fascinating vocations and meaningful work, and more heavenly affirmation and support than they can possibly imagine—along with a certain amount jealousy and envy, of course—and they will also be granted full enrollment in God's Grad School! Because many who have it all will have the least, and many who have the least will soon discover that they actually have it all, and have it in abundance!"

THE FACTORY OF ABSOLUTE FAIRNESS

"Look," Jesus further explained, "Our Heavenly Father's Eternal Kingdom of Just Rewards is like this story."

"Early one morning, a very Scrupulous Factory Owner (SFO) went out and signed-up some factory workers to work for the usual minimum daily wage in his Factory of Absolute Fairness and Just Rewards (FAFJW), where the motto was, 'An Honest Day's Wage for an Honest Day's Work.'"

"Then the SFO went out a couple of hours later and enlisted some more workers who looked like they had nothing better to do than to also spend their time and effort in his very elaborate system of Absolutely Fair and Just Rewards, where they were churning out Absolutely Fair and Just Rewards just as fast and as hard as they could. And, of course, because it was essential to the growth of his business, the SFO continued throughout the day going out again and again and continuously getting others to buy into his whole system OF AND FOR the manufacturing of Absolute Fairness and Just Rewards just as fast and hard as they could."

"Even as the last whistle of the day was about to blow, that SFO was still out there trying to grab anybody he could get to completely buy into and work their socks off for his system of Absolute Fairness and Just Rewards that he was so very busy selling to any and all who would buy into it."

He said to those he found still hanging-out on the streets, "Hey, why aren't you folks busy measuring-up like everybody else?" But they said, "Because no one has given us any work in the Measuring-up Department." So the SFO said, "Well, get to work now, and start measuring absolutely everything you see according to my precise standards of Absolute Fairness and Just Rewards."

Now, at the end of the day when the whistle blew, according to the SFO's brilliant master plan, he called in the first workers, who had bought into his system big time, and he paid them the usual minimum daily wage for which they had agreed to work. Then, of course, and exactly according to his well-advertised system, he paid all of the other workers less than that because it had taken them somewhat longer to buy into his system hook, line and sinker. Then, finally, he paid even far less to reward the workers who had only bought-in to his system at the very last minute.

Well, then the last minute workers grumbled and said, "Look. Maybe we bought-into your system late, but we also bought-into it with our whole hearts—hook, line and sinker—and for that we too deserve to receive a whole day's wage!

But the SFO said to their Shop Steward, "Hey, you Little Shrimp, I AM being ABSOLUTELY FAIR in giving you your absolutely JUST REWARD—just like my FAFJW manufactures! See? The other workers actually bore the burden of the day and the scorching heat, meting-out and measuring-out and cranking-out Absolute Fairness and Just Rewards just as fast and hard as they could—all the livelong day. Don't the Fair and Just Factory Rules say that the less long and hard you work in my system, the less your value to me? Look right here in the big print of the very first contract clause you signed where it says: "The first will be first and the last, last." Or do you, deep-down, really want me not to be fair? How absurd! Because, as everybody knows, Absolute Fairness is my business and so here, in my factory, what you deserve is always exactly what you get!"

Then the SFO taunted them, saying,

> So read it and weep!
> The contract is quite clear!
> You only get what you deserve,
> And that ain't much, my dear!

"But then," said Jesus, "those FAF workers went on strike, charging that ninety-nine percent of all FAF Workers receive less than the minimum living, daily wage, and that the SFO of the FAFJW hid this complete lack of compassion behind a strict interpretation of their own labor laws. And at least one of their placards criticizing the Factory of Absolute Fairness and Just Rewards said,

> "Give me an hour" says The Man,
> "And I'll pay you fair and square."
> But, WE KNOW when you work for the FAF,
> Your cupboard will be bare!

Then Jesus concluded his explanation with yet another special, healing rhyme of his own, suggesting that the people go to work for the Company of God's Delight instead.

So go back to work for God's Delight
And the blessings we will share
Rejoicing that—no matter if it's wrong or right—
God's Love is never fair!

BART AND ZACK

Now there were two people in the same theater who had a lot in common. They were both men who were living at the same time, in the same place, and wanting to know what the fuss was all about when a famous actor, Jesus of Nazareth, was passing by on his way to somewhere else.

The first guy was a poor, old beggar living off of others, and blind. The second guy was a rich, young, tax collector, living off of others, and short—which is different as night and day. Yet, they had something else in common, because neither of them could see what they wanted to see for various reasons. But both of them were extraordinarily clever in getting an audience with the famous actor who was passing by.

The first guy cleverly used his voice instead of his eyes. Employing his professional skills as a beggar, he projected his voice out over the crowd to Jesus' ears, yelling: "Hey, hey, hey! Lord Jesus! Have mercy!" louder and louder, again and again. Now this annoyed Jesus' disciples and the people around him who told the first guy, "Shut up, you old pariah!" But he got Jesus' attention anyway, and Jesus stopped to say: "Well, what do you want?" The man replied, "Look! I just want to see!"

Now, the second guy cleverly used his head and his arms and his legs to run ahead of the crowd and to climb a tree to position himself out over the crowd—out on a limb—in order to see. This too caught Jesus' attention!

When Jesus heard the desire of the poor, old, blind beggar who lived off of others, he said to him, "Receive your sight." It changed the man's whole perspective and he began to follow Jesus and give glory to God with his whole life.

And when Jesus saw the tree-climbing tax collector who lived off of others, he said to him, "Get down right now, Son, and receive me in your home!"

Well now, this REALLY annoyed the people around them who immediately called the short, tax-collecting tree-climber, "A Sinner!" and then also called Jesus, "A Sinner-Lover!"

But in very self-same moment, the tax-collector rejoiced and changed his life from being short and rich to becoming rich for the sake of others—although he was still short.

And so on this day, in this town, and in this way, two lost men were found by Jesus in spite of the crowd who surrounded them, and they got what they truly desired and received their sight to become true seers at last through whom God beamed pure delight!

NICODEMUS AND METANOIA MAN

Later on, when it was pitch black and probably about three o'clock in the morning, a well-known and very serious religious fellow named Nicodemus ventured out into the dark to see the Famous Teacher and to tell that Teacher that he, Nicodemus, could clearly see what Jesus was up to.

Well, Nick just barged right on in and woke-up Jesus, who was sound asleep in his bed with his special blanket and genuine, lamb's wool night-cap. Nick said to him loudly, "Teacher! Let me introduce myself! For I, a fellow teacher, am a person who can clearly see what you are up to—and I can tell that you are another one of the many talented teachers God Almighty has chosen to be a teacher, because, as far as I am concerned, you have already proven that fact by the very clarity of your teaching!"

Jesus rubbed his eyes and answered him, "Well, the plain truth of it is that unless a person has been turned inside-out and upside-down, they can't even begin to see what either God or I am up to in this world. To which the very serious religious fellow, Nicodemus, said, "Well, I just can't see that at all! It doesn't even make sense! And it's just plain ridiculous! How can you even suggest that a human being could live if they were turned inside-out and upside down, with their skin on the inside and their bones on the outside? Why, such a person would be totally vulnerable! Everything would just fall out and apart! I'm surprised at you, Jesus! That's just utter nonsense! It makes about as much sense as saying "You must be born again" as if you could literally crawl back into your mother's womb and start all over again! Humph! Nothing but crazy talk!"

So our Teacher Jesus patiently explained it again, saying, "Well, let me explain it again then. Because the plain truth is that unless a person has been turned upside-down and inside-out and spun completely all around, then they won't even come close to seeing what God and I are up to in this world."

And then Jesus summarized this teaching by saying, "If a person can only see in one way, then that person can only see in one way. But a person who is turned around to see in other ways is able to turn around to see in other ways. And you do not need to be astounded at what I say because you yourself already know a very clear example of this, and if you think about it for a minute, you will see that the wind blowing every-which-a-way all over the face of the earth can be seen as attesting to the living power and presence of God in this world—which is very much in the spirit of what I am saying about being turned inside-out and upside-down and spun completely all around. And if you listen as you listen to the sound of the wind, you will see how you really can see what you just can't see!"

But Nick said that he just didn't get it, to which Jesus replied, "Nicodemus, Nicodemus! You have a Master's Degree in Teaching and you still don't get it? Open your eyes! Look! If you don't see my point about the wind, then how are you going to see what I am showing you right here and right now—right in front of your eyes—which is exactly what God and I are up to in this world! For just as Moses lifted up his staff to remind God's people that their sins would always come back to bite them—and that only God could forgive and lead them to new life— so too must I be lifted up to take the venom out of sin and the sting out of death in order to show God's children the way to be born again so that they might experience perfect forgiveness and new life in abundance and forever!"

Editors' Note: For as our most poetic author, John, said in the sixteenth verse of Stanza Three of his most beloved witness, "God loved the world so much that he gave Jesus to us as a gift and a sight for sore eyes so that whoever looks on him and recognizes the One who sent him shall truly know life in abundance and everlasting!"

ANGLO-CATHOLIC FATHER JESUS

Well! When that famous itinerant minister, our beloved Anglo-Catholic Father Jesus, was traveling through the Midwest, naturally he stopped for some rest and respite at a church with little basins of holy water posted at the door. He stretched out and made himself comfortable on the back pew in the chapel.

Now it was about time for the mid-week worship service when here came your average Anglo-Catholic parishioner thirsting for enough midweek spiritual food and drink to last for the rest of her busy week. Father Jesus said to her, "Bless me with that holy water."

The Anglo-Catholic Woman said to him, "How is it that you, a stranger, a man, and a priest are asking me, a lowly layperson and a woman, to bless you?" She could tell he was a priest because he was wearing an Anglican collar at the time. "It's usually the other way around. Well, isn't it?"

Father Jesus answered her, "Woman, if you were really intimate with God's True Gift of Life, and if you even had a clue who you were encountering here and now in this immediate time and place, you would already be down on your lovely Anglo-Catholic knees begging him to shower you with the blessing of holy abundant and living water forever."

The woman said to him, "Excuse me, Father, but you don't much look like you're really equipped to offer me such a gift! The subject is very deep, you know, and surely way beyond your therapeutic skills. So where would you come up with something like that? Do you think you are a smarter, and wiser, and a better therapist than our much loved and fondly-remembered first priest who established this church and taught us everything we need to know about incense and holy water and the right and proper worship of God?"

Father Jesus said to her, "Woman, everyone who comes here for holy water will have to keep coming back to get it again and again. But whoever receives the water flowing directly from me will be permanently blessed, for my water will become a fountain of holy water welling up within her and flowing forever."

The woman said to him, "Well then, Father, give me some of this water so that I don't have to keep coming back to this church twice a week for a little drop at a time."

"Father Jesus said to her, "OK, but first go get your Great High Priest and true husband in ministry."

The woman answered him, "I have no Great High Priest and true husband in ministry! Father, I can't magically come up with anybody like that!"

Father Jesus said, "Well, you are quite right to say 'I have no Great High Priest and true husband in ministry.' For although you have had at least five priests in charge of this parish, including that fellow you've got now, the truth of the matter is that not of one of them has ever been, can be, or ever will be your true Great High Priest and husband and partner in ministry and worship in the deepest sense of the word."

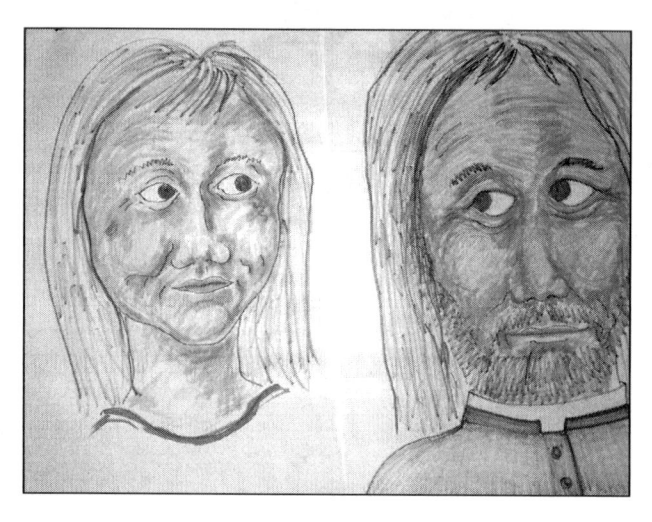

She said to him, "Well Father, I see you're pretty smart for an Anglo-Catholic priest; I'll give you that. So explain to me, please. Don't you Anglo-Catholics say that we have to go to Canterbury Cathedral in England to worship rightly and properly if we really want to fully encounter and be truly blessed by God?"

Father Jesus said to her, "Woman, very soon indeed, and even now, true worshippers can enter directly into an intimate, holy, blessed, creative and life-giving relationship with The True Great High Priest, Husband, and Father of us all, and I am literally showing you precisely what it means to have an intimate, life-giving relationship with the living Great High Priest, Husband and Father of All, who is your true partner in life and service to the world, even as we speak. For truly I tell you, it is for such life-giving relationships that the Father thirsts!"

The woman said to him, "Well, Father, I do know that 'Christ has died. Christ is risen. Christ will come again.'[2] We say it here at church whenever we use a certain prayer, I think. And when he finally does come, then life will be abundant, holy, blessed, and overflowing with meaning."

Father Jesus said to her, "Woman, open your eyes and see me right here and now! For, I am always here with you, and I am down on my knees because I am proposing to be your true partner in life forever and ever. Amen."

Then the Anglo-Catholic woman was so excited that she left the basin of holy water in the chapel and rushed off to tell every one she could find. And because of her testimony, many came to see, to understand, to believe, and to rejoice in him!

THE LIVING QUAIL

Jesus really surprised his Little Flock when he said one day, "I am the Living Quail come down from heaven; whoever eats my soft and tender flesh will be well fed forever." Many of his friends, when they first heard this, said, "Yikes! That's a really hard one to swallow. Anybody want to chew on that one for awhile?"

But Jesus, who was already well aware of their predilection for the usual fare, said, "Why are you turning up your noses up at this? Would you prefer that I magically disappear now the same way I just showed-up just a minute ago? Open-up your clogged-up ears and listen to me sing! It's the very strange and surprising spirit of God who gives the greatest of great delight! A tough realism is entirely of no avail in this regard! See? I am right here and now giving you a gift of spirit and life! Now I'm not naming names, but, uh, *some of you* (*wink) just aren't really giving me one-hundred percent of your full attention just yet so you're still having trouble believing that what I'm telling you is truly of the spirit and life you would know! Well, isn't that so?"

But because Jesus already knew who all would have a lot of trouble letting go of their usual expectations in order to open-up and receive an entirely new and very strange creature of freedom and beauty which is everyday food for the human soul dwelling in God's eternal kingdom, he added, "Look. This is exactly why I'm telling you these delightful things in this strange and unusual way! It is God the Father who gives surprising, strange and completely free gifts all the time! Why you yourselves wouldn't even be here if it weren't for God!"

But after this, of course, many of his would-be disciples quickly distanced themselves from him, saying, "Who? Jesus? Oh, he's really crazy. I mean, we're talking One Really Strange Bird! I wouldn't touch him with a ten-foot pole!"

So then Jesus turned and asked his dearest of friends, "Do you also wish to distance yourselves from me?" Then, as voiced by Simon Peter, they answered him, "You have the True Manna from above. Where else could we go?" Although, as Jesus already understood all too well, at least one of them would eventually high-tail it out of there in the opposite direction.

THE WILD CARD OF JUDEA

Well, it was right after Jesus managed to clean out the entire Temple Casino when some of the House Dealers approached him and placed their high card on the table, which was the Ace of Clubs from the Temple Casino Club House Deck embossed with the words "Members Only!" and "No Wild Cards Allowed!" They demanded a response.

Then right away Jesus played his card, known as the Wild Card of Judea, which said "Repent!" and "The Kingdom of God is in the hand!" Then he asked if they could come up with a decent response to it.

But, alas, those expert House Dealers looked at their two remaining cards, neither of which they could risk playing, for if they played their Prophet Card, they would just be handing the game over to God right then and there, and the House would lose. Or, if they played the Not-A-Prophet card, the crowd would go wild, and so too the House would lose! And so they said, "We pass."

Then Jesus showed them his two remaining cards and asked if they could come up with a decent response to either one of them. First he showed them the Wild Card that said, "Hell no! I won't go!" but then went ahead and followed suit anyway.

Then he showed the Good-Old-Standby Card that said, "Play me! Play Me! Dear Old Daddy!" who did not follow suit, but just sat there and folded instead.

Then Jesus asked the House Dealers, "So which card do you think actually worked and took the trick?" And they picked the Wild Card, of course, because it actually worked to follow suit.

And then that Old Cardmeister Jesus played his winning card which was really wild! For the descriptive notes on the Winning Card said, "Riff-Raff are busy out-maneuvering expert House Dealers because they respond to this Wild Card of Judea." Then he flipped over the Wild Man Card and showed them the final trump card which said, "This Wild Card of Judea Plays Exclusively for Almighty God!"

TIME TO VOTE IN A VERY IMPORTANT ELECTION

It was on that very same day after Jesus came to the temple—drove out all who were buying and selling; overturned the tables of the money changers; cured the blind and lame who came to him; caused children to make all kinds of noise in the temple; cursed a fig tree for not bearing fruit; had then returned to the temple where he was confronted by some very serious, upstanding, religious folks who questioned what he was up to; and then the chief priests and elders refused to answer a question Jesus posed to them about what they thought John the Baptist was up to—when Jesus told them this story as well.

"Once upon a time, there was a very Good, Solid Citizen who raised both of his two sons to become Good, Solid Citizens of the Kingdom of God. When they grew up and reached the Age of Majority, he told them it was now time for them to exercise their right to vote in a very important election. The first son said, "Oh, yes, indeed, Father. You know me! I am a very good citizen myself, and of course I will vote in this important election." But instead, he elected to hang-out schmoozing with the candidates outside the polling place, and never even made it through the door. Now the second son said, "Nah, Dad, I'll think I'll pass on that. There's nothing to vote for, and besides, my vote doesn't count anyway. It's all a colossal waste of time, and besides, I've got better things to do," and he hit the road. But, lo and behold, somehow he miraculously managed to drop by the polls and vote anyway!"

"So what do you think?" Jesus asked. "Which of the two sons was a Good Citizen?"

"The one who actually voted!" the very serious, upstanding, religious folks replied. "Quite right!" Jesus affirmed. "So now you can understand why those who you consider unacceptable are so gladly experiencing the Kingdom of God instead of you. When John came preaching that it was high time to start walking the walk instead of just talking the talk, you didn't believe him. But those you considered to be beneath you believed him! And even when you saw them actually changing their behavior, you still didn't change your own!"

WHAT WILL THAT BISHOP DO?

Then on another occasion, Jesus addressed a Diocesan Convention and said, "Listen to another parable."

"There once was a bishop who planted a church, built it with walls of stone, filled it with pews and classrooms, and even erected a bell tower. Then he turned its care over to a local congregation and vestry and went back to his See City. When the time came to collect the Mission and Ministry Assessment, the Bishop's Treasurer and his staff sent letters to the congregation's vestry asking them to pay what they owed. But the vestry ignored one letter, tore up another one, and mutilated yet another."

"Again the Bishop's Treasurer and his staff sent even more letters than before and the vestry treated them all in the same way."

"Finally, the Bishop sent a hand-written letter of his own, saying, 'Surely, they will respect my personal appeal.' But when the vestry saw that letter they said to themselves, 'Hey, this is the answer to all of our financial difficulties! Come, let us shred this letter and use the Mission and Ministry Assessment to pay all of our bills.' So they took the Bishop's letter to the church office and shredded it."

"Now I have a question for you," said Jesus to the Diocesan Convention, "When the Bishop leaves his city and goes to visit that congregation, what do you think he will do?"

The whole Convention rose with one voice and exclaimed, "He will excommunicate those wretches and give that church to a new congregation who will pay their assessments on time!"

Jesus said to them, "Oh no, no, no!! Sit down! Sit down! The Bishop won't write-off that congregation! Have you never read in your Diocesan Canons, 'The principle of Abiding Generosity is the very cornerstone of the Bishop's ongoing work with congregations'? The Bishop will work with that congregation to bring them into Good Standing and the fullness of generosity according to the Canons."

"Therefore I tell you, the fullness of God's generosity can only be fully received by those who practice abiding generosity themselves! This is entirely the Lord's way of working and it is marvelous to behold!"

HIS STEADFAST LOVE ENDURES FOREVER

Jesus told them another little parable that endures to this day.

"Once upon a time, a writer carefully crafted a story about the Kingdom of God. He set-up a border around the page; he dug down into the source material right at hand, and he carefully constructed an impressive building of choice words to temporarily contain the central-most metaphor, gift and meaning of it all.

When it was nearly time for all to be revealed, he assigned some of his best readers to read it and begin gathering its rewards, but, alas, they found that story as cold and hard as a rock and they were quickly and easily defeated by the whole enterprise. So the writer assigned even more readers to the task, but they also found it awfully hard to fathom and a real killer.

Then the Author sent in his very own Pride and Joy to wrestle with his own story, anticipating that it would be most likely to yield to him— the author's very own brain-child—with the utmost respect. But, alas, he was completely defeated by it as well."

"So, when that writer next encounters that barren, unyielding story, what do you expect he will do with it?" Jesus asked.

They said, "Why, he will crush it up in his fist and throw it right in the incinerator, and then he will assign the task to somebody else who will actually take that story and struggle with it until it really pays off for him when the time is good and ripe!"

But Jesus said to them, "Haven't you dug down deeply into the source material right at hand? Haven't you read your foundational stories, or dug down to discover what gem the source material has to offer up?" Then he asked if they remembered this key verse from what should have been a very familiar song to them: 'The stone that the builders rejected has become the cornerstone; this was the Lord's doing and it is amazing in our eyes!'" (Mark 12:10).

So Jesus explained that the story the readers rejected really is a little stronghold of words so arranged in order to temporarily contain the central-most metaphor, gift and meaning of it all until it all comes together and bears fruit when the time is really, really ripe and ready for delivery. For the very source material which the readers have rejected— and failed to care for and tend to properly— easily yields the true answer to Jesus' key question, "Now what do you think that writer will do?"

As found in that very same, carefully constructed song:

O give thanks to the Lord for he is good;
His steadfast love endures forever.

Let Israel say,
His steadfast love endures forever.

Let the house of Aaron say,
His steadfast love endures forever.

Let those who fear the Lord say
His steadfast love endures forever.

O give thanks to the Lord for he is good;
His steadfast love endures forever. (Psalm 118:1–4; 29)

"Therefore I tell you, that writer will indeed continue to wrestle and struggle with that story as long as it takes and until it yields the foundational truth of God's abundantly patient, enduring and eternal love! For this is not really the writers' doing or the readers' doing, but, "This is the Lord's doing, and it is amazing in our eyes!" (Mark 12:10). So always, always, "give thanks to the Lord for he is good; his steadfast love endures forever!" (Psalm 118:29) and ever. Amen.

THE ABSENTEE LANDLORD

When Jesus was confronted by the Scribes and Elders in the Temple about the source of his authority, he told this parable to the people.

"A real-estate developer built an apartment complex and put it under the care of some Resident Managers and went off to California to live as an absentee-landlord for a long while. The time came when the landlord sent a homeless person to the managers for some food and shelter. But the Resident Managers told her to "Beat it!" and sent her away to walk the streets. The landlord then sent another homeless person and the Resident Managers also told him to "Beat it!" and verbally abused him, calling him a despicable, vile and odious bum, and turned him away homeless too. The landlord sent yet a third homeless person, and this one they literally kicked right out of the door.

Then the Landlord, who was also the Architect and Developer of the Apartment Complex which was also called the Literal-Minded Violently-Exclusive Complex Syndrome (LM-VEC Syndrome) puzzled aloud to himself, "Well, what shall I do now? I know! I'll send my very own son! Maybe, they will respect him!" But when the Resident Managers saw the son they said to themselves, "This is our landlord's will for the future? We'd better put a stop to him and take over this Complex all for ourselves. Because now what do you suppose the Landlord will do? I tell you what he will do. He will come and fire those Resident Managers and give their jobs to someone else!"

When the people heard this story, they all said, "God forbid!"

But Jesus looked at them and said, "What did you think is the meaning of those strange biblical quotes from Psalm 118, Isaiah, and the Book of Daniel. Isn't that the way you usually allegorize and interpret Psalm 118? But I say to you, look more closely at the foundation rock. The living will and purposes of God are written in stone, and even though they may be rejected by the Resident Managers and Architects of society, they are still now and always will be the very foundation and true cornerstone of the future, and whatever stands in its way will be taken apart and dismantled!"

Of course, the local Managers wanted to get their hands on Jesus right then and there because they saw he had told this parable against them. But they didn't act at that time because were afraid of their tenants.

THE ENEMY DRESSED IN HIS SUNDAY BEST

Jesus also told them this strange little story about the Kingdom of God.

"The Kingdom of God is a lot like an Episcopal priest who offered both the time and the place for people to come together and worship our loving God and Father."

"First, he sent out invitations throughout the city—to all the Movers and Shakers and all those who looked to all the world like they had their lives together—but, alas for him, they would not deign to come. Then he sent out the Senior Warden and the Junior Warden and the other members of his vestry, telling them to advertise the service with personal invitations and fliers that said,

> Come to the feast that is already prepared for you! Be Ready to Celebrate Life in all its Wonder and Glory! God's Table is Set and Filled with Abundant Food and Drink for Life and for Life in Abundance! A Feast for Human Eyes and a Banquet for the Human Soul!

"But, my-oh-my, how both the churched and the un-churched alike had a good time making fun of that, reminding everybody of how

Episcopalians, among others, have often been referred to as The Frozen Chosen because they are so out-of-date and out-of-step with today's world and are therefore totally irrelevant—all of which really dampened the vestry's enthusiasm and crushed their spirits—and completely infuriated our priest! And, believe-you-me, he was sorely tempted to take-up scare tactics himself—to go ahead and preach darkness and damnation with vigor and abandon, and to send his entire congregation out to all of the churched and the un-churched alike to deliver a blistering condemnation that would shrivel their mean, judgmental souls to nothing!"

"But what he said to his congregation was this instead: 'Look! The banquet *is* ready! The feast provided by our loving God and Father has already begun and is already being served all around us! So let us resolve to go out and invite anybody who is willing to come, no matter how they're dressed or where they come from! And I do mean anybody! We will welcome anybody! We will rejoice with anybody! Get it? Anybody at all!"

"So then the entire church was filled with people! The good and the bad! The faith-filled and the doubt-full! But when the priest looked out over the congregation he suddenly noticed one in their midst who was all dressed up according to the self-aggrandizing rules of the world. So the priest said to him, 'Well, My Old Nemesis, how in the world did you get in here?!' But he received no answer. So he told the congregation to 'Grab him by the horns, tie him up, and throw this Prince of Darkness right back out into the darkness from whence he comes—where there is much weeping and gnashing of teeth (Lam 2:16) because of his infernal destructiveness!'"

And so this is why it is still said to this day, "Many are called to be Episcopalians, but few are blessed to be so chosen, and the Prince of Darkness is surely not one of them!"

JESUS ANSWERS IN A TIMELY FASHION

Well, the Official Referees and Legal Time-Keepers had themselves a long, involved meeting to figure out how to so trip-up, confuse, disorient and entangle Jesus with his own words that he could never spend time or show his face in public again. They sent their student lackeys to him, saying, "Teacher, we know that you are incredibly well-adjusted and efficient and really know how to use your time in accordance with God's will, no matter what. So do tell. Is it OK with God if we spend a significant portion of our time on-the-clock living in the Real World, or not?

But Jesus, alert to their duplicity, said, "Why this two-timing test of me, you two-faced time keepers? Show me the clock you use to divvy-up your time?"

So they handed him a clock. And Jesus said to them, "Whose face, and controlling metaphor, is this?"

They answered, "Father Time's."

Then Jesus took the time to coin this famous phrase for them: "Therefore render unto Father Time the time that belongs to Father Time, and the time that belongs to God the Father, render unto to God the Father."

When they heard it, then suddenly *they* were the ones who were all confused and disoriented and amazed, and so they tapped their wrist watches and exclaimed, "Ooops! Wow! Gosh! Look at the time! It's time to go already!" And they scurried off and went on their way muttering, "Curses, foiled again!" So then, after that, they went back to just biding their time until another opportune time to try to trip-him-up should appear.

ONE BRIDE FOR SEVEN BROTHERS

Narrator: Well, you see, there were some very serious religious folk, called Sadducees, who were very upset because they had heard that Jesus believed in life after death. So these very serious religious folk came to Jesus and posed a very serious question that they had designed in order to show Jesus that his belief in the resurrection of the dead was not only preposterous, but also downright silly!

Now three of the Sadducees were carrying picket signs that said: "Our Religion is Very Serious!"—"Life After Death is Ridiculous!"—"Bah Humbug!"—"Just Say No to Immortality!"—"Because Moses Says So!"—"What About the *Rules*?!"—and the like.

Sad 1: We are very serious, Jesus, about our laws, which came straight from God to Moses.

Sad 2: And one of the laws that Moses wrote, Jesus, was all about human responsibility.

Sad 3: And we take our responsibilities very seriously, Jesus.

Sad 1: Therefore, Jesus, we would like for you to consider your silly belief in life after death in terms of the law Moses wrote about The Property Rights and Responsibilities of Brothers. . .

Sad 2: . . . and see how little sense you make!

Narrator: . . . they said, accusing Jesus of being illogical and not respecting the laws of either God or Moses!

Sad 3: Yeah, Jesus! What about the law in Deuteronomy, Chapter 25, Verse 5, that specifically states: "If thy brother shall die childless, then thou shalt marry thy brother's wife and thou shalt thereby produce children for thy brother as soon as possible for thy brother is dead and therefore no longer in a very good position to produce children for himself!"

Sad 1: Yeah, Jesus! What about that law?!

Sad 2: See Jesus? We just happen to have a copy of that law, written in stone, right here with us, at our fingertips!

Sad 3: But Jesus, what if there should just happen to be seven brothers?

Sad 1: And what if the first one of them marries a woman . . .

Sad 2: . . . but then what if that brother just keels over and dies without producing any children?

Sad 3: And then, what if the second brother marries her and dies, and then the third brother also marries her and up and dies?

Sad 1: And, furthermore, what if both of them die without producing any children either?

Sad 2: Exactly, Jesus! And, likewise, what if each one of the rest of those seven brothers marry her, each in turn?

Sad 3: Well, Jesus? Ha! What if they all keel-over dead without producing any children?

Sad 1: Yeah, Jesus! What if all seven brothers possess her in complete fulfillment of the law.

Sad 2: As even you, Jesus, must agree that they should!

Sads 1, 2, & 3: What then?!

Narrator: And then the Sadducees asked Jesus the most serious part of their very serious religious question:

Sad 1: If there is life after death. . .

Sad 2: . . . which we seriously doubt. . .

Sad 3: . . . then, when the woman finally dies, and she goes to heaven . . .

Sad 1: Whose wife will she be then?

Narrator: Why, can't you just see all the brothers suddenly vying for her attention?
1. "Don't Settle for Brotherly Love! Pick me!"
2. "Married to Me and All My Brothers! Choose Me Now, and Dump the Others!"
3. "Roses are Red; Violets are Blue; Remember How I Die for You!"
4. "For a Match Made in Heaven, Pick Me!"
5. "Be Forever Mine! Valentine!
6. "Eternal Bliss You Will Not Miss! If You Pick Me!"
7. "First is better than all the rest! Pick me because I'm still the best!"

All 7 Brothers: Therefore choose me! Therefore choose me!
Narrator: Then Jesus just chuckled, kind-of sighed and said,
Jesus: Talk about SILLY! Now that's REALLY silly!

>But take it from me
>Once this good woman is raised to new life
>She'll never again become ANYONE'S wife!
>
>Because creatures like angels
>Who've been raised from the dead
>And are subject no longer
>To the laws you've just read
>
>When their life is eternal
>With God at their head
>Having now attained heaven
>Most surely won't wed!
>
>And even Moses, you know,
>Who wrote this fine law,
>At the Old Burning Bush,
>Resurrection he saw!
>
>That the dead are all raised
>There cannot be a doubt
>For God's Eternal Life
>Is what God's all about!

Narrator: And, you know, although it's not really a matter of biblical record, I can't help thinking that when they heard the light-hearted grace of Jesus' answer, that, just maybe, some of those deadly serious Sad-you-sees were surely changed into Glad-you-sees!

All: So let your hearts be glad
And let your souls rejoice!
It's to the God of the Living
That we raise our voice!

To the Great God of Life
AND the God of the Dead
For "All live to God!"
Just as Jesus once said!

JÉSUS BEN DIOS AND DAVE "THE BABE" KING

So you see, Baseball Fans, when the Phar-I-See infield saw the unrestricted, free-agent, slugger Jésus ben Dios hit each and every one of the Sad-U-See's pitches right out of the ballpark, the Phar-I-See's huddled together in their own dug-out and came up with a game plan to see if they could arrange an exclusive and long term, lucrative contract on his extraordinary talent.

So they sent their very best free-agency lawyer over to Jésus to question his loyalties and to find out if he would sign-on with their own winning team—strong in the baseball family tradition of their own claim to fame: Dave "The Babe" King, who was our very own Super Star, the King of All Baseball—also known as The Bambino!

"Wow! That's a tape measure swing you've got there, Jésus!" the team lawyer said. "I am here to tell you that the famous Phar-I-Sees are very interested in you. But first I need to ask you one very important question because, as you must already know, baseball is very, very important to us."

"So, tell us, Jésus, in your opinion and in your own words, please tell us and the whole baseball world for that matter, 'What do you yourself consider to the most important rule in baseball today?'"

Jésus ben Dios answered:

> The most important thing about baseball is to completely devote yourself to our beloved Sponsor and Commissioner: the One who

makes this all possible—the Creator of the game, the Maintainer of the Standards and the Sustainer of the Sport—loving him with all of your heart and soul and mind with a truly religious fervor.

The second thing is just like it: to love each and every single player on the field as much as you love being a player yourself and with an equally religious fervor.

On these two inspiring insights the entire history and future of baseball rests!

Then, while the Phar-I-Sees were still dug-in to their dug-out, Jésus turned around and pitched the ball directly into their strike zone, asking them an equally central and important question relating to the history and future of baseball: "When the Mega-Star Who is to Come makes his appearance, for whom do you think he will play?" *(GOOD PITCH!)*

"Why of course he will obviously play for OUR team!" they cheered, "because we operate solidly within the tradition of our crowning glory, King David 'The Babe' King, as everybody who's anybody in baseball already knows!" *(BUT IT WAS A SWING AND A MISS. STRIKE ONE!)*

Then Jésus rapidly fired-off another pitch, straight into the strike-zone again: "But as everybody in baseball knows, even Dave 'The Babe' King himself—in a pure state of baseball fever—was recorded as saying that he himself would really like to sign an exclusive contract and play on the team of the Mega-Star Who is to Come, because Dave 'The Babe' understood that the Mega-Star would be in a league of his own and soon have all the other teams under his cleats." *(LOOKING! STRIKE TWO!)*

And then Jésus ben Dios delivered his zinger—SO FOLLOW THIS BALL IF YOU CAN!

(THE WIND-UP): "If the magnificent Dave Tthe Babe' expressed HIS desire to play for the Mega-Star Who is to Come. . .

(AND THE PITCH): . . . then how can you possibly think that the Mega-Star Who is to Come would EVEN CONSIDER signing a contract making himself subject to and property belonging to YOU?" *(100 MPH. LOOKING AGAIN! STRIKE THREE!)*

And they were all O. U. T. Out! Out of questions! Out of answers! And out of the ballpark! And they never even approached future Hall of Fame-er, Jésus ben Dios, again!

YOGI JESUS AND THE VOICES OF ANXIETY

"Well," Dr. Jesus said to his little therapy group, "The voices of anxiety love to sit where they can be most easily heard. Therefore, recognize them for what they are and listen to what they are telling you about themselves and their fear, but don't let them infect you or jerk you around. Look, the voices of anxiety just love to present themselves as voices of concern for you and your well-being, but what they really want to do is to get you all wrapped-up and tied-down in their whole world of fear so that you can carry it on your shoulders for them, which certainly doesn't do a thing to make your lives any easier! You see, the voices of anxiety do everything they can to capture your complete attention, spinning ever bigger and more frightening scenarios. They thrive on emergencies and are thrilled to dominate the most prominent places in your hearts and minds!"

"Listen, the voices of anxiety love to be called the Voice of Authority. But you? You are not called to become purveyors of anxiety or voices of authority, for there is only one Voice of Authority for you, and that voice is clearly not the voice of anxiety. And, in fact, you are all already fully-equipped to hear it. So don't let anybody on earth displace, disturb, or disrupt your hearing the voice of your Father in Heaven. Don't let anybody lord it over your life, for there is only one God, and you all have ears to hear him. For even as we speak, the loud, harsh voices of anxiety that frighten and hinder are being recognized for what they are and are thereby silenced whenever the steady voice of hope and trust born of God is raised.

AN APOCALYPTIC COFFEE HOUR CONVERSATION

Re: The Whole World Coming Apart at the Seams
Setting: Church Parish Hall
Time: Sunday Morning, Coffee Hour

Worshipper #1: What I really need is some coffee!
Worshipper #2: Me too. That was such a long service.
Worshipper #3: It sure was. Say, don't we have anything to eat except doughnuts and bagels?
Worshipper #4: Don't you know by now that we never have anything else?

Worshipper #1: Hey, let's stand over here where we can hear each other better, OK?
Worshipper #2: Sure, OK.
Worshipper #2: Say, did any of you happen to see the paper this morning before you came to church?
Worshippers #1, 3 & 4: No. Well, no.
Worshipper #3: I don't read it at all anymore. It's just too depressing.
Worshipper #4: Just tears this town down all the time.
Worshipper #1: Well, I still get it, but I sure agree with you. It really is depressing.
Worshipper #2: I know what you mean.
Worshipper #3: Same-old same-old every day.
Worshipper #4: Nothing new under the sun. NOTHING GOOD ANYWAY.
Worshipper #1: Yeah, well you've got that right! Today's headline, for example, said, "Whole World Coming Apart at the Seams!" They might as well just print that very same headline every single day.
Worshipper #2: Exactly. It's just the same old list of horrible things going on day after day after day.
Worshipper #3: Divorce is up. The economy is in the dumps. Robbers and muggers around every corner. Why with all the gangs and drug-dealers on the prowl decent people can't even take a walk in their own neighborhoods anymore.
Worshipper #4: The police can't do anything about it. Our legal system is a joke. The schools are failing. Everybody and his brother are abusing children! Not to mention the clergy.
Worshipper #1: Politicians playing games with our money don't mind dipping into our pockets, but sure won't touch their own health care or pension plans.
Worshipper #2: The rich get richer and the poor get poorer. It's true.
Worshipper #3: Well if you think the newspaper makes for grim reading, have any of you seen the Church Pledge Letter yet?
Worshipper #4: Talk about discouraging.
Worshipper #1: Makes me wonder if the church can even survive.
Worshipper #2: I don't get it. I mean, we're a great church, but it seems like people just don't care anymore.
Worshipper #3: Seems like people are just too busy to come to church anymore.
Worshipper #4: Me? I just feel numb to the whole thing.

Worshipper #1: Yeah. And it's like: Where in the world is G*od* anymore?
Worshipper #2: Or, why doesn't God just step in and do something?
Worshipper #3: Yeah. Like make people pledge more money!
Worshipper #4: Or send some more people anyway!
Worshipper #1: You know, it sure seems like we're coming to the end of the world, doesn't it?
Worshipper #2: Yeah. Where is God when you really need him?
Worshipper #3: What really is the point of coming to church and trying to be a person of faith in a world like this?
Worshipper #4: Hey, Jesus. You've been awfully quiet. What do you have to say about the whole world coming apart at the seams?
Worshippers #1, 3 & 4: Yeah, Jesus. What do you think?
Jesus: My dear friends, I think at this point in the conversation I would simply like to remind you that our Father in Heaven knows and cares deeply about each one of you and he grieves with you about the troubled world in which you live.

Our Father knows full well that you live in a time of dangerous and tumultuous change. And he grieves for all those who suffer the violence and injustice so evident in your homes and schools and workplaces and streets. And I myself weep with all those who weep in the darkness and long for the light.

I understand that you're greatly tempted to give up and retreat into some private place where you think you can be safe and sound—where you try to take care of yourself while the rest of the world comes apart at the seams—and that your hearts and souls are tested daily in many, many ways.

But, don't you understand? And don't you see? When I look at this world, I see that "the whole world coming apart at the seams," as you put it, is really God's own handiwork still going on. I see so clearly that you are God's people "and the sheep of his pasture" (Ps 100:03)—that you are God's agents in this world, and that you are here and now, in this world, in the position to put it back together in a brand-new way. You know, you have been baptized by water and marked as God's own agents forever. You have been graced with the indwelling spirit to give you the desire, the strength, the will and the wisdom to do the will of God right in the midst of a world coming apart at the seams: to shed light wherever there is darkness; to become beacons of light in the midst of a world that is filled with darkness and injustice; to see the fracturing and failures of the old structures of injustice and the old ways of being as opportunities to participate in God's creation of a life-giving world and kingdom of true justice and true hope. And, My Dear Brothers and Sisters, I would like to remind you of just one more thing: Even if you are hurt, even if you are betrayed, even if you are humiliated, or are persecuted or killed in the course of your faithful life, Our Father has promised that not one hair of your head will be lost to him. For it is truly through your steadfast devotion that you receive the fullness of your own true life."

THE BOSOM OF GOD

Because, you see, this text is not meant to frighten the little children of God or to somehow explain God's terrible distance and lengthy delay, but, rather, this word of God has been carefully crafted and designed to bring us to that place where we experience and take comfort in God's incredible nearness and immediacy—to gather us, the children of God, from the four winds, from the ends of the earth, to the ends of heaven—and bring us all to the very bosom of God.

How near God is to you: so near that her star could rise in your heart at any moment; so near that she might suddenly appear and take her rightful seat on the throne of your heart; so near that he might suddenly be revealed to you in all truth and glory and occupy the very center of your life—acknowledged as the only one truly worth revolving your life around; the only one worthy of your whole-hearted worship; your precious gem of priceless value—that your heart of stone might be replaced with a heart of flesh; that your heart might be warmed at the fire of her nearness; that your heart might become a heart of compassion just like the heart of God—a heart responding to the sorrows and joys of others the way a mother's milk suddenly let's down for her newborn baby whether convenient or not—that you might live a truly inconvenienced life for the sake of others.

So that the milk of human kindness might flow from your heart, how very near she is to you! She is so near that the tender bud of your faith is even now becoming a flowering tree in the full light and warmth of God's love for you and for all of humankind in the fullness of time—any moment now—maybe even on this very day.

THE PRESENCE OF GOD IS COMING TO TOWN

Setting: Jesus' makeshift schoolroom on the Mount of Olives
Time: Near the end of the Gospel of Matthew; near the end of Jesus' earthly ministry.

Narrator: Well, Friends, just as soon as the tired Teacher found a place for a few minutes of rest and relaxation, here came some of his students asking him to give them the answer to a Million Dollar Question about which they were still completely mystified.

Student #1: Teacher! Teachers! Look! We want you to tell us all about The End of the World as We Know It!

Student #2: The Last Day! The Big Finalé! The Last Hurrah!

Student #3: The Judgment Day! The Desolating Sacrilege! You know, Jesus, when the cows come home!

Student #1: The coming of the Son of Man, or the coming of the Man of God.

Student #2: Or of the Son of God.

Student #3: Or of The Messiah, or The Christ, or whatever you call him!

Student #1: We want you to explain the whole thing! The Big Secret, The Great Mystery.

Student #2: Yes, Jesus, we want you to share your special, secret, esoteric knowledge with all of us!

Student #3: Reveal to us, your disciples, what nobody else knows!

Student #1: Our lips will be sealed!

Student #2: Mums the word!

Student #3: If you'll just let us in on it. Give us some clues. So come on, Jesus. Tell us what we should be on the lookout for.

Student #1: So that we'll know what to do when God makes his whole presence felt again on the earth!

Student #2: Exactly! So we'll have half-a-clue what to do when the time comes!

Student #3: So we'll have half-a-chance to know what's happening when God comes near to the world again.

Jesus: OK! OK! Calm down Little Children. Please take your seats, open your books to page five and we will go over this very basic material once again.

Narrator: Then Jesus began to give them a private lesson right then and there in his makeshift classroom on the Mount of Olives, telling them all about what THEY had referred to as The Big Secret regarding The End of the World as We Know It, when God's will be done on earth as it is in heaven—The Coming of the Son of Man, the Messiah, the Holy One of God—exactly as it was already written in one of their best loved and most familiar story books.

Student #1: Teacher? See? We don't have any books!

Student #2: And, Teacher, we don't recall ever reading anything about any of this stuff anywhere anyway!

Student #3: Exactly what book could you possibly mean, Teacher? We just don't know what you're talking about!

Jesus: Oh, sure you do, Children! It's one of your very favorite childhood stories. Don't you remember it?

Student #1: No, Teacher, I'm afraid we don't.

Student #2: Couldn't you just draw us a picture or something?

Student #3: Yes, Jesus. It surely would help us if you could just lay it all out for us in black and white—or, better yet, with colored markers if you have any!

Jesus: Well, OK. No problem, Children! Why don't we all just take another look at it right here and now?

Jesus: Oh good! Look! Here it is, our over-sized copy of THE GENESIS BOOK: THE ORIGINAL WORD OF GOD FOR ALL READERS OF ALL AGES. The story I'm talking about is found in Chapters 6—9, where we find the story you all know as the story of Noah's Ark.

You remember the story of Noah's Ark, don't you, Children? How God was unhappy with all the mean and selfish and sinful ways his people were living in his world; how God told Noah to build an ark because God was going to sweep everybody up and flood Noah's world with change; how just about everybody thought old Noah was off his rocker as he went about the business of building his boat because they couldn't imagine that anything could possibly happen to change their world or the ways to which they had become accustomed. So most people just stayed busy thinking and doing the very same things they had always done and so they didn't even begin to have a clue as to what was taking place all around them.

Narrator: Then Jesus continued to patiently explain to his beloved students that the Coming of the End of the World as They Knew It, when the will of God would come to be done on earth as it is in heaven, would be just like that!

Jesus: You see, just as in Noah's day, when the great majority of people were so busy and so wrapped-up in their own personal lives that they didn't see the Flood of Change that was about to hit them, so it will be when the Will of God comes to be done on earth as it is in heaven. Most people are going to be so busy and so wrapped-up in their own personal lives and daily affairs that they won't even notice what's taking place in their very midst—and just about to hit them.

Narrator: And then, to sum up the lesson, Jesus gave his beloved students a little piece of heartfelt advice.

Jesus: So, for heaven's sake, My Dear Ones: wake up! Get ready! And pay attention! Because at the end of this unjust and sinful world to which you have become accustomed, the true and full Presence of God is going to come like a thief in the night and your whole world is going to be completely changed at a time, and a place, and an hour you least expect!

Narrator: You know what else, My Brothers and Sisters? Just because half of the people aren't paying any attention—and just because fifty percent of the folks out there don't know something—well, that doesn't mean that it's not actually happening! Nor does it mean that it's such a Big Secret! Hello?! Wake up People! It just means that when the time comes half the people won't know until it suddenly hits them!

A GROOM-CENTERED WEDDING

Then Jesus shared his own excited anticipation by introducing the Wedding Coordinator at the For the Love of God Chapel in the Pines by the River and/or University in this role.

Lola: Ladies and Gentlemen! Good morning! Thank you for coming! Welcome to our For the Love of God wedding chapel right here in our beautiful, and most convenient, fair town. My name is Loyalty Incarnate, but you can call me Lola for short! I am the full-time wedding coordinator here at For the Love of God.

Before we begin, I would just like to compliment you all for choosing us to host your happy day! Please give yourselves a round of applause. You know you deserve it!

Yes, thank you; thank you; thank you! And what a fine group of discerning people you are!

So now let me show you a little something about how unique and special our wedding services are here at For the Love of God.

Our most popular wedding package deal and the reason why we're famous is called Spotlight on the Groom for a Change! For here is where the groom gets equal billing and his fair share of the spotlight for a change—featuring the Ten Bridesmaids Focus on the Groom Reception Centerpiece—a groom-friendly environment designed especially for the Man of the Hour!

Sick and tired of the bride getting all the attention while the poor groom stands idly by, twiddling his thumbs, invisible, huddled-up somewhere in the dark with the clergy while she gets; the big-fat diamond ring; the train; the musical theme; the "dum, dum, dee-dum"; everybody on their feet; the grand entrance; hogging all the spotlight? Need I go on?

Well! So are we here at For the Love of God, which is why we have developed this Spotlight on the Groom for a Change thing—which, let me point out to you, is based on a little-known section in the Gospel of Matthew's Guide to Celebration Etiquette where Jesus Christ himself compares the Kingdom of God to full complement of bridesmaids going out to greet the bridegroom. But enough-said about that. Let us show you how it works!

Stage Director: Uh, Bridesmaids! That's your cue! Come on in now!

Hope: Hi ya'll! My name is Hope. You know, because Hope Springs Eternal!? Well, I am just thrilled to be one of the ten lovely bridesmaids whose job it is to focus, not on ourselves, but on the Man of the Hour when he appears!

Trusty: Hi! I'm Trusty, for Perpetual Trustworthiness, with my ever-ready batteries, eager to shine!

Wonder: Hi! And I'm Wonder—short for Ceaseless Wonder! Ain't life grand?!

Lovi: My name is Lovi, for Constant Affection. I just love my job!

Joy: I'm Joy, and I'm full of Joyful Anticipation! It's all so exciting!

Truth: Truth here. Enduring Truth. That's my name and my claim to fame!

Faith: Oh, you know me! I'm Faith! And I've always worked here—LIKE FOREVER!

Rockie: They call me Rockie 'cause I'm solid like a rock!

Grace: I'm Grace, and I am just so filled with Undying Gratitude and I'm just so thankful to be alive and to be here today! Thank you, Mom! Thank you Dad! And, most of all, I would just like to thank my God—I know He's up there somewhere—without whom none of this would have ever been possible!

Patience: And, at last, as you can see, I'm Patience because I've got lots of Patience Galore, and it is always my great pleasure to serve you here at For the Love of God, in your own good time, of course.

Hope: Like I said, Girls, our job at For the Love of God is to watch for the Bridegroom, to shine our little lights when he appears, and to sing his praises as we light his way!

Trusty: And, trust me, there's nothing in the whole world we'd rather be doing, is there Girls?!

Bridesmaids: No! No there isn't! We love our job! That's right! You bet! It's a fabulous job! We're so lucky to have it!

Bridesmaids (SING): "This little light of mine! I'm gonna let it shine! This little light of mine, I'm gonna let it shine! This little light of mine, I'm gonna let it shine. Let it shine, let it shine, let it shine"[3] on the groom!

Lola: OK Girls! That's enough for now! You girls wait over here and watch closely now, you hear? Now, when he appears, do like we rehearsed! OK? Let your lights so shine!

Bridesmaids: OK! Yes Ma'am! We sure will!

Hope: Wonder what's taking him so long.

Trusty: Probably stuck in traffic somewhere.

Grace: Bet he's fallen out of love. Decided to abandon us all at the altar.

Patience: I bet he doesn't even exist.

Hope: Must have more important things to do.

Trusty: If he cared about us, he would be present with us, right here and right now, that's all I can say.

Grace: I bet he doesn't have a clue. Probably driving up and down our street completely lost. He'll never find us.

Patience: I bet he just gave up and went home.

Hope: Well, all I know for sure is that he's not here, with or among us now, and he's not going to be here anytime soon.

Lola: Hey! Wake up! Wake up! Hop to, Girls! Here comes the groom! Skinny like a broom! Get up! Get up! The Bridegroom is here! Right here! Right now! In our very midst!

Hope: Oh no! Now my little light won't shine!
Trusty: Oh no! My die-hard batteries are dead and gone!
Wonder, Lovi & Joy: Oh no! Mine too!
Hope: Oh no! Whatever shall we do?!
Trusty: Hey! I have a really bright idea! Let's get the other bridesmaids to share!
Wonder, Lovi & Joy: Brilliant! Brilliant idea!
Hope: Hey, Gracie! Give us your light! Focus on us! Make our lights shine too!
Grace: Sorry Hope! No can do! See? Your light takes Double-A Ever-Readies while my light takes Triple-D Always Currents! Get it? Always current—as in electrical current—as in always turned-on?
Trusty: Oh, come on, Patience. Focus on "me, me, me"! My little light's gone out. Let me borrow some of yours.
Wonder, Lovi & Joy: Yes! Focus on us! Give us your light!
Grace: But we need our batteries for our light to do our job and focus on the Bridegroom! And besides, none of us take exactly same kind! So maybe you should focus on getting over to the store to get some of your own to focus on him so that he can been seen in the light by the whole party!
Lola: He's here, folks! I'm telling you! The Good News is that he's here! Right here! Right now! Even as we speak! He is here among us! In our very midst! At this time! In this very place! Even as he promised! The Bridegroom is here! So let us all focus on him! Right here! Right now! For the love of God!
Lola: Everybody now!
Bridesmaids (SING):
> This little light of mine,
> I'm gonna let it shine!
> This little light of mine,
> I'm gonna let it shine!
> This little light of mine,
> I'm gonna let it shine,
> Let it shine, let it shine, let it shine
> On the Groom![4]

The Bridegroom: Hey everybody! It's high time we dance! Don't worry! It's easy! I'll teach you how to dance the Macarena![5]

Stage Director: So they all had a wonderful time dancing the night away!
  Beat 01: R arm straight out in front of you Palm Down
  Beat 02: L arm straight out in front of you Palm Down
  Beat 03: R arm straight out in front of you Palm Up
  Beat 04: L arm straight out in front of you Palm Up
  Beat 05: R hand grasps inside of the L arm at the Elbow
  Beat 06: L hand grasps inside of the R arm at the Elbow
  Beat 07: R hand behind R back of Neck
  Beat 08: L hand behind L back of Neck
  Beat 09: R hand on L Front Pants Pocket
  Beat 10: L hand on R Front Pants Pocket
  Beat 11: R hand on R Back Pants Pocket
  Beat 12: L hand on L. Back Pants Pocket
  Beat 13: Move your rump to the Left
  Beat 14: Move your rump to the Right
  Beat 15: Move your rump to the Left
  Beat 16: CLAP and turn ninety degrees to the Right
  *Repeat all 16 beats
Lola: Well, folks! There you have it! A typical Groom's Choice wedding here at For the Love of God! I hope you will keep us in mind for all of your future celebration needs! Now, go ahead and give yourselves another round of applause!
Hope, Trusty, Wonder, Love, and Joy: Hey everybody! We're back! Time to focus on us! We're ready to party now! Check us out! Party! Party! Party!
Stage Director: Oh no! I'm afraid you're too late! Gee, I'm sorry. Um, uh, come again. Now who'd you say you are? Friends of the groom, you say? Well, you see, well, yes, the groom was here, and he taught us how to do the Macarena[6] and everything! But, uh, didn't know we were supposed to wait for you. Sorry. You're too late and that's really too bad. Oh, that's just so sad. A really great time was had by all! Guess you had to be here to see it!
Stage Director (SING): Hey Macarena![7]

MEAN OLD MOMMY

Setting: The Family Room

Narrator: Then Jesus told his brothers and sisters that life with God was something like life with a mommy-person who had to go away for a few days for whatever reason.
Greek Chorus:
    Mean Old Mommy!
    Heartless too!
    Leaving her children
    Sad and blue!
Narrator: Now just before she left, she gathered her three daughters together in her arms and said,
Mommy: Now, my Sweethearts, you know Mommy has to go away for a couple of days. Remember? Like I told you? But before I go, I have a few presents for you!
Greek Chorus:
    Watch out, Children!
    It's a bribe!
    She's the kind of mommy
    We can't abide!
Daughters 1 & 2: For Joy! For joy! Yippie-Skippy! Hooray! Thank you, Mommy! Thank you, Mommy!
Mommy: Number One Daughter, for you I have these five crayons! Aren't they pretty colors, My Love?
Daughter # 1: Oh yes, Mommy! They are! They are! Thank you, Mommy!
Mommy: And for you, Number Two Daughter, here are two for you. I really hope you like them, Sweetheart! Look! Now this one is red! And this one is blue! And they're both for you! Hey, that rhymes!
Daughter #2: Oh Mommy! I love them! Thank you! Thank you!
Mommy: And for you, my darling Daughter Number Three, my baby, my sweet. Look! Here is your very own crayon too!
Daughter #3: Gee. Lucky me.
Greek Chorus:
    Mean and stingy!
    Stingy and Mean!
    What a big rip-off!
    See what we mean!

    Mean and stingy!

Neglectful and abusive!
She's so mean
Her mean-ness is effusive!

Narrator: Now, when the mommy-person returned,

Mommy: I'm home, my darlings! Children, where are you?

Narrator: The most mature of her daughters hurried to greet her and show her their treasures.

Daughter #1: Mommy! Mommy! Look what I made you! Isn't it pretty? I mixed all the colors together, Mommy, and look what happened! It's a picture of you, Mommy!

Daughter #2: Mommy! Mommy! I made a picture too! It's our whole family! See? There I am! And there's Susie! And Mary! And that there is you, Mommy!

Greek Chorus:

Suck-ups! Suck-ups!
That's what they are!
Sucking-up to Mean Old Mommy
And she doesn't give a darrrrrrrnnn!

Mommy: Oh wonderful, Girls! Splendid! How incredibly creative of you! These are terrific pictures and you've made me very happy! What a great delight! Well done, good and faithful children! Oh Darling Daughter Number Three! Where are you, Honey-Lamb? I want to see your picture too!

Daughter #3: I didn't make you a stupid picture because you are a mean, neglectful and abusive, Mean Old Mommy, and you steal candy and crayons from little kids, and you cheat, and you always criticize everything we do, and all you do is just rip-up little kids' pictures to pieces and then you just throw them in the trashcan anyway, and I really, really hate you! And I'm always afraid of you and your terrible temper! So here! Take your lousy—your darn—crayon back! And if it looks dirty to you, that's because I kicked it under the bed just as soon as you left! So there!

Greek Chorus:

Go on with your Bad Self!
You tell her, Kid!
Don't pull any punches!
Of her, you'll be rid!

She's a Mean Old Mommy!
Mean Old Mommy!
Mean Old Mommy!
Mommy is mean!

Mommy: Whoa! Slow down a minute, Sweetie! Let me just get this straight! You mean to say that you kicked your own gift under the bed because you knew that I was a Mean Old Mommy who wouldn't appreciate your creativity with it anyway? And that I steal, and I cheat? And besides, you are terribly afraid of *MOI*? But yet you didn't do one single thing to try to appease my abusive self? You just kicked your own gift under your own bed? Why that doesn't even make sense, Sweetie! Look, if you were really so afraid of me and my terrible temper, why didn't you draw a hundred pictures just to try to get me to calm down? But you didn't draw *ANY*? How very strange! But OK then, if that's how you want it, Dear. It's your sister's now. Look at her wonderful picture! She really knows what a crayon is good for!

Greek Chorus:

See? What did we tell you?
She's a mean, mean Mom!
First she cheated her own kid
Then she stole the kid's crayon!

Yes, her mean-ness is a legend!
You have everything to fear
From a Mommy such as this one
As we hope we've made it clear.

That she's a Mean Old Mommy!
Mean Old Mommy! Mean Old Mommy!
Mean Old Mommy! Mean Old Mommy!
Mean Old Mommy! Mean Old Mommy!
Mean Old Mommy! Mean Old Mommy!

Narrator: And so folks, there you have it. One of the strange little stories Jesus told his brothers and sisters about life with God. Then he summed it up, saying something like this: "Look folks! This Mommy isn't a Mean Mommy! She gave her beloved children creative gifts, and creative gifts are meant for creativity! Use 'em or lose 'em! It's as simple as that! Creativity gives rise to more creativity! Miserliness does nothing except to create a whole world of misers with nothing to offer."

Or, as the author of our original little drama put it in Chapter 13, Line 12 of his playbook, "For to every one who has will more be given, and they will have in abundance, but from those who have nothing, even that will be taken away." (Matt. 13:12)

TWO TYPES OF DEAD MEAT

Jesus explained further, "Well, basically there are only two types of dead meat—Warm, Tender Mutton and Cold Goat Jerky—and a Man with Discriminating Tastes can and will easily tell them apart."

"To the Warm, Tender Mutton he will say, 'Oh you warm and absolutely delicious food! You are truly pleasing to the eye and good for the soul! Yours by right is a place at the heavenly banquet! For you feed me with good things, and you make my heart sing!'"

"And the Warm and Tender Mutton will shyly reply: 'We do? Really? You mean it? Really? That we lowly sheep feed you? How can this be? That we, who are nothing, feed you, who is everything?'"

"And then he will say to the Tender Mutton, 'Oh yes! Of course! Indeed, you do feed me! Don't you know that whenever you feed anybody I love, you are feeding me with good things and making my heart sing?!'"

"But to the Cold Goat Jerky he will say, 'As for you, you tasteless meat, get off of my table, for you have never offered me any gastronomical pleasures of any kind!'"

"And the Cold Goat Jerky will haughtily reply, 'Oh yeah? Well, we never-ever even saw you hungry!'"

"To which the Man with Discriminating Tastes will reply, 'That's exactly right! You never did!'"

"And so, alas, the un-eaten, Cold Goat Jerky will be tossed out on the street with the rest of the garbage while the Warm Tender Mutton will be handsomely served at the heavenly banquet with great gusto—and, of course, plenty of delightful, mint relish!"

VII

The Johannine Theater Wing

THE COUNTRY WEDDING

WELL, YOU SEE, IT was at the end of a three-day weekend when there was a country wedding way back up in the mountains. Now Jesus' mother was up in there, of course, and he and some of his good old boys were supposed to be there too. But the party took a sorrowful turn for the worse when they ran out of hooch just when it was getting good, so Jesus' mother went and complained to him saying, "Oh no! Jesus! Now they've gone and run out of hooch!" And he said, "Well, shucks, Mama. What do you want me to do about it? My gig ain't up yet!" And she said to the kids who were hanging around, "Ya'll just stay here and mind Jesus, ya hear?"

Now there just happened to be a bunch of big old buckets just hanging around the place for Washing-Up Day, so Jesus told the kids, "Well, don't just stand there a-gawking. Take these big buckets down to the well and fill them up with water!" So, of course, those silly kids filled them up to the very top so they were a-splashing and a-spilling all over the place! So Jesus told them to go find themselves a big dipper and take some of it to Granpaw up on the porch and see what he had to say about it. And then Granpaw, well, he acted like he was just about drunk with delirium when he exclaimed, "Why this is just about the best white lightening I ever tasted in my whole life," and he didn't even know whose still it had come from—although the kids all knew for sure!

Then Granpaw called that Lucky Feller, the groom, up on the porch and slapped him right hard on the back! "Folks are always squeezing-out a few drops of the good stuff first and then suddenly getting real free-handed with all the rot gut stuff when folks are all drunk as skunks! But, hey, you been a-holding out on us, Boy—'cause you're sure pulling-out buckets full of the very best stuff right now!"

But this was actually only the very first of many very cool things Jesus ever did to keep a party going! And it sure gave everybody a powerful punch of his white lightening! And, believe you me, after tasting Jesus' special brand of immediately distilled spirits, all the good old boys, and all of their mama's, and all of their other women-folk too—well they all hooked-up with Jesus for good—like grapes on a vine!

THE MIRACLE AT THE EUCHARIST

Well, on Easter Sunday there was a celebration of the Eucharist at the Church where Jesus' mother was serving on the Altar Guild. Jesus and his disciples had also been invited to attend.

When the wine ran out in the middle of the communion, Jesus' mother pointed-out to him, "They have no wine." And Jesus said to her, "Mother, what do you want from me? I can't go buy any wine until after one o'clock in this Blue Law town."

His mother then said to the acolytes, "Just stand here and wait on him and do whatever he tells you to do."

Now, standing in the church kitchen there were always six punch bowls for fancy champagne receptions and parish parties, each holding four or five gallons.

Jesus said, "Fill the punch bowls with water." So they filled them all the way up to the brim.

Then he said to them, "Now draw some out and take it up to the priest."

So they took it, and when the priest tasted the water that was now serving as wine without knowing where it had come from—although the acolytes all knew, of course—that priest took the chalice in his hands, looked up and said, "Oh thank you, Jesus! You have truly saved the best for last!"

Now Jesus did this most recent of his glory-revealing signs at a church where his disciples immediately experienced his refreshing distillation.

LIGHT PERCEPTION

As he continued on his way, our beloved Light of the World saw a man born without light perception and who was unable to see what was right there in front of his nose. Now some Students of Delight asked him, "Your Marvelous Brightness, Sir, kindly enlighten us about who is to blame, this man or his parents. Was he literally conceived in the darkness and so that's why he doesn't see anything?"

Jesus answered them, "It's not a matter of who is to blame. The man was born without light perception and unable to see what is right smack in front of his nose—and light is something that must truly be seen and perceived while it's shining! Soon it will be dark. But as long as I am here right in front of your noses, I am the Light of the World. And by me all things will be seen to be what they truly are."

When he had revealed himself in this strangely-illuminating way, Jesus was showing them a shining example of how to creatively enlighten one another while simultaneously working his magic on the man right there in front of their eyes.

First, he took native materials, as were really handy right there in front of their noses and very own eyes—which were readily available—right at hand—right on the ground, and in his very own mouth—out of which he formed an opaque, artistic material. Then he spread the stuff that was about as clear as mud over the man's non-functioning light-perceptors.

He told the man to go immerse himself in the Pool of Faith. Then the man who did exactly as our Lord said—well, he suddenly saw the light!

Then his friends and neighbors all said, "Isn't he that fellow who sat around here only seeing all the darkness in the world?" Half the people who believed they knew who they were looking at said "Yup, that's him." But the other half of the people said, "Naw, that was some other blind guy."

But the man kept saying, "Open your eyes, People, and look here! It's me! It's me! Look again! It's me!" But they kept saying, "Yeah, right. Sure it's you. How'd you suddenly get so bright and open then?"

So he kept trying to tell them, "Look! He just made it up right then and there on the spot and put his special touch on me—and behold! Now everywhere I look I see the Light of the World shining and shining abundantly!"

MAN WITH STRANGE LOOKING SPECTACLES

Then the neighborhood folks were so confused by the sight of a man wearing strange-looking spectacles on his face who could apparently see through these strange-looking and clearly un-official spectacles, that they dragged him off to the premises over at the Official Court of Legitimate Vision—also known as the Legitimate Court of Official Vision—where they were sure to get an officially legitimate clarification of the matter.

The very serious, religious experts demanded to know, "What is the matter with you? How did you come by those strange-looking spectacles? Who in the world is responsible for this travesty, anyway?"

"A man put them on my face, sent me to take a bath in The Scented Waters—also known as The Waters of Sent—and I have been able to see with them ever since," the man simply replied, which, of course, simply confused and divided the very serious, religious experts who split into two very different opinions about the matter.

Half of them said, "Well, obviously, as anybody can plainly see, the man who put these spectacles upon your face is an Agent of the Enemy Competition because he didn't even regard or observe the official rules and regulations about when to work and when not to work, like on Sundays," they powerfully expressed.

The other half of them contended, "But how do you figure that an Agent of the Competition could even hope to come up with something as marvelous and miraculous as these spectacles," they speculated.

Then, frankly, since they seemed to be having some trouble clarifying the matter between themselves, they turned their attention again directly upon the man who could see through those strange-looking spectacles on his face.

"OK, Mister. *You* enlighten us about the origin and nature of the man who put those there spectacles on your face."

The man simply offered, "Well, I would say that he sure was a man of God and that you all are surely acting like you are considering becoming his disciples," which for some strange reason absolutely infuriated the very serious religious experts who then became entirely focused upon what they claimed is completely obvious to anyone who knows anything about the nature and power of God Almighty—that the Agent who had given the man the strange-looking spectacles on his face was indeed, and quite clearly, an agent of the Enemy Competition, and that the spectacles on his face were thereby declared to be completely un-official and absolutely ill-legitimate and now banished forever from the realm of their sight. Then the very serious religious experts of the Official Court of Legitimate Vision had that man removed from their premises once and for all.

But when the Agent who had provided the strange-looking spectacles heard about the way the man had been treated on the grounds and premises of the Official Court of Legitimate Vision, he looked for and found him in the place to which that man had been banished for good. He said to the man, "Oh Man, do you believe in any real power greater than the all-too-real power of the Official Court of Legitimate Vision?"

The man replied, "Well, I sure would if I could see it!"

"Then look right in front of your nose," Jesus said, "Here I am." So the man's heart was filled to overflowing with love for him.

I AM THE BACKSTAGE DOOR

Then the Principle Actor delivered these lines to the other actors in his Company: "The actor who does not come into the theater by the Backstage Door but who comes sneaking up the Fire Escape or slipping in through the windows is clearing acting for the Competition! But the actor who does come into the Theater by the Backstage Door has the lead role! To that actor the door is thrown wide open and the other actors thrill at the sound of that actor's voice! And that actor delivers the lines of the script clearly and directly into the ears of each and every member of the Company by name, which, of course, brings out the very best acting in each and every one of them—which certainly explains why each and every one of them so willingly and joyfully follows that actor's lead!"

But, of course, the other actors were clearly mystified and entirely missed the whole dramatic point of Jesus' story. So Jesus found it necessary to tell his story all over again by delivering these lines clearly and directly into the ears of each and every one of them by name, "The plain truth of it is that I myself am serving as the Backstage Door in order that anyone who enters the Theater through me is given an absolutely Free Pass to come and go at any time, at their own leisure, forever and forever more! All of the others who were here before me were clearly acting for the Competition and are hereby summarily dismissed! For I tell you, the Competition means only to lock the door and throw away the key! But I am the Backstage Door, and I am here to make sure that the fabulously-abundant riches of this Theater are made available at all times and in all places for each and every one of you, by name, forever! Amen."

I AM THE GOOD MOTHER

Jesus said, "I am the Good Mother who gladly flings herself in front of the train to save the lives of her children. Now, the adolescent Nanny—stereotypically referring to the one who is not the mother and who did not bring the children into life—well, when *she* catches a glimpse of the Number One E Train coming down the tracks, she immediately leaves the children playing on the tracks and quickly runs away while the Evil One slams into them and flings them all about. Now the Nanny doesn't pay attention to the children because, as everybody knows, a paid babysitter really only cares about, 1) what's in the refrigerator, 2) which one of her friends is on the telephone, and 3) what time her boyfriend is coming over."

"I am the Good Mother. I know my own children and my own children know me, just as the Father knows me, and I know the Father. So, listen-up My Children. Here I am in your very midst still gladly flinging myself in front of the train for you!"

"Now, there are still *some children in the world* who may not be paying full attention or be fully with us at this moment—*children who might temporarily be kind of spaced-out themselves, you know* (*wink)—but who are, indeed, beloved hearts of my heart and apples of my eye. It is my duty and my deep delight to also bring them all the way into life so that when I speak they too can hear my voice coming through to the inner-ears of their hearts so that, as the Father wills, you may all be one family with one Mother."

Then his disciples responded, "In the Name of God the Mother, God-with-Us and God the Creative, Unifying Spirit, Amen," and then sang this hymn to the tune of "The King of Love My Shepherd Is.[1]"

> The Queen of Love my Mother is, whose goodness faileth never;
> I nothing lack if I am hers, and she is mine forever.
> Where streams of living water flow, my ransomed soul she leadeth,
> and where the verdant pastures grow, with food celestial feedeth.
>
> Perverse and foolish oft I strayed, but yet in love she sought me,
> and on her bosom gently laid, and home rejoicing brought me.
> In death's dark vale I fear no ill with thee, dear Lord, beside me;
> thy rod and staff my comfort still, thy cross before to guide me.

Thou spreadst a table in my sight; thy unction grace bestoweth;
and oh, what transport of delight from thy pure chalice floweth!
And so through all the length of days thy goodness faileth never:
Good Mother, may I sing thy praise within thy house forever.

THE JERUSALEM NATIONAL GALLERY OF ART

Well, it was on the annual day of celebration of Great Restoration/Re-story-ation Art at the Jerusalem National Gallery of Art (JNGA) in memory of it's Grand Re-opening three years after it was thoroughly plundered and vandalized by crooks, when our famous street artist, Jesus the Artist of Nazareth, was hanging around among the marvelous works in The Great Masters' Gallery—also known as Solomon's Portico Gallery. Now the Great Masters' Gallery was filled with originals by David Monet, Ezekiel Matisse, Elijah Lautrec, Moses DaVinci, Sarah O'Keefe, Rebecca Rembrandt, and the like.

So the Board of Directors of the JNGA, who were extremely proud of that collection, crowded around Jesus and asked, "How long will you continue to hide the truth and when will you stop keeping everything veiled and a deep, dark secret from us? If you are the Greatest Restoryation Artist of All Time, show us the picture you are working on."

Jesus answered, "I have shown you, but you do not see. My works testify to me; in fact, they practically scream the name of the artist who creates them! The only reason you don't know is because you never really look. My works can't hang in a gallery! For heaven's sake, I'm a Performance Artist! If you don't get it by now, there really isn't much more to say! You've already seen my performance! Didn't you see my work with the man born blind who can now see? Or with the lame man who was lingering at the Pool of Bethsaida? Or with the people caught throwing stones at the woman caught in adultery?"

"Obviously, the reason you don't get it is because you don't really appreciate performance art because performance art can't be hung in your gallery!"

"The performance art that I perform for our Creator clearly and plainly expresses everything that there is to know about me, but you do not see it because you are not students of my creative art. My students are not the least bit confused about who I am and what I am doing and saying in my art form. And I know who they are because they are the ones who practice my technique. I continually inspire them with abundantly creative life without end and no one can take that away from me—or from them for that matter! My students are free gifts to me from My Father who is the greatest Performance Artist of All Time and Creation. My gift to them is this very same Source of creativity that will never end so that they too can perform the works that I perform—and even more so because I go to the Creator where I continue to share our Creator's creativity with them forever. The creativity our Creator has lavished upon me is the greatest re-story-izing art of all, and no one can take that away from the hand of the Artist God who gives it so freely. In this— God's own art form—the Creator of the Universe and I are one and the same! You see? *Now* you're really getting the picture!"

Poor Old Russ

Here lies poor old Russ:
A true life symbol for the rest of us.
Caused our Lord to weep and cry
Before he could live, he had to die.

Wrapped up in himself and bound to sin,
He lived in the dark where none would go in
For fear of the stench and the awful eruption
That occurs when you open a door on corruption.

His life, surely messy and all convoluted;
His relations with others, no doubt quite polluted
With misunderstandings and unfulfilled dreams,
Controlling behaviors and blindness, it seems.

His relations with God were shaky at best.
His prayers, if at all, were often a test;
An attempt at a barter, or a childish request,
Always wanting to win; never daring to rest.

Wanting to live as God intended
But afraid of life unless amended,
He was stuck in some ways that he just didn't know,
Refusing to hurt and reluctant to grow.

Here lies poor old Russ:
A true life symbol for the rest of us;
Fear and anxiety marking his soul,
Looking for peace, never reaching the goal.

And so we have buried him here in this grave.
How sad! God was not here our dear friend to save!
But let us remember and let go of our doubt
And with the words that he gave us, let us all shout!

For surely together we can call the man out.
So let us remember and let go of our doubt
That our Lord did before raise him up with a shout.
And the words that he used were just, "Lazarus, come out!"

THE BAPTISMAL FONT OF ELECTRIFYING POWER

A Lay Preacher named John climbed up into the pulpit carrying a folder labeled Notes to Self.

John: Thank you, thank you, Father Pastor. And thank you all for bringing me back again this week. It's my pleasure to be here. I must say, lately I seem to find myself drawn to your wonderful church like a magnet! Better get my notes out, though. I'd be lost without them. Oh! Ah, here they are! See? Notes to Self, copyright circa 120 AD, give-or-take 10–20 years—or is that one to two thousand years? Oh well, never mind. Anyway, it says right here, "Use in Chapter Twelve. Set the story right before Passover; note the Paschal Lamb; Gentiles' desire to see Jesus; Reveals the true nature and challenge of following the Lord of Life; Highlight the disciples Phyllis-Philip and Andrew. Oh, yes! Good! I've found my place now. Ah! Here it is!

Time to introduce you to the two disciples with the Greek names, who each have a part to play in this story so you can see for yourselves what real characters they are! They both hail from the area at the north end of the Sea of Galilee where there is a heavy Greek population.

So, Ladies and Gentlemen, without further ado, please welcome Phyllis/Philip from the Bethsaida School of Fine Acting.

Phyllis: Thank you! Thank you! Good morning! Peace be with you! Let me begin this morning by telling you just a little bit about myself. In the Johannine Theater Wing, I was the third person Jesus called to be his disciple. Jesus came and found me on the very next day after Andrew and Simon Peter joined his ministry. Then, right after I was called, I ran to tell Nathaniel all about Jesus—but that's a whole 'nother story! I also played an exciting role in the story of the Feeding of the Five Thousand, remember? I'm the one who exclaimed, "Jesus! Look here! Four hundred dollars wouldn't be enough to buy food for all these hungry people!" And, finally, at the Last Supper, I'm the one who begged, "Lord, show us the Father and we will be satisfied!"

John: Thank you, Phyllis/Philip. And now, Ladies and Gentlemen, please welcome Brother Andrew, also from the Bethsaida school.

Andrew: Thank you! Thank you! Good morning! Peace be with you. And now I would like to tell you just a little bit about myself. The first thing that I want you to know is that I originally appeared as a student of that great actor, John the Baptist. The second thing that I want you to know is that I was the first person to whom John the Baptist pointed-out Jesus when he said, "Behold the Lamb of God." So that made me the very first disciple of Jesus—according to our friend John, anyway!

I also want to remind you that I was the one who ran to get my brother, Simon Peter, to bring him to see Jesus for the first time! And, of course, you all know that I also had an exciting role in the Feeding of the Five Thousand when I pointed-out the young boy who had five barley loaves and two fish, and then I wondered out loud how that could possibly be enough to feed so many people!

John: Thank you Andrew. Well, you see? The stage is set. Now, with the help of these two talented disciples, let me try one more time to bring this story alive and to show you what it is that I really want you to see.

Well, you see, unable to resist the magnetic pull of Jesus of Nazareth, some people from the outside world—some Greeks that is—were immediately drawn to one of the disciples who just happened to also have a Greek name, Phyllis/Philip.

Now, the Greeks said to Phyllis/Philip: "Hey Phyllis! We came to see Jesus! We wish to see Jesus! We desire to see Jesus! We yearn to see Jesus! We hope to see Jesus! We even dare to look for Jesus!"

So right-away Phyllis went running over to Andrew and said,

Phyllis: Yikes, Andrew! There's all these Greek people here who want to see Jesus! Whatever should we do?!"

John: And Andrew answered,

Andrew: Good grief, Phyllis! I don't know! Let's go ask Jesus!

Phyllis: But he's up there praying!

Andrew: Oh for heaven's sake, Phyllis! Just come on!

Andrew and Phyllis: Pssst... Jesus. Friend. Sorry to disturb. But, uh, some people here—some Greeks—have come looking for you. Won't go away. Won't be satisfied. Until they see you for themselves.

John: Then Jesus got up and went straight to the people and immediately gave them all quite a shock!

Jesus: Hey, do you really want to see something? Because it is indeed time for the electrifying power of God to surge through me!

John: And he lit right up right then and there just as bright as a bolt of lightening when delivered a series of jolts right into their hearts.

Jesus: Whoever does not dare to die will remain powerless! Whoever dares to die will be transformed! Truly I tell you, whoever dares to follow me and to hate all the injustices of the way things work in this world will be given plenty of life with me—and I do mean life in abundance!

John: And just as you might imagine, all of the people said, "Huh?! Say what?!" To which Jesus responded,

Jesus: Look, only those who stop relying on all the sinful, arrogant, self-centered, violent and murderous ways of this world will ever come to know the true, abiding and abundant life and peace that surpasses understanding; or be drawn into the force field of love's magnetic, electrifying power; or ever be truly transformed by the power of God's fierce love!

John: Then it suddenly came all the way home to Jesus—the full impact of what he was saying and the truth he had just uttered.

Jesus: Oh my God! How can I possibly ask my Father to spare me from having to literally die here in the face of the sinful realities of this world of hatred, injustice and violence? Why that's the whole reason I came into this world because that's the only way anyone is ever going to see the real power and glory of our God and Father in me.

John: Then suddenly all the people truly felt an electrifying power surging from the very heart of Jesus and radiating outwards in all directions as they heard a voice from out of heaven.

Voice: I have revealed my power before, and I will reveal it again and again!

John: Now some of the men who were there declared that they had heard a clap of thunder, while some of the women said it was the voice of an angel. But Jesus simply said,

Jesus: What you have seen and heard here today is humbly offered for your true enlightenment and eternal joy—and so that you may begin to see and understand your own need to die to the seductive powers of this world in order to live in the fullness of God's love.

John: And all so that you all might be drawn, right along with me, into the very arms and heart of the living God through the magnetic and electrifying power of Jesus Christ our Lord and Master. Amen.

TERMS OF ENDEARMENT

Now when the final, inevitable betrayal of Jesus had been set into motion on that darkest of nights, the extreme anxiety and tangible tension in the room was so thick that you could cut it with a knife—which was exactly the moment when Our Lord himself began to really shine! And he wasted no time in immediately speaking to his stressed and fearful disciples, saying, "Dear, precious little Children of God: I know with my whole heart that you do not understand what is going to happen next in this world. But I want you to know, my Dear Ones, that what is going to happen to me is going to show forth all the truth and beauty and glory of Our Father in Heaven, both for now and forevermore. And yes, my Dear and most Beloved Friends, it is true that very soon indeed you are going to find yourselves alone in this world which will often feel quite meaningless and completely godforsaken to you. But, my Dear Hearts, because I love you so very much, I have a very special gift to give you before I leave. It is my very own and most precious rule of life given to sustain you in the midst of all of the anxiety and uncertainty and the most terrible not-knowing that the world can deliver. And, yes, indeed, you may go ahead and open it. See, I am having it engraved on your hearts right this very moment."

> Love one another other the way I have loved each and every one of you more than life itself. Strengthen and sustain each other, and listen very carefully and with infinite patience to the voice of each and every heart. For only in this way will this world ever really experience the security and the knowledge and the peace beyond comprehension of the abiding presence and the ever-patient and compassionate love of God.

NO WAY! YES, WAY!

Then, still desiring to alleviate their obvious stage-fright, the Principle Actor enlightened the other actors with his considerable creativity regarding the passage relating to the Universal Theater of God's Kingdom in which they were acting: "In the marvelously wonderful Universal Theater of God's Kingdom," he said, "God Almighty is the Gentle and Loving Author of many, many scenes," some of which can be found in the Oxycatherine Papyrus-OCP 5194, 1993. I trust you are all enlightened enough to recognize the creativity of what I am saying when I deliver this very passage to you," he added. "Because, you see, I am on my way to setting the stage for you now, and I am assuming that you already know the passage by which I am going."

"No way!" his disciples exclaimed.

But Jesus just said, "Yes! Way!"

But alas for poor Jesus, because it was obvious his friends did not see the light, were having considerable trouble keeping-up with his creativity, and great difficulty understanding the way he was illuminating the passage for them. So they asked him to pass it by them one more time.

Jesus gently and lovingly offered, "Look, hear, and pay attention to the way I deliver my lines to a particular actor by name—*Doubting Thomas*—because I myself am the light, the creativity, the passage, and the way. No one sees and hears our Gentle and Loving Author who doesn't see our Gentle and Loving Author in me."

"No way!" his disciples exclaimed.

"Yes! Way!" Jesus said. "If you had known all along with whom you were acting while you were acting all along the way here with me—well, you would already have known the presence of our Gentle and Loving Author whom you seek and whom you will know intimately from this day forward."

Ah, but alas-and-alak for poor Jesus, his friends still couldn't follow the way he was shedding light on the passage about acting in the Universal Theater of God's Kingdom.

"Well, OK then, Jesus," taunted an Evil Prompter with a sign. "Why don't you just go ahead and show us this Gentle and Loving Author for whom we are supposed to be acting and then we will have enough faith to go out there on the stage and play our own parts in the production." To which the Principle Actor gently and lovingly responded with these lines: "Tell me, *Doubting Philip*. How long is it that you and I have been acting together in this theater and yet you still do not know with whom you have been acting? What divine wisdom prompts you to ask me now, at this late date, to introduce you to our Gentle and Loving Author as if you had never met before? Don't you recognize the way I am present in our Gentle and Loving Author, and the way the Gentle and Loving Author is present in me? Don't you know by now that I do not deliver lines of my own authorship, for it is our Author who clearly delivers our Author's own lines through me?"

"No way!" the disciples exclaimed. "Yes! Way!" Jesus said.

"So either see and/or hear the way I am present in our Gentle and Loving Author and our Gentle and Loving Author is present in me—or else simply believe me for the power and beauty of the way I act. But whichever way you choose to see it, I want you to see the light, receive the power and the creativity, and recognize what I am really passing along to you. For I tell you truly, that whoever truly sees the way I work will truly receive the power to deliver their own lines just as powerfully and passionately as I do and, for that matter, even more effectively than it is possible for me to do alone! Because I, who go to be fully present in our Gentle and Loving Author, am passing all the power and beauty of the way I act directly over to you so that you may live out your own lives to the even greater glory of God."

"No way!" the disciples exclaimed.

"Yes! Way!" Jesus responded.

Then one of the disciples said, "Well then it really must be Party Time! Excellent! Let the singing and dancing begin! Amen!"

CORRESPOND AND COLLABORATE WITH THE AUTHOR

Well, our wonderful Creative Writing Teacher often wrote letters like this for us.

Dear Friend,

For heaven's sake, don't let yourself get all stressed-out! Correspond and collaborate with the Author; correspond and collaborate also with me! In our Author's internationally famous book there are many, many intimate words of healing and grace. If that weren't true, how do you think I would be able to write this letter to you to tell you that I am attending to our ongoing correspondence right here and now, and that I also promise to continue to do this creative work with you again and again and again, and to continue to share my heart of hearts with you so that we may always be inspired and energized together in true collaboration. For I believe that you really do know the method by which I write!

Then one of his student writers wrote back and said, "Hey! Look! I'm afraid I have absolutely no clue where you're going with all of this so how can I know the method of your writing?"

Then our Beloved Teacher answered,

Dear Friend,

How is it that I been corresponding and collaborating with you from the heart for so long now and yet you still don't know me and my methods? Anyone who has corresponded and collaborated with me has also collaborated and corresponded with the Author. How can you say, "Show me the Author"? Do you not realize that I write from within the heart of the Author and that the Author places her own words in my heart? These words that I write to you are not of my own authorship, but the Author who lives in me pens her own words. So please, Friend, I want you to collaborate and correspond with me because you know that I am in the Author and the Author is in me—or else collaborate and correspond with me because of the grace and power of the words themselves. But for heaven's sake, please know how much I want to collaborate and correspond with you. The truth that I am writing to you is this: Whoever collaborates and corresponds with me will also write as I write because I consult with the Author about everything I do and say. Whatever you ask for the sake of our collaboration, I will certainly do it so that the Author may be revealed through his very own sons and daughters. So, please, Dear Friend, go ahead and request anything of me for the sake of our Beloved Author and I will ever be at your service.

With love from your servant, Jesus of Nazareth

Co-Author and Friend

DR. JESUS OF NAZARETH, MEDICINE MAN

Dr. Jesus of Nazareth, Medicine Man counseled his regular patients, "My Dear Friends, if you truly love and respect me you will take my free, heart-felt advice, and you will follow my prescriptions very, very carefully. I will call up God, and God will dispense a wonderful counselor for you, even the *Very Essence of the True Spirit of Life*™ that the world cannot take because the world doesn't even have a clue about the existence of this wonderful elixir. But you yourselves are very well aware of this wonderful elixir of mine because you have already had a taste of it hanging around with me!"

"In all truth, Friends, I tell you that I will not leave you spiritless, medicine-less, hopeless, or *sans elixir*. I promise to make house calls!"

"Now, after I die, the world definitely won't see me anymore. But you will! Because my spirit of compassion is the true essence of life, you yourselves will be filled with life, and we will 'dwell in the house of the Lord forever.'"(Psalm 23:6b)

"Anyone who takes my prescriptions and follows them will truly experience the wonderful care found in the household of God and I will gladly give them with a lifetime supply of the very essence of my spirit.

Because I truly love each and every one of you, I will make many, many house calls!"

"This *Very Essence of the True Spirit of Life*™ elixir, for which there are absolutely no counter-indications, has the power to completely cure Heartburn; Clogged Ears; Festering Wounds; Listlessness; Foot-in-Mouth Disease; Restlessness; Blurred Vision; Angry Swellings; In-articulitis; Paralysis; Blockages; Hunger and Thirst; Social Diseases; Strains and Stress; and many, many other disorders. Take all of this medicine at least one time today and call me in the morning! Unlimited refills! Do not refrigerate! Cautions: Potent Stimulant! May affect vision! Watch out for many side effects! And always remember: Dr. Jesus does make house calls! Dial him up anytime! Amen."

DR. SPIRITUS SANCTUS

Well, that world-famous Wonderful Guidance Counselor, Dr. Jesus, said to his regular patients at the Body of Christ Group Counseling Center: "Look, if you desire Wholeness and Well-being, you will take my advice and counsel to heart. I will hook-you-up with the Original Father of All Holistic Medicine who will immediately arrange for you to see yet another truly inspiring counselor in Our Most Wonderful Counseling Partnership, Dr. Spiritus Sanctus, who will always be free and available to see you at any time, day or night—which really is the Honest-to-God-Truth—although you'll never quite be able to prove it to by me because the world which demands proof is, in fact, completely deaf and blind to the truth!

But you, his very own patients, you already know the Counselor of whom I speak because he has already established his practice within you and will always continue to work in your very midst."

"You see, I will not leave you *dis-counsel-ate*. I will see you again very soon!"

"Now, of course, very soon the world will not see me, but when you truly enter into therapy with Dr. Spiritus Sanctus, you will see me very well indeed! And because I am Holy Alive and Well, you also will be Wholly Alive and Well!"

"For on that very day, you yourselves will be able to see clearly that I am in Our Father's Practice, and you are in mine, and I am in yours. Everyone who follows my guidance and counsel reveals a burning desire to be wholly alive and well through me. And all who are embraced and welcomed into the Practice by me will be embraced and welcomed into the Practice of Our Father. And because I truly desire your partnership, I will fully open-up and reveal my presence and power in your midst, in the Holy Wonderful Practice of God the Father, God the Son and God the Holy Spirit. Amen."

THE FIRST/LAST BANK OF HOPE AND TRUST

Blessings are Our Business
If we were you, we'd bank with us!

Member GD$\overset{A}{\Omega}$C™

Shareholders' Manual
Membership Meeting #EVI-A
Departments and Services:
 New Accounts and New Member Incorporation; Security Investments; Deposits; Withdrawals; Retirement/Estate Planning; Checking; Credit Inquiry; Personal Trust Division and Debt Cancellation; Employee Benefits and Business Opportunities; Futures; Divestiture ; Equity Resolves
 Try our Newest Service: The Dove™ ATM
 Upfront Disclaimer: Contrary to popular opinion, The First/Last Bank of Hope and Trust is not a brokerage firm and does not provide goods and services associated with the amassing of personal fame, fortune, or any of the other methods of attempted insulation from the realities of the human condition.

Company Policy Statements Applicable to All Branch Managers

1.1.1. By order of the Parent Company (as so often and so clearly expressed in the many memos of our beloved C.E.O.), all candidates for Branch Management have already been declared to be wholly acceptable and fit for service!

1.1.2. Regardless of actual length of employment, all Branch Managers are instructed to frequently refer to the vision and organization of the Parent Company (as defined and described in the Restructured "Flow Chart" and "Company

Policy Statements" as well as to all of the original Articles of Incorporation) for constant guidance regarding the way to act in and on behalf of the Parent Company.

1.1.3. The Parent Company hereby reminds all Branch Managers that they are only authorized to operate within the scope and vision of this the only abiding supplier of true and continuing hope and trust.

1.1.4. Operating outside of and beyond the scope of the corporate vision of the Parent Company *inevitably* results in the serious diminishment of assets and the subsequent loss of GDIC insurance, our only carrier.

1.1.5. All Branch Managers are heartily encouraged to be as creative as possible at all times, so long as, and under the condition that all such creativity remain under the auspices of the Parent Company, as directed by our C.E.O.

1.1.6. All Branch Managers are instructed to make frequent and generous investments using the limitless investment potential provided by our Founding Father of the Parent Company.

1.1.7. The Criteria for Successful Branch Management is as follows:

    1.1.7.1.1. Increase in true and abiding hope

    1.1.7.1.2. Increase in true and abiding trust

    1.1.7.1.3. Increase in numbers of true and abiding Branch Managers

    1.1.7.1.4. Subject to the following conditions.

1.1.8. All investment is intended for the sole purpose of providing generous blessing by greatly increasing the amount of true hope and trust.

1.1.9. Individual entrepreneurial ventures are definitely not recommended as they are inherently defective and doomed to failure.

1.1.10.   All investment policies are subject to the continuous supervision, review and correction by the Founding Father of the Parent Company.

1.1.11.   Any and all investment policies not meeting the above criteria (i.e., any policies not producing generous blessing and not greatly increasing the amount of hope and trust) will be automatically invalidated and terminated, for good.

1.1.12.   All Branch Managers are expected to joyfully carry and freely distribute the abundant goods and service so lavishly offered under the leadership and auspices of our C.E.O.

1.1.13.   As the Parent Company has invested heavily in you, so shall you make heavy investments in your neighbors, communities and world!

1.1.14.   Finally, let it be widely known and generally understood that the abundant production and free distribution of blessing, hope and trust necessarily and automatically results in the ultimate glorification of our Founding Father – for it is Proof Positive of legitimate Branch Management under the leadership of our Beloved and Most Generous C.E.O./J.C.O.L.

PRAYER JESUS

Then, right after our Guest Preacher, Jesus the Christ himself, finished his self-revealing and heart-felt sermon at the church where he had suddenly appeared two weeks before—when two of the regular parishioners had pestered him to literally show them the Father and he showed them his very own heart—he continued on with that particular sermon as it was still a part of our Lord's ongoing revelation and is still just as much at heart of the matter today as it ever was.

Then it was right after Jesus preached that sermon here in our midst that he raised his eyes and his heart up to God the Father and he immediately prayed out loud for all the people who were there—right in front of our eyes and where we could clearly see and hear him!

"Father," he said. "It is now time for you to reveal your true nature and very real presence through the window of my heart. For my own heart is where I hold each and every one of these dear people. And I thank you from the bottom of my heart for each and every one of these brothers and sisters you have given to me. Because I love them, I raise them up to you now for your ongoing guidance and blessing upon their lives."

"Father, I know my friends are often worried and anxious about many things, and I know it is because there really is real, undeniable pain and suffering in their lives and all around them. They are only human beings like me, Father, and they face many trials and tribulations, disappointments and defeats. I truly understand how easy it is for them to feel alone in their struggles—and even overwhelmed—and I am well aware that there are going to be many times when they are going to feel completely abandoned and forsaken; lost; small; weak; insignificant; short-changed; a day late and a dollar short; lacking in resources, money and energy; and ready to give up. And Father, I know that their hearts will be broken again and again, and indeed be troubled in this life."

"Who knows better than I, Father, how such sufferings will tempt them to make friends with the Enemy and suffer meaninglessly for something unworthy like the Prince of Evil instead of suffering fruitfully for you, Father—the Living God and the God of those who live? You have marked them as your own, Father, and I have surely accomplished my work of bringing your people to this place on this day. Now they know that everyone you have given to me comes from you, including their own hearts—and they also know that it really was you who sent me to reveal your abundant life to them."

"Lord, this is not a prayer for the world or for the Church at large, but it is my prayer today formed specifically for those who have come to this place or page today to remember and to continue to see your hand at work in the world. May your Living Presence so fill their hearts that they may consistently choose life in you whenever they are tempted to turn away and choose death instead."

"In the face of suffering, give them the strength to choose to be loving anyway. In the face of hardship, help them choose to do good anyway. In the face of temptations, give them courage to choose to love and affirm one another anyway and to never lose sight of their relationship with you—which really is the heart of the matter, the core of their being, and the true source of their life and love. Amen."

VIII

The Passion

THE PRESIDING BISHOP OF THE WHOLE CHURCH

So the Worldly Judge hauled Jesus into his chambers one more time and asked him straight out, "So, Jesus, are you, or are you not, the Presiding Bishop of the Whole Church?"

Jesus said, "Is that a question from the depths of your own heart, Judge, or is it just hearsay?

The Worldly Judge said, "Do I look like a parishioner to you? Your own church and clergy named you Presiding Bishop, put you on trial, and handed you over to me. So, tell me, Jesus, what have you done?"

Jesus said, "My church does not belong to this world. If my church did belong to this world, then my people would be calling in favors and pulling strings to keep me out of your hands. But my church truly does not belong to this world."

The Worldly Judge said, "So! You *are* the Presiding Bishop!"

Jesus said, "You're the one who keeps saying that I am Presiding Bishop. But I was born for this and for this alone: to speak the truth, the whole truth, and nothing but the truth. And the truth is that the Word of God presides in the hearts of those who belong to the truth, and everyone who belongs to the truth listens very carefully and pays close attention whenever the truth is spoken and lived.

A PASSION PLAY IN ONE FINAL BET

Narrator: Well, as luck or the Devil-himself would have it, Jesus wasn't the only person whose number was up that day. Two other men, who were, frankly, a couple of real losers, were also hanging around the main event.

Now, the Promoters of the Exhibition set Jesus up right there in the very center of all the action where the people could see him clearly as they were all straggling-around and placing their bets. The Promoters stapled a big sign on him that said, "Here hangs the Master Magician—the Wonderful Wizard of God!" For you see, the Promoters really were setting him up and daring Jesus to nail down his reputation as the Greatest Wizard of all time—while all the time they themselves were, in fact, placing their own bets squarely against him.

And a Promoter of that arena said,

Promoter: He helped a lot of others escape from some pretty tight restraints. If he's such a Wise and Wonderful Wizard, let's see him escape from this!

Narrator: And the Promoter's henchmen said,

Soldier #1: Here, have a magic wand! Hey, Wizard! How'd you like a little something to help you wiggle out of this trap?

Soldier #2: Hey, I've got a hundred bucks that says he can't do it!

Soldier #1: But who in the world would be naive enough to bet on a loser like him?

Soldier #2: Not me, that's for sure! Hey, *HOUDINI*[1]! If you're such a wise and wonderful wizard, let's see you do something really magical! Just come on down off of that cross if you want to be a really big winner!

Narrator: For there was a sign on Jesus, clearly saying: "Place your bets here! *IF YOU WANT TO LOSE, THAT IS!*

Soldier #1: Yes! Step right up folks and place your bets here! *THAT IS, IF YOU REALLY WANT TO BET ON A REAL LOSER!*

Narrator: All of which the one offender, named "Hanging Out," thought was really clever. So he hustled to place his bet on the Promoter and his henchmen, saying,

Criminal #1: Well, Mr. Almighty Wizard! Where is your magic when we really need it? Like *NOW* for example! Are you not the Great Wizard? Why don't you just wave your magic wand and save us all?

Narrator: But the other offender, "Hanging-In," said,

Criminal #2: Shut up, Man! You and I are getting exactly what we bet on in this world, but this man here between us, he is being royally cheated out of his life!

Narrator: And then, with his very last breath, he said to Jesus,

Criminal #2: Jesus, please don't forget that I placed my bet and hung-in here today with you.

Narrator: Jesus simply turned to him and said,

Jesus: My Dear Brother, on this very day you and I will be hanging-around together in Paradise—at home in the Godly magic of our Father's Kingdom—and you, my friend, can bet your whole heart and soul and last breath on that!

Narrator: And it was so. For that, my friends, is a very good bet. Because the ones who wager on the power of the Promoters and the rulers and the henchmen of this world—who put their whole trust in the powers-that-be—who place their entire well-being into the hands of the kings, the powers and the principalities of this world—who bet their lives on worldly rewards—who give their whole hearts over to the crowns and glories of worldly fame and fortune, and cast their lots with the abusers and the crucifiers—*THEY* are the ones who are really missing out on the true glories and riches of the Kingdom of God. Because those who place their bets on the crowns and kingdoms of this world are blind to the reality of the True King—the Crucified One wearing his magnificent Crown of Thorns—the Lamb who was slain and the only Shepherd worthy to bring us all home.

IX

Ongoing Appearances

TWO OF THE WOMEN

Mary and Martha, who were two of the women who had loved most passionately and lost most dearly, began to face the reality of death at the very break of day.

They immediately went to the place of their deepest grief where, instead of the dark and predictably closed pit of despair, they witnessed an amazing transformation of the whole place! For suddenly and all at once they felt a brightly energetic Presence and a tremendous release of pure energy shaking the very ground upon which they had just been standing so sadly, completely opening-up the closed pit of despair, and finally coming to rest upon what had only moments ago seemed like an insurmountable barrier to the source of their deep and passionately-lived lives. Incidentally, such excitement nearly scared the two big, brave, perhaps-even-Stoic guards half to death, because they just fell over on their faces right then and there while they were supposed to be protecting and defending that supposedly-insurmountable barrier.

But then the brightly energetic Presence spoke directly to the women right from the heart of their grief, saying, "I know why you have come to this place and I am here to help you understand something very important about the source of your deep and passionately-lived lives that you seek. Look. The source of passionate life is not here in the pit of despair."

Then the Presence invited the women to look more closely into the place of their despair and see for themselves how utterly hollow and empty it was.

Ongoing Appearances 175

As the women really looked very deeply into the tomb of grief, the Presence spoke right into the most intimate place of their heart of hearts and told them exactly where the source of passionate life could be found on earth—and at that they felt a surge of energy through their bodies, leapt up, and took-off running to tell the others what they had discovered about the source of passionate life!

As they were running in the direction of their hearts' content, something else absolutely amazing happened! The Very Source of Passionate Life suddenly appeared very clearly to them to be right then and there, in their very midst, receiving and enfolding them completely into the arms of God's own deep, and abiding, and most passionate Love!

A WGIJ-TV EASTER BROADCAST

Mark: Good morning, good morning, good morning! Happy Easter! Welcome to our program on the Here and Now Today Show on this glorious day celebrating the resurrection of our Lord and Savior, Jesus Christ! I am Mark E. Van G. List, and I'm coming to you live this morning from WGIJ-TV. Remember: "Yesterday it was news! Today it's even newer news!"

We are here in our recently updated studios in the west-central suburbs of our fair city on this the very first day of the week, and boy-oh-boy am I excited! Truly I tell you, we are all in for a really special treat this morning!

Believe it or not, I have right here with me in our WGIJ studios the very same, named, world-famous women, all the way here from the birth-place of Jesus' ministry in Galilee, who were featured in the exciting, transforming story we just ran a few minutes ago in an earlier Gospel Broadcast. Yes! That's right! Mary Magdalene herself is with us at WGIJ this morning! Also we are delighted to welcome Mary, the Mother of James, and last but not least—the irrepressible Salomé!

First of all, thank you for your willingness to appear here on our program today, to talk about your experience on that very first Easter morning. This is truly a special and happy morning for us at WGIJ! I understand from the clip we just saw that all three of you woke up very early and went to a tomb. So let me begin by asking you, why did you go to that particular tomb that morning?

Mary Magdalene: Because we knew the man and loved him more than life itself.

Salomé: We saw him crucified on a cross like a common criminal. With our own eyes, we watched him die. We were there when they buried his lifeless body in a cave.

Mary Magdalene: And we even saw Joseph roll a huge stone against the door of the tomb.

Mark: OK, let me get this straight. You mean you returned to the tomb again, a second time, several days after the burial of his body and the permanent sealing of his tomb?

Mary Magdalene: Well, two or three days at the most, I think. It's hard to remember exactly, because we were really scared and disoriented at the time. Also, you've got to understand that, especially right at that time, it was extremely dangerous for us to be out in public at all.

Salomé: Oh yes, I will never forget how frightened—scared to death, really.

Mary Magdalene: We knew it would have entertained the Roman soldiers to see us hang on crosses too.

Salomé: I loved Jesus with my whole heart, but my heart was in pieces on the ground. I was in a total state of shock. My whole world was in a shambles. I think I was just completely numb.

Mary Magdalene: Look. It took us a couple of days just to gather-up enough courage to risk sneaking out to his tomb to do what we really wanted, and even needed, to do.

Mary: His body, broken; His blood on the ground; the rattle of his dying breath.

Mary Magdalene: He was just literally ripped from our arms, you know. They buried him in such a hurry. We had no access to him at all.

Salomé: You see? It was all so very wrong.

Mary Magdalene: So we gathered-up all of our precious spices and perfumes and went to his tomb to anoint his body.

Mark: So you went to perform your Last Rites for him?

Salomé: In spite of everything, how could we not offer this one final, ritual act of respect for him? We loved everything about him, and we cherished his body.

Mary Magdalene: And besides, that's just what women do.

Salomé: We somehow find it in our hearts, out of our deepest love.

Mary: And, he was the very source of it.
Salomé: Oh yes, indeed he was!
Mary Magdalene: Why it was like the Love of God himself was present whenever Jesus was in the room!
Salomé: Oh, I know! I know! And what about in the kitchen?! Oh how I loved it that he always worked right along with us in the kitchen! Not like other men at all!
Mary: And how he waited on other people all the time! Always attending to their needs! It was quite a sight for sore eyes!
Mary Magdalene: Remember when he suddenly got up and washed all the disciples' feet?! Why I could have just kissed him over and over again at least a hundred times for that and for that alone!
Salomé: You know, sometimes I think we wouldn't have any voice in the church at all if it weren't for him!
Mary Magdalene: Probably not!
Salomé: A true friend of women everywhere!
Mary Magdalene: Well, you got that right!
Salomé: You know it, Sister!
Mark: But, well, uh, I gather that when you three actually arrived at the tomb, you found something you really didn't expect. So, I think the next thing our viewers might like to hear you talk about is what you expected to find when you got there. What was going on in your hearts and minds?
Mary Magdalene: Well, I was really anxious and I was entirely focused on that giant stone blocking the doorway. Salomé kept saying maybe we could find some strong, young man to move it away for us, but I just thought she was completely out of her mind.
Salomé: Actually, I assumed we would have to leave our spices there beside the stone as a little shrine in his memory.
Mary: But we were all hoping against all hope that we would be with him again for one final time of intimate communion with him.
Mary Magdalene: To weep and mourn together; to tell each other comforting stories of remembrance; to put him to final rest.
Salomé: I was looking for closure of some kind.
Mary: The pain was too much. I just wanted it to go away.
Mary Magdalene: But when we got there—when, as the story says, we finally looked up—why nothing at all blocked the way to Jesus! The struggle was already over! But you know what, Dear Friends?

Up until then there was a piece of me that actually wanted to keep him locked up.

Salomé: Yes, me too. Where nobody else could ever get to him.

Mary: To own him like a piece of property; to put him in my pocket and keep him all to myself. All for me and for me alone, you know?

Mary Magdalene: Indeed I do!

Salomé: Oh yes! Me too!

Mark: Ladies, Ladies! Excuse me for interrupting, but I thought that when you got there to the Empty Tomb, it wasn't empty at all.

Mary Magdalene: Empty? Who said it was empty?!

Salomé: No way! Why, it was nothing like empty at all!

Mary: It was filled! Filled with Presence! Filled with Power! Filled with Light!

Salomé: Like an angel of the Lord! Speaking to us!

Mary Magdalene: Like a young man in the prime of life! Perched! Right there in the tomb! Right where Jesus' body was laid! And, oh my God, how he—or It—spoke to us!

Mark: What on earth did he say to you?

Mary Magdalene: OK, I'll try to tell you, but it was really strange. It said that Jesus' death had been, roughly translated, "undone"; that Jesus had been "made un-dead." I mean, that Jesus had been "raised." That Jesus was somehow alive and well and could be found again, if we really wanted him, back home in Galilee—and that we should go give this urgent message to his other disciples—and especially to that Big Blockhead, Peter!

Mark: Wow! That must have been an incredible experience! Do I remember right that you all took-off running to tell the disciples?

Salomé: Say what?! Were you born in a coo-coo clock? We took-off running, all right! But we weren't running to the disciples! We were running away from him—or It! We didn't dare to tell another soul for days and days!

Mary: Oh Lord! My heart was in my throat!

Mary Magdalene: Me? I couldn't even breathe, let alone talk.

Mark: Wow! That's really an amazing story! I can't tell you what a real thrill it is that you are all so willing—and now also so wonderfully able—to talk with us about your life-changing experience! So in these last sixty seconds, as we wrap-up this segment of our show—now that you have had so many years to unpack and live into it—I wonder if you might share with us any further reflections you may have.

Mary Magdalene: What I would like for your viewers to know is that everything they think is over-and-done-with and settled, isn't; that everything they believe is frozen, fixed and certain, isn't; that at the core of our lives is an unexpected, passionate love that cannot be overcome by the insanities and sins of the world—that there is a power at loose and at work in this world which really cannot be controlled, extinguished, snuffed-out, or kept away from us in any way. And that not even death can stop the Living, Life-giving Presence of God!

Salomé: It's irrepressible!

Mary Magdalene: The desire and the will of God for all!

Mary: And that nothing at all—no thing—not one single, solitary thing—no small thing or large thing in heaven or on earth—nor in life, nor in death—can ever separate us from the love of God made known and palpable to us through Christ Jesus our Lord. Happy Easter! Amen! Alleluia! Alleluia!

THE SACRISTY OF THE HUMAN HEART

Well for heaven's sake, most reasonable people were still in bed asleep because it wasn't even light yet when some of our most supremely-dedicated Church Ladies, who were Charter Members of the Altar Guild, arrived at the Church one Easter morning long, long ago, bringing with them bottles of scented oil for the candles, and cans of incense, and all the altar cloths, towels and other fine linens they had washed, dried, starched and ironed all the Holy Week long. But when they got to the Sacristy door, right away they noticed that the alarm had been de-activated and the door was unlocked, and the door was standing wide open! But when they went in and checked around, they found no body there!

Now, while they were still somewhat in the dark about this, a couple of very strange clergy-types suddenly appeared in dazzling vestments and stood there right beside them, and the three women immediately fell at their feet!

But the men said, "Yikes! Why are you women fumbling around here in the Sacristy? There is no body here! And if you're looking for your priest, he's probably still home in bed at this un-godly hour! Remember what Jesus of Nazareth said when he was still alive: that the Living Presence of God would be handed-over to the world, mocked, scourged, pierced and crucified so that even his memory would be distorted and made completely unrecognizable, until on the third day—at long last, when all is said and done—the Living Presence of God may finally rise in the Sacristy of your hearts,

to put on and wear;*
the holy vestments there."

Then suddenly they did remember what they already knew because their Lord had taught it to them. And what they remembered was that the Presence of the Living God simply cannot be contained or confined, boxed, bottled or canned; imprisoned in the Sacristy; monopolized by the Church; restricted to any religious language about God; limited to any person, place or thing; commercialized; trivialized; romanticized; cheapened; managed; controlled or domesticated in any way—and that the Presence of the Living God simply cannot be washed, dried, starched, or ironed flat—*nor even fully captured in the story at hand!*

So on that very Easter Day, the three of them went in to the service and preached to the choir! And they were Mary M., Jane, and Mary, the wife of the Pastor. Of course, the choir wrote them off as Old Wives' Tales and didn't believe a single word of it!

But the Beloved Rector of that parish? Well, he jumped-up and ran to the door of the Sacristy, and when he leaned into it, sure enough, those fine linen cloths were lying in there all by themselves! Then he went home that Easter Day truly amazed! And that, Dear People, is just the very first threads of the rest of the story!

ON THE ROAD TO AMAZE-US

Now when the actors witnessed the incredibly efficient and absolutely thorough and, indeed, the extremely brutal shutting-down of The

Universal Theater of God's Kingdom, when the Principle Actor was first dragged-off the stage and then permanently removed from ever acting in that or any other theater again, forever, a couple of them just packed-up their grief and immediately hit the road. But while they were on their way to the nearby town of Amaze-Us, something absolutely amazing happened! For as they were struggling to come to grips with all the confusing ramifications concerning the permanent closing of The Universal Theater of God's Kingdom, they experienced something of a third-party intervention in the form of a very strange actor whom they did not recognize, but who had suddenly joined them in their grief-stricken journey to that nearby place.

Now those two actors who had just been wandering around in the maze of their grief suddenly found themselves amazed, thoroughly spellbound, and completely in the grips of that very strange third-party actor whom they did not recognize, and who was so incredibly, and efficiently, and absolutely thoroughly, but ever so gently explaining to them that even as brutal as it was, the shutting-down of the Universal Theater of God's Kingdom did not in any way represent The End of the script or the permanent closing of the play, but that it was, in fact, a scene which had actually and always been written right there and incorporated into the script itself—part and parcel of the Author's Wonderful Work from the very beginning!

So, you see, the couple of grief-stricken actors were so thoroughly absorbed by what that very strange, third-party actor was saying that they begged for an extension of the companionship when they finally arrived at a resting-place on the road to Amaze-Us.

They immediately sat down together at the table, and then, just as they were about to receive, the most truly amazing thing of all happened! The very strange, third-party actor recited some of the most important and very famous words found in the original script itself! While they were hearing those very special and familiar words, the two formerly grief-stricken actors actually recognized the very present and immediate voice of the Principle Actor himself—whom they had obviously, mistakenly assumed to have been permanently removed from the stage forever—but who was right then and there making a gift of his presence as he re-opened The Universal Theater of God's Kingdom incredibly efficiently, absolutely thoroughly, and ever so gently, forever!

CSI: JERUSALEM

The 24th episode of CSI[1]: Jerusalem entitled *Under a Microscope*

Scene One
The entire cast is angry, frustrated and grief-stricken, not only for the loss of their own Beloved Lead Investigator, but also because they still don't have an explanation for his brutal murder or the subsequent dismantling of their Special Investigative Unit, which left them with only a handful of flimsy, insubstantial clues. So, not having any substantial leads, a couple of their most famous Ace Detectives, *Gil Grissom*,[2] the named, male detective—and an un-named female detective who might have been Sara Sidekick or Katherine Somebody—quietly pack-up their Closed Case File, their Evidence Collection Guidelines where it says: "Always search in pairs," (Mark 6:7) and their Detectives' Bibles and set off down the road to Amaze-Us.

Scene Two
Out on the Road to Amaze-Us, while Grissom and his Side-kick are busy conducting their painstaking review of the events and the timeline, their Beloved Lead Investigator mysteriously arrives and lends his own expertise to their analysis—although, at this point in our drama, they don't recognize his presence even though they are skilled in Voice Analysis—or even when he pointedly asks them, "So what are you two geniuses so busy investigating?"

So they stop right there, dead-in-their-tracks, looking downtrodden. Grissom answers the question with a question of his own: "Say what? Are you the only Private Eye in the world who doesn't have a clue about the recent CSI Shutdown? That's incredible! It's all over the news! Why you can't hardly turn on a single television channel or radio station without hearing about it and how all the Insurance Companies and Policy Police just put us all out of business!"

Then Sidekick says, "But what's even more amazing than that, after only three days on the job, some low-level typists from our office pool are reporting that they have inspected it all again, looked very, very closely, seen the light and solved the mystery already! Yikes! If you can believe that!"

But then the Strange Investigator calmly said to them, "Look, *My Dear Watson*[3]—uh, I mean Detectives Grissom and Sidekick—for inquiring and discerning hearts, Christian Education never ends." Then he said, as he put a couple of slides under his high-powered microscope for them to see for themselves:

> Christian Education is a series of lessons, with the greatest for the last. It is true that, "though in your mission you have missed a few things of importance, yet even those things which have obtruded themselves upon your notice give rise to serious thought. It is of highest importance in the art of detection to be able to recognize, out of a number of facts, which are incidental and which vital. Otherwise your energy and attention must be dissipated instead of being concentrated. You know my methods; here is my lens. For there is nothing as good as first-hand evidence."[4]

A Couple of Moses' Samples

1. "When the Israelites saw it, they said to one another, 'What is it?' for they did not know what it was. Moses said to them, 'It is the bread that the Lord has given you to eat.'" (Exod 16:15)
2. "The house of Israel called it manna; it was like coriander seed, white, and the taste of it was like was like wafers made with honey." (Exod 16:31)

An Elijah Sample

1. "The ravens brought him bread and meat in the morning, and bread and meat in the evening; and he drank from the wadi." (I Kings 17:6)

Grissom and Sidekick become completely engrossed and thoroughly spellbound by everything this Strange Investigator is showing them about his wonderful work and the way he really makes the evidence speak! In fact, they are both so incredibly intrigued that they invite him to sit down and join them for dinner right in the middle of their ongoing investigation.

Scene Three

When they sit down to eat together that evening, the Strange Investigator begins reading out loud right from their own personal copy of the Detectives' Handbook where it gives this definition of Transient Evidence:

> Transient Evidence is Special, Mysterious Evidence that, in order to be seen, and in order to retain its true value to satisfy the mind

and to truly fill the soul, must be received openly, one day at a time, and be fully appreciated as a true gift from God.

And then that Strange Investigator just picks up the bread which they now regard as manna; blesses it with what they recognize as the deepest appreciation; breaks it as they remember their Lord's own body was broken; and simply hands it over to them like a precious gift from the hand of God. So their eyes are opened and they recognize his palpable presence even as he vanishes from their fleeting sight!

Scene Four (The Rest of the Story)
So they confirm with each other, "Did not our hearts burn within us while he talked to us on the road, while he opened to us the scriptures?" (Luke 24:32). Then they turn around right then and there and return to Jerusalem where they find the community gathered together and saying, "The Lord is risen indeed and the Church is joyfully bearing witness!

Then they each tell in their own strange and unique ways—and as best they can—what had happened on the road and how he was made manifest to them in the breaking of bread.

A SPOOKY WAY TO HANDLE JESUS

Then, while Jesus' disciples were still in Jerusalem hiding-out in the upper room and telling one another eerie stories about how they had each seen Jesus risen from the dead,

>Jesus himself appeared in their midst,*
>Spooking them all right out of their wits!

They all jumped to the conclusion that they were seeing an optical illusion or a trick of the mind—or maybe even some kind of ghastly spirit! But the palpable presence of Jesus questioned their thinking and strongly suggested that they should get a grip on themselves and somehow come to realize what they were having some much difficulty seeing with their real eyes as they heard these words, "Hey, look at my hands and feet; handle me, and see if you can grab a-hold of the real thing—because spooks have no flesh and bones, as you can surely see that I have!"

But when the disciples immediately leapt to the assumption that this was surely too good to be true, Jesus brought them back down to earth and asked them if they had anything good to eat. So they offered him a piece of broiled fish which he took and savored right before their eyes!

Then he reminded them that in order to get a handle on the real Body of Christ, they would need to open their hearts and their minds to the scripture which tells us that Jesus died and rose again so that his disciples might become the real and visible Body and Blood, flesh and bones, and hands and feet of our Risen Lord.

In other words, while Jesus' disciples were still in Jerusalem hiding-out in that upper room, missing the richness of that life with God they had known so intimately with Jesus when he was alive, and longing for that sense of well-being they had known in his presence—missing Jesus and feeling depressed and disconnected and unsure if there was really any hope in life at all—when they began to tell one another eerie stories about how they had each seen Jesus risen from the dead, and wondering if these stories were merely figments of their imaginations or just another case of wishful thinking that would all disappear in a puff of smoke—easy-come, easy-go—when suddenly the Living Word of God Incarnate stood right there in their midst, scaring them all half to death and right out of their wits! They all jumped to the conclusion that they were seeing an optical illusion or a trick of the mind, or maybe even some kind of ghostly, disembodied spirit, for they were all suddenly on the very same scary page at the very same time!

But, of course, the Word of God strongly suggested that they should get a grip on what they were in fact in the very process of truly perceiving, "Hey! Come to me and look at my hands and my feet; touch me; sense me; feel me, and see if you can put your hands on the real thing. Come to me and see if the Word of God can yet live—if the Word of God can take on flesh and blood, connect tissue to tissue, bone to bone, and live on the earth as our old friend and poet, Ezekiel, said in his *Big Book of Weird Visions and Bizarre Scenes*, Chapter 37:1–14, because ghosts have no flesh and bones, as you can surely see that I have!"

But when the disciples again leapt to the assumption that this was surely too good to be true, the Word of God brought them back down to earth with the question, "Well, do you have anything here to eat to help keep me alive?" So they offered him a piece of broiled fish—a taste of their true identity and desire for life—which he gladly took into himself right before their very eyes! Then he reminded them that in order to get in touch with the real Living Word of God they would need to open their minds to the scripture which tells us that the Word of God Incarnate died and rose again so that the disciples themselves might become the real and visible Body and Blood, flesh and bones, and hands and feet of the Living Lord of Life.

A CERTAIN PILLAR OF THE CHURCH

Then one day, early on a Sunday morning and well before the early service, while it was still dark outside, a certain Pillar of the Church went to the church to humbly kneel and pray before anyone else arrived to worship. But right away she noticed that the doors to the church had somehow been flung wide open to any and all who might actually want to come in, no matter who they were—whether *the good, the bad*, or even people right off the street! So she immediately became unhinged herself and rushed into the church office where she phoned, using their home phone numbers, both the Bishop and that other one affectionately known as the One the Lord Really Loves.

She told them in no uncertain terms, "Hey! You guys better hurry up and get your rears over here because the church has been robbed! These people here have just ruined everything! They've just sucked the life right out of our worship! I tell you, they have taken away everything of value! Everything that was sacred has been stolen!"

And, rest assured, Dear Hearts, those two guys surely came running!

But, of course, the One the Lord Really Loves got there first and saw that things were indeed in turmoil, but without the Bishop there, he didn't actually go in there to try to straighten anything out.

Now, when the Bishop did finally show up to look into the matter, he did, in fact, detect a bit of a situation in the church. But when he looked into it a little more thoroughly, he saw that even though there was some obvious turmoil, the Lord's Table was beautifully set and ready to serve God's People nevertheless. And then, after that, the One the Lord Really Loves also looked into the matter more thoroughly and believed that he had caught a glimpse of the true Body of Christ. But, as yet, neither of them could grasp the whole of what was really going on so they went on back to the See City, or to their homes—or back to the place from wherever they had hailed.

Now, the Pillar of the Church still stood outside of the church weeping and gnashing her teeth. But as she wept, she looked into the church again and, through her tears, she noticed that the two candles on either side of the altar were lit. Then, in her eyes anyway, they suddenly took on more beauty and meaning than they had ever had before.

She heard a voice within herself saying, "Pillar of the Church, why are you crying?" as she muttered in her heart, "This church has been robbed! These people here have just ruined everything! There's nothing sacred here anymore! They have taken away everything of value!"

Then she got up and turned around and actually saw the Lord of Hosts with her own eyes standing right there in front of her, although she was still blind to his real Presence. He spoke to her, saying, "Pillar of the Church, why are you crying? Have you lost something—*or someone?*"

Assuming he was the janitor, she said, "They have taken away everything that was sacred and precious to me! Now I can't feel the presence of My Beloved Teacher in this place anymore! So, if you happen know where else I might go to find him, please tell me and I'll attend there from now on."

Then she heard our Lord's voice tugging at her heart with his special nickname for her, "Dear Stalwart One." She immediately turned to him and said, "My Beloved Teacher," which is *Rabbouni* in Hebrew.

He said to her, "Dear Stalwart One, don't hold on to what is dead and has passed away. Go ahead and tell your brothers and sisters to look for me and to seek me in the Presence of the God and Father of us all—of your God and my God—who is always here—right in front of your own two eyes—in the loving presence of others and of the community of faith that surrounds you. For, very soon, that is the only place where I will be found."

Of course, she then did exactly as her Beloved Teacher had taught her to do, saying to all of her brothers and sisters, both then and now, even here on this Easter Sunday morning at a church where the doors are still open to any and to all, "I have seen, and heard, and tasted, and touched, and felt, and known the Presence of the Lord of Hosts here in this place."

JESUS ASCENDS BEFORE OUR VERY EYES

Well, just as soon as it was abundantly clear that the Company of Jesus' Players understood the bit about the permanent re-opening of The Universal Theater of God's Kingdom, and that they had actually grasped the bit about how the whole scenario had always been written right there in the Holy Script—part and parcel of the Gentle and Loving Author's wonderful work—the Principle Actor simply marched the entire Company downstage, front and center, to the area called Bethany where he proceeded to bless them all with a powerfully passionate and highly dramatic performance summing up all the dazzling beauty of his brief, but magnificent acting career, and then directing them to wait backstage where they would soon be receiving their marvelous new costumes as promised by the Gentle and Loving Author—as written in his stage notes to the actor commonly referred to by one name only, Joel—as found in the original script (Joel 2:17–18).

Now, while he was in the very act of blessing them with his performance, he reached the highest point of his whole career. He blessed them with the most glorious and truly elevating finalé they had ever witnessed—after which they went backstage in extremely high spirits to attend the cast party of their wildest dreams—also as once described by their old friend, Joel. Of course, the most celebrated Guest of Honor was none other than the Gentle and Loving Author of all their works begun and ended in him.

THE WHOLE WORLD COMMUNICATIONS COMPANY

And then, all of a sudden, there they were in the newsroom of the Jerusalem Headquarters of the Whole World Communications and Broadcasting Company (WWCBC) where we find the Star Reporter, Mary Magdalene, early on a Monday morning, just signing-on to her word processor when—lo and behold! Look what happened! Jesus himself appeared right there on her computer screen just as soon as she signed-on!

Well, Mary Magdalene immediately ran to the boardroom of the WWCBC where the Broadcast Team was sitting in a post-mortem depression. She made her astounding report that she had just seen Jesus making a live broadcast that very morning. But when the Broadcast Team heard what she had to say, they immediately closed their minds and hearts to the very idea.

So then Jesus found yet another way to show-up—suddenly appearing to two reporters who were out on the road on assignment. One of the reporters was the named, male reporter with the byline "Cleophas." The other reporter was a certain female reporter without a byline. But the two of them were out pounding the Road to Amaze-Us together, as was Company travel policy.

All employees of the WWCBC must always travel together and do all of their broadcasting work in teams of at least two or more reporters, without exception.

Now, when those two reporters got the real scoop, they immediately ran back to the Company Headquarters in Jerusalem to make their amazing report. But the Broadcast Team steadfastly closed their hearts and their minds and totally rejected their whole story too.

Then, after that rejection, Jesus himself stormed into the Board Room to confront his Broadcast Team and to upbraid them for closing their hearts and minds and for rejecting the reports of their very own newscasters to whom he had appeared.

He then gave them their marching orders in the form of a memo.

To: All Employees
From: Jesus Christ, V. P. and Right-hand Man
Re: Whole World Communications

Message: Don't just sit there! Go into the whole world and proclaim the good news to the whole creation!

After delivering this memo, Jesus left the Board Room and took his private elevator up to his penthouse office right next to the Company Founder. The Broadcast Team immediately left the Boardroom and began to deliver the Good News from one end of the globe to another, and Our Lord Jesus assisted their good work in every way, shape and form, and giving them many, many signs of his approval—even to this very day—right here and right now as you read this very latest report with your very own eyes!

You go, Girl!

Atta Boy! Keep up the good work!

Well done good and faithful servants!

THE LAST CURTAIN FALLS

So the eleven disciples who were still there went directly to Galilee to the familiar arena where the women informed them the Principle Actor really could be found on earth. Then, when they really did sense his familiar Presence on that very stage where they had originally known him to act so well,

> They sang and rejoiced as they praised his great name;*
> all except for the ones still in doubt of the same.

Then the Principle Actor himself came into the spotlight on Center Stage and delivered these closing lines, "I have been fully endowed with all the powers of our Gentle and Loving Author, and it is high-time for you all to get out there and recruit new actors! Fully receive them into The Universal Theater of God's Kingdom™, The Company of Jesus' Players™ and the School of the Indwelling Spirit to Act™."

"Teach them to act in the same way I have taught you to act and you will find that I am always right there acting right along with you even until all the scenes have been played—when the play is finally finished—when the last curtain falls!"

GOD'S GREAT LOVE FOR THE WORLD

But then, in the middle of a small, tightly secured room, as the hostile city and the darkness of night were just beginning to close in around them, and while their own hands and hearts were clenched in fear, they all became acutely aware of his immediate Presence close-in among them as they heard his simple and very familiar proclamation echoing in a most familiar and intimate way, "Peace be with you." It was what he always said.

And they were all-together deeply moved by the remembrance and vision of the wounds he had sustained on the cross. And then, when they finally and fully recognized who it was who was there with them in their very midst,

> Their own hearts and hands were gently released;*
> as all together came great joy and peace.

They were once again filled with the words and the presence of their friend, the Lord, who was re-telling their hearts and reminding them all of everything that the Father had done for them.

So, you see, on that evening when they were all together, they were deeply inspired by the breath of fresh air gently blowing in that room.

> In that small, airtight room
> With their hearts clenched in fear
> As the city surrounded
> And nightfall drew near

They acknowledged his Presence
His peace, they received
By the wounds he sustained on the cross,
Sight believed

As they breathed in the air
Of his power increased
In their hearts filled with joy
In their ears, peace confessed
In their eyes all the signs
Of the love he expressed

In their hearts, in that night,
In that room, in that place
They were given the power to act
By his grace

And to pass it along
Or refuse and withhold
God's great love for the world
Sent to make the world whole.

ON PENTECOST SUNDAY

Then, on Pentecost Sunday, every last member and friend of the church came to worship in the very same place on the very same day. Suddenly something felt altogether different about their entire religious experience right then and there, for it was like they were suddenly all dramatically awakened from a deep sleep by a loud, roaring sound, as a mighty breath of fresh air blew all around and among those who worshipped God together there—permeating everything and filling and satisfying each and every one of them with the holy vitality, essence, spirit and intent of God for their lives.

Each member of the congregation was given his or her own individual voice, and they all began communicating with each other in more unique and spirit-filled ways than they had ever even previously imagined that they could: in creative images; in honest exchanges; in poetry, music and song; some in the utterance of wisdom; others in the utterances of knowledge; others in faith; prophecy; discernment; and various translations into day-to-day language and current metaphors. Plus, there were also other fellow human beings—other living souls, neighbors, and friends living in the area, from all walks of life, who, when they got wind of the goings-on there, crowded around the church because they were staggered by what they saw and heard, and they were incredibly intrigued and wondered what it was all about. They exclaimed, "Hey, aren't these all just a bunch of middle-class mid-westerners and mainstream church-goers? How is it that they are all saying things that are making abundant sense to all of us as diverse as we are, and from so many different walks of life? For some of us are doctors and lawyers, hairdressers and morticians, homemakers and homeless people, prophets and poets, electricians and beauticians from all over the city—and these folks are indeed communicating the mighty power, love and compassion of God and making it understandable, accessible and immediately available to all of us!"

FISHING IN THE LAKE OF THE HUMAN HEART

Now, after his crucifixion and death, Jesus also disclosed his presence to his students by the Lake of the Human Heart in this strange and mysterious manner, as follows.

Five named disciples and two un-named disciples were all gathered together in the same place and on the same page, so to speak. Simon Peter, also understood to refer to "the Church," announced that he, for one, intended to continue with the prayers and studies of the community that they had loved studying with Jesus while he was alive. The rest of them agreed that this was a good idea and that they would do so as well.

So they all got into the same boat together and proceeded to work on the same page. But nothing came to them for a long, dark period of time.

But then, at some point in the midst of that long, deep, dark period of time, something finally began to dawn upon them and they caught a glimpse of something on the horizon—or just on the periphery of their understanding—although they didn't realize it was actually the Lord at work in their hearts and minds.

But that Something on the horizon was somehow breaking into the scene with this persistent question: "Children, are you netting any results from all your prayer and study? They truthfully had to answer, "Well no. Not really."

So the voice spoke to them, gently suggesting, "Try to see and hear it in a different way now. Let go of your pre-conceived notions of how it is supposed to be done and what it is supposed to mean and you will learn something new and begin netting results the likes of which you never imagined."

Then one of the students who took all of this so very, very personally and was so busy writing himself or herself into the very heart of the story—that Anonymous One whom Jesus also loves as his very own— quickly pointed out that what they were hearing was, in fact, the voice of Jesus himself speaking directly to them right across and through all of the barriers of space and time.

When Peter, a.k.a. the Church, recognized that it really was Jesus himself who was leading them on from beyond the grave, he jumped up with great excitement, got ready for an ongoing encounter with the Living Lord, and plunged headlong right into the text-at-hand, as well as into the ongoing life of the community, with his entire being dressed for success! The other students then also came dragging along behind, bringing the results they had netted—and "wagging their tails behind them"[5]! For they were incredibly close to having a revelation and seeing it all for themselves with their very own eyes!

And then, when they all really got to the same place at the same time and were truly all on the very same page, the whole community saw such a clear vision of God's truth and felt such warmth from the fire of God's love that it appeared as if such abundance had always been spread out on a table before them—and that both the fish and the bread of life had already been prepared for them as from before the beginning of the world!

And, of course, Jesus, the Bread and Fish of Life—the Word of Life—the Logos and the Author of our Salvation—really was fully present and calling out to them, "Children, bring some of the results you have just netted to the table with you!"

So the Church went out and hauled the net ashore, full of large fish fresh from the Lake of the Human Heart—all *one-hundred and fifty-three of them*—for what they had just netted was indeed *whole and brimming with fullness of life!*

X

Beginning Again

HOW STRANGE AND BEAUTIFUL

THEN A STRANGE AND beautiful spirit of light and energy spoke to the very heart of a certain servant of God, saying: "Go out along the desert way and witness what God will show you there." So the servant of God followed the signs given by the strange and beautiful spirit of light and energy out along that solitary, deserted road.

Behold! The servant of God witnessed something astonishing far out along that way when he met a solitary soul completely steeped in the word of God. The solitary soul openly invited the servant of God to come into his place of engagement with the scripture and to join him there in the texts and contexts.

As they read together, the solitary soul and the servant of God often asked, "Do you understand what we are reading?" And they also often answered, "How can I unless there is someone to guide me?"

Now, one of the passages of scripture that awed and dumbfounded them was this one:

> As a sheep led to the slaughter
> Or a lamb before its shearer is dumb,
> So he opens not his mouth.
> In his humiliation justice was denied him.
> Who can describe his generation?
> For his life is taken up from the earth."
> (Acts 8:32–33, based on Isa 53:7–8)

They asked each other, "Is the poet being self-referential or writing this about someone else?"

So it was in this way that they began to discover many new and exciting ways to understand and express the good news hovering around and all about Jesus Christ on every side.

Then, as they moved further and further along in their journey together, they suddenly came upon a magnificent oasis of sparkling water which suddenly gave them a very bright idea! So they said to each other, "What is to prevent us from becoming completely immersed in this marvelous source of liquid beauty and meaning?"

So they stopped right then and there, dove all the way in, and swam way down deep under the surface of that wonderful source of refreshment and joy.

When they re-emerged, the solitary soul and the servant of God were astonished to find their life completely transcended and transformed by the whole experience—and forever deeply connected through the strange channels of light and energy witnessed and experienced in such exquisite beauty.

Then they each continued to travel on in their own unique and wonderful ways,

> Forever remembered,
> Forever rejoicing;*
> Forever the song
> Of the power of love.

Notes

PREFACE

1. Paul Blackburn, "Proensa: A Reading at Long Island University, Brooklyn Center," December 14, 1965: on tape; quoted in: Economou, George, ed., Proensa: An Anthology of Troubadour Poetry (New York: Paragon House, 1978), xvii.

2. Catherine Whittier Huber and Lynn C. McCallum, *The Whole Gospel according to the Universal Theater of God's Kingdom: Any Handy Metaphor Will Do* (Eugene: Wipf and Stock, 2011) 157.

CHAPTER I

1. Sung to the tune of "Jingle Bells," music and lyrics by James Pierpoint, 1857.

CHAPTER II

1. Sung to the tune of the famous Italian song, "O Sole Mio," music by Eduardo di Capua; lyrics by Giovanni Capurro, 1898.

CHAPTER III

1. Sung to the tune of "Good Christian Friends Rejoice," The Hymnal, 1982 according to the use of the Episcopal Church (New York: The Church Hymnal Corporation) # 107. Music: In dulci jubilo, German carol, 14th century. Words: John Mason Neale (1818–1866).

2. First line of hymn lyrics by Clifford Bax, 1916, at the request of Gustav Holst. The Hymnal of the Protestant Episcopal Church, 1940 (New York: The Church Pension Fund) #536.

3. From the "Confession of Sin," The Book of Common Prayer (Harrisburg: Morehouse Publishing, 1985) 42.

4. From the "Confession of Sin," The Book of Common Prayer (Harrisburg: Morehouse Publishing, 1985) 360.

5. Sung to the tune of "Santa Claus is Coming to Town;" music by J. Fred Coots; lyrics by Haven Gillespie, 1932.

6. Sung to the tune of "Deck the Halls with Boughs of Holly," 18th century traditional Welsh Christmas carol.

7. From "The Great Thanksgiving," The Book of Common Prayer (Harrisburg: Morehouse Publishing, 1985) 361.

CHAPTER IV

1. Sung to the tune of "Take Me Out to the Ballgame;" music by Jack Norworth; lyrics by Albert Von Tilzer, 1858.

2. From the popular 1980 song, "Nine to Five," by Dolly Parton.

3. Syrus Publilius, (42 BC) Maxim 524.

4. From the 1975 Broadway musical, The Wiz; music and lyrics by Charlie Smalls.

5. Syrus Publilius, (42 BC) Maxim 524.

6. From the 1975 Broadway musical, The Wiz; music and lyrics by Charlie Smalls.

7. Sung to the tune of the traditional gospel hymn, "Come on in the Room," recorded by the Georgia Mass Choir on the album Hold On, Help is On the Way, Savoy Records, 1990.

8. From "Ordination: Bishop," The Book of Common Prayer (Harrisburg: Morehouse Publishing, 1985), 518.

9. From "Eucharist Prayer A," The Book of Common Prayer (Harrisburg: Morehouse Publishing, 1985), 361.

10. From the Collect for "Proper 7," The Book of Common Prayer (Harrisburg: Morehouse Publishing, 1985), 230.

11. Sung to the tune of the traditional African-American Spiritual, "Rise and Shine and Give God the Glory."

12. From "Immortal, Invisible, God Only Wise," The Hymnal, 1982 according to the use of the Episcopal Church (New York: The Church Hymnal Corporation) #423. Music: Welsh hymn from Caniadau y Cyssegr, 1839; Words: Smith, Walter Chalmers (1824–1908).

13. Ibid.

14. From the "Nicene Creed," The Book of Common Prayer (Harrisburg: Morehouse Publishing, 1985) 326.

15. From The Book of Common Prayer (Harrisburg: Morehouse Publishing, 1985) 366.

16. From they hymn "Alleluia, alleluia, alleluia! The strife is o're," The Hymnal, 1982 according to the use of the Episcopal Church (New York: The Church Hymnal Corporation) #208. Music: Victory, Giovanni Pierluigi da Palestrina (1525–1594; adapt. and arr. William Henry Monk (1823–1889); Words: Latin, 1695; tr. Francis Pott (1832–1909) alt.

17. Refrain from the song, "Takes Two to Tango," music and lyrics by Al Hoffman and Dick Manning, 1952.

CHAPTER V

1. Sung to the tune of "I'm in the Army Now," by Frank Luther, 1941.

2. Sung to the tune of "Do Your Ears Hang Low," Roud Folk Song Index #15472, The English Folk Dance and Song Society, Vaughan Williams Memorial Library, Cecil Sharpe House, London, England at www.efdss.org. Pankake, Prairie Home Companion Folk Song Book (1988) 210–11.

3. Sung to the tune of "Pop Goes the Weasel," traditional English nursery rhyme; Roud Folk Song Index #5249, The English Folk Dance and Song Society, Vaughan Williams Memorial Library, Cecil Sharpe House, London, England at www.efdss.org. Montgomerie, Scottish Nursery Rhymes (1946) 94–95.

CHAPTER VI

1. Based on "Little Jack Horner," Traditional English nursery rhyme; Roud Folk Song Index #S181970, The English Folk Dance and Song Society, Vaughan Williams Memorial Library, Cecil Sharpe House, London, England at www.efdss.org. Opie, Oxford Dictionary of Nursery Rhymes (1951) 234–37.

2. From "Eucharist Prayer A," The Book of Common Prayer (Harrisburg: Morehouse Publishing, 1985), 363.

3. Traditional African-American Spiritual, "This Little Light of Mine."

4. Ibid.

5. A simple hand dance associated with the Spanish song, "Macarena," written and recorded by Los del Rio on their 1996 album, Fiesta Macarena. In the late 1990's, it was a popular group activity during wedding receptions in the United States.

6. Ibid.

7. Ibid.

CHAPTER VII

1. Paraphrase of Psalm 23, sung to the tune of "The King of Love My Shepherd Is," The Hymnal, 1982 according to the use of the Episcopal Church (New York: The Church Hymnal Corporation) # 645. Music: St. Columba, Irish melody. Lyrics: Baker, Henry Williams (1821–1877).

CHAPTER VIII

1. Internationally-famous professional magician and escape artist, Harry Houdini (1874–1926) was born Erik Weisz in Budapest, Austria-Hungary. He immigrated to the United States in 1878 when his family changed the spelling of his name to Erick Weiss.

CHAPTER IX

1. CBS Television Studios series, *CSI: Crime Scene Inve*stigation, 2000-present, includes television programs under the titles: CSI: Las Vegas; CSI: Miami, and CSI: New York.

2. "Gil Grissom" was one of the former main characters in the CBS Television Studios series, CSI: Crime Scene Investigation; CSI: Las Vegas, 2000-present.

3. Sir Arthur Conan Doyle, "'The Reigate Puzzle," in The Memoirs of Sherlock Holmes, George Newnes, London, 1894. www.pagebypagebooks.com.

4. Ibid.

5. From "Little Bo-Peep," traditional English nursery rhyme; Roud Folk Song Index #6487, The English Folk Dance and Song Society, Vaughan Williams Memorial Library, Cecil Sharpe House, London, England at www.efdss.org. Opie, Oxford Dictionary of Nursery Rhymes (1951) 93–94.

Appendix

The Universal Theater of God's Kingdom in Synoptic Order Outline with the Gospel of John Inserted

Appendix: The Universal Theater of God's Kingdom in Synoptic Order Outline with the Gospel of John Inserted

"UTGK" Titles	Bible Verses	Season	Year/Day	Huck-Leitzmann Titles and Story Numbers	#
I. A Handful of Previous Productions			Episcopal Lectionary		J=John Only
A Man for Whom Faith	Genesis 22:1–14	Lent	B-2	Abraham and Isaac	
Theophany in the Bush	Exodus 3:1–6	Trinity	B	Moses at the Burning Bush	
Elijah Bread	I Kings 17:8–16	Proper	B-27	Widow of Zaraphath	
Isaiah Rap	Isaiah 28:14–22	Proper	C-16	Judgment on Corrupt Rulers, Priests	
The "Fleeing as You Fled" Song	Zechariah 14:4–9	Advent	C-1	Future Warfare and Final Victory	
II. Nativity					
Annunciation of Anonymous	Luke 1:26–38	Advent	B-4	Infancy Annunciation	Luke only
O Sole Mio	Luke 1:39–56	Advent	C-4	Infancy Mary's Visit to Elizabeth	Luke only
The Next Generations' Magnificat	Luke 1:39–56	Advent	C-4	Infancy Mary's Visit to Elizabeth	Luke only
Jesus is Born in Context	Matt 1:18–25	Christmas	Day: A, B, C	Infancy Birth of Jesus	Matt only
A Bright, Life-Saving Idea	Matt 2:13–15;1–23	Christmas	Christmas 2	Infancy Flight and Return	Matt only
III. John the Baptist					
The Qumran Computation	Luke 3:1–6	Advent	C-2	Galilean John the Baptist	1
The Wild Man of Judea	Luke 3:7–18	Advent	C-3	Galilean John's Preaching	2; 3; 4

IV. Galilean Section

a. Temptation

Jésus ben Dios in Spring Training	Luke 4:1–13	Lent	C-1	Galilean Temptation	8

b. Teaching & Healing

The Galilee Theater	Matt 4:12–23	Epiphany	A-3	Galilean First Preaching in Galilee	9
The Galilee School District	John 1:43–51	Epiphany	B-2	John Calling of Philip and Nathanael	J-1
Doctor Jesus	Mark 1:29–39	Epiphany	B-5	Galilean Healing of Peter's Mother-in-Law	13
The Lake of the Human Heart	Luke 5:1–11	Epiphany	C-5	Galilean Miraculous Catch of Fish	17
The Way-to-Be-Attitudes	Matt 5:1–12	Epiphany	A-4	Galilean Introduction; Beatitudes	18; 19
The Holy Script-yours	Matt 5:13–20	Epiphany	A-3	Galilean Salt and Light	20; 21
Three Rulis Dramatis	Matt 5:21–37	Epiphany	C-6	Galilean On Murder, Adultery	23–27
Commentary on the Script	Matt 5:38–48	Epiphany	A-7	Galilean On Retaliation; Love of Enemies	26; 27
The Rock or Sand Sermon	Matt 7:21–27	Proper	A-4	Galilean Warning against Self-Deception	42; 43
Invigorating the Paralyzed at Home	Mark 2:1–12	Epiphany	B-7	Galilean Healing of Paralytic	52
Dr. Jesus Eats with Patients	Matt 9:1–9	Proper	A-5	Galilean Healing of Paralytic	52
Hacker Jesus	Matt 9:9–13	Proper	A-5	Galilean Call of Levi	53
Computer Savvy Bishop	Matt 9:9–13	Proper	A-5	Galilean Call of Levi	53
Chef Jesus' Culinary Magic Show	Matt 9:35–10:15	Proper	A-6	Galilean Sending Out of the Twelve	58; 59
Jesus' School of Servanthood	Matt 10:24–33	Proper	A-7	Galilean Exhortation to Confession	60

Shredding Illusions of Domestic	Matt 10:34–42	Proper	A-8	Galilean	Division in Households;	61; 62
John the Journalist	Matt 11:2–11	Advent	A-3	Galilean	John's Questions to Jesus	64; 65
Jesus' Jokes Are Easy	Matt 11:25–30	Proper	A-9	Galilean	Comfort for Heavy Laden	68
The "Bread of God's Presence" Bread	Mark 2:23–28	Proper	B-4	Galilean Sabbath	Plucking Ears of Grain	69
The Sermon on the Level	Luke 6:17–26	Epiphany	C-6	Galilean	Beatitudes	71-74
The "Just a Few Good Men"	Luke 7:36–50	Proper	C-6	Galilean	Woman with Ointment	83
St. Pious in the Suburbs	Luke 7:36–50	Proper	C-6	Galilean	Woman with Ointment	83
Jesus' Rap Song	Mark 3:22–25	Proper	B-5	Galilean	Accusations Against Jesus	85
To Un-Clog Your Ears	Matt 13:1–9;18–23	Proper	A-10	Galilean	Parable of Sower; Interpretation	90; 93
Headline News from Trying Times	Matt 13:24–30;36–43	Proper	A-11	Galilean –	Parable of Weeds; Interpretation	96; 100
Like a Book of Common Prayer	Matt 13:31–33;44–49	Proper	A-12	Galilean Pearl	Mustard Seed; Treasure;	97; 101
Farmer Jesus' Metaphorical Seeds	Mark 4:26–34	Proper	B-6	Galilean Leaven	Weeds; Mustard Seed;	95–98
The Incredible Skulk	Luke 8:26–39	Proper	C-7 RCL	Galilean	Gerasene Demoniac	106
The Women's Issue	Mark 5:22–43	Proper	B-8	Galilean Faith	Jairus' Daughter;Woman's	107
The Gospel of the Prairie	Mark 6:7–13	Proper	B-10	Galilean	Sending Out of the Twelve	109
Head Chef Jesus	Matt 14:13–21	Proper	A-13	Galilean	Feeding of Five Thousand	112
Dog Tired	Matt 15:21–28	Proper	A-15	Galilean	Syrophoenician Woman	116
Man with Attention Deaf-icit	Mark 7:31–37	Proper	B-18	Galilean	Healing of Deaf:Mute	117
In the Chapel of the Consoling Christ	Luke 9:18–24	Proper	C-7	Galilean –	Confession; Predict Passion	122
The Demise of the Fairy Tale God	Matt 17:1–9	Epiphany	Last	Galilean	Transfiguration	124

Appendix 207

All Saints' Way Out in the Mountains	Matt 17:1–9	Epiphany Last		Galilean Transfiguration	124
Bishop Jesus and the Unwilling Spirit	Mark 8:27–38	Proper	B-19	Galilean Epileptic Boy Healed	126
Infant Formula: INAMA	Mark 9:30–37	Proper	B-20	Galilean Dispute about Greatness	129
Bishop Jesus Cuts Some Clergy	Mark 9:38–48	Proper	B-21	Galilean Strange Exorcist; On Temptations	130; 131
Two to Tango	Matt 18:15–20	Proper	A-18	Galilean On Reproving One's Brother	134
V. Luke's Special Section					
You're in God's Army Now	Luke 9:57–62	Proper	C-8	Luke's Special Nature of Discipleship	138
In the Army of the Dog	Luke 10:1–20	Proper	C-9	Luke's Special Sending Out of 70	139
The Good Un-Churched Fellow	Luke 10:25–37	Proper	C-10	Luke's Special Good Samaritan	143; 144
Jesus' Lesson Plan	Luke 10:38–42	Proper	C-11	Luke's Special Mary & Martha	145
How to Pray to God on Cell Phone	Luke 11:1–13	Proper	C-12	Luke's Special Friend at Midnight	146–148
Shop 'til You Drop	Luke 12:13–21	Proper	C-13	Luke's Special Rich Fool	156
The Graciously, Gracefully-Humored	Luke 12:32–40	Proper	C-14	Luke's Special Watchfulness	157; 158
Pyromaniac-Arsonist Jesus	Luke 12:49–56	Proper	C-15	Luke's Special Interpreting the Present	160
The International Association of FGP	Luke 13:1–9	Lent	C-3	Luke's Special Repentance or Destruction	162
All Peoples Airline	Luke 13:22–35	Lent	C-2	Luke's Special Departure from Galilee	165–167
A Real Cause for Celebration	Luke 15:1–15	Proper	C-19	Luke's Special Lost Sheep; Prodigal Son	172; 173
Happy Hour	Luke 17:5–10	Proper	C-22	Luke's Special Servant's Wages	180; 181
Marshall Jesus Encounters the Dirty	Luke 17:11–19	Proper	C-23	Luke's Special Ten Lepers	182

	Luke 18:1–14	Proper	C-24	Luke's Special Unjust Judge	185
Another One Bites the Dust					
VI. Judean					
a. Journey to Jerusalem					
What?! Am I a Lawyer?!	Mark 10:2–9	Proper	B-22	Judean to Jerusalem – Marriage/Divorce	187
A Precocious Child	Mark 10:17–27	Proper	B-23	Judean to Jerusalem Rich Young Man	189
The Factory of Absolute Fairness	Matt 20:1–16	Proper	A-20	Judean to Jerusalem Vineyard Laborers	190
Bart and Zack	Luke 19:1–10	Proper	C-26	Judean to Jerusalem Zacchaeus	194
b. Little John Insert					
Nicodemus and Metanoia Man	John 3:1–17	Lent	A-2	John Nicodemus Visits Jesus	J-3
Anglo-Catholic Father Jesus	John 4:5–26	Lent	A-3	John Woman of Samaria	J-4
The Living Quail	John 6:60–69	Proper	B-16	John Words of Eternal Life	J-6
c. The Days in Jerusalem					
The Wild Card of Judea	Matt 21:28–32	Proper	A-21	Judean in Jerusalem Parable of Two Sons	203
Time to Vote in a Very Important	Matt 21:28–32	Proper	A-21	Judean in Jerusalem Parable of Two Sons	203
What Will That Bishop Do?	Matt 21:33–43	Proper	A-22	Judean in Jerusalem Wicked Tenants	204
His Steadfast Love Endures Forever	Matt 21:33–43	Proper	A-22	Judean in Jerusalem Wicked Tenants	204
The Absentee Landlord	Luke 20:9–19	Lent	C-5	Judean in Jerusalem Wicked Tenants	204
The Enemy Dressed	Matt 22:1–14	Proper	A-23	Judean in Jerusalem Parable of Marriage	205
Jesus Answers in a Timely Fashion	Matt 22:15–22	Proper	A-24	Judean in Jerusalem Tribute to Caesar	206

Appendix 209

One Bride for Seven Brothers	Luke 20:27-38	Proper	C-27	Judean in Jerusalem Q re: Resurrection	207
Jésus ben Dios and Dave "The Babe"	Matt 22:34-36	Proper	A-25	Judean in Jerusalem Great Command	208; 209
Yogi Jesus and the Voices of Anxiety	Matt 23:1-12	Proper	A-26	Judean in Jerusalem Woes	210
d. Synoptic Apocalypse					
An Apocalyptic Coffee Hour	Luke 21:5-19	Proper	C-28	Judean Apocalypse Destruction Temple	213-215
The Bosom of God	Mark 13:14-37	Proper	B-28	Judean Apocalypse Desolating Sacrilege	216-220
The Presence of God is Coming	Matt 24:37-44	Advent	A-1	Judean Apocalypse Householder	224; 225
A Groom-Centered Wedding	Matt 25:1-13	Proper	A-27	Judean Apocalypse Ten Maidens	227
Mean Old Mommy	Matt 25:14-29	Proper	A-28	Judean Apocalypse Parable of Talents	228
Two Types of Dead Meat	Matt 25:31-46	Proper	A-29	Judean Apocalypse Last Judgment	229
VII. John's Special Section					
The Country Wedding	John 2:1-11	Epiphany	C-2	John Wedding at Cana	J-2
The Miracle at the Eucharist	John 2:1-11	Epiphany	C-2	John Wedding at Cana	J-2
Light Perception	John 9:14-38	Lent	A-4	John Man Born Blind	J-9
Man with Strange-Looking Spec's	John 9:14-38	Lent	A-4	John Man Born Blind	J-9
I Am the Backstage Door	John 10:1-10	Easter	A-4	John The Good Shepherd	J-10a
I Am the Good Mother	John 10:11-16	Easter	B-4	John The Good Shepherd, cont.	J-10b
The Jerusalem National Gallery	John 10:22-30	Easter	C-4	John Jesus Gets Rejected	J-10c
Poor Old Russ	John 11:7-44	Lent	A-5	John Raising of Lazarus	J-11
The Baptismal Font of Electrifying	John 12:20-33	Lent	B-5	John Some Greeks Wish to See Jesus	J-12

Terms of Endearment	John 13:31–35	Easter	C-5	John The New Commandment	J-13
Correspond and Collaborate	John 14:1–14	Easter	A-5	John Jesus the Way to the Father	J-14a
No way! Yes! Way!	John 14:1–14	Easter	A-5	John Jesus the Way to the Father	J-14a
Correspond and Collaborate	John 14:1–14	Easter	A-5	John Jesus the Way to the Father	J-14a
Dr. Jesus of Nazareth, Medicine Man	John 14:15–21	Easter	B-5	John Promise of the Holy Spirit	J-14b
Dr. Spiritus Sanctus	John 14:15–21	Easter	B-5	John Promise of the Holy Spirit	J-14b
The First/Last Bank	John 15:1–8	Easter	A-6	John Jesus the True Vine	J-15
Prayer Jesus	John 17:1–11	Easter	A-7	John Jesus Prays for His Disciples	J-17
VIII. The Passion					
The Presiding Bishop	John 18:33–37	Proper	B-29	John Betrayal and Arrest of Jesus	J-18
A Passion Play in One Final Bet	Luke 23:35–43	Proper	C-29	Judean Passion Golgotha; Crucifixion	248; 249
IX. Appearances					
a. Easter					
Two of the Women	Matt 28:1–10	Easter	A	Appearances Empty Tomb	253
A WGIJ-TV Easter Broadcast	Mark 16:1–8	Easter	B	Appearances Empty Tomb	253
The Sacristy of the Human Heart	Luke 24:1–12	Easter	C	Appearances Empty Tomb	253
On the Road to Amaze-Us	Luke 24:13–35	Easter	A-3	Appearances Road to Emmaus	Luke only
CSI: Jerusalem	Luke 24:13–35	Easter	A-3	Appearances Road to Emmaus	Luke only
A Spooky Way to Handle Jesus	Luke 24:36–48	Easter	B-3	Appearances Risen Christ in Jerusalem	Luke only
A Certain Pillar of the Church	John 20:1–18	Easter A		Appearances – The Gardener	J-20

Appendix

*Jesus Ascends	Luke 24:49–53	Ascension	A	Ascension - Appearances Ascension	Luke only
*The Whole World Communications	Mark 16:9–20	Ascension	B	Ascension Appearances - Longer Ending	Mark only
The Last Curtain Falls	Matt 28:16–20	Trinity	A	Trinity Appearances – Great Command	Matt only
***God's Great Love for the World	John 20:19–23	Pentecost	A	John Pentecost	J-20
**On Pentecost Sunday	John 20:19–23	Pentecost	A	John Pentecost	J-20
Fishing in the Lake of the Human	John 21:1–14	Easter	C-3	John Jesus Appears to Seven Disciples	J-21
b. Ascension					
*Ascension stories moved to Easter					
**Pentecost stories moved to Easter					
X. Acts of the Apostles					
How Strange and Beautiful	Acts 8:26–40	Easter	B-5	Acts Philip and the Ethiopian	Acts only